SHARING PASTS

DUTCH AMERICANS THROUGH FOUR CENTURIES

Sharing Pasts: Dutch Americans through Four Centuries

Edited by Henk Aay

Janny Venema

Dennis N. Voskuil

Van Raalte PRESS
Holland, Michigan

Van Raalte Press is a division of Hope College Publishing

Editorial Address: A. C. Van Raalte Institute
                       Theil Research Center
                       9 East Tenth Street
                       Holland, MI 49423

Mailing Address: PO Box 9000
                       Holland, MI 49422-9000

                       vanraalte@hope.edu
                       www.hope.edu/vri

Printed in the United States of America
ISBN 978-0-9891469-4-4

Editor-in-Chief: Jacob E. Nyenhuis
Copy Editor: JoHannah Smith
Cover Design: Nella Kennedy and Russ Gasero
Page Layout: Russ Gasero

Papers from the Twentieth Biennial Conference of the Association for the Advancement of Dutch American Studies, a Joint Conference with the New Netherland Institute, Albany, New York, held 17-19 September 2015.

Charles T. Gehring and Robert P. Swierenga

Trail-blazing scholars and visionary leaders

for the study of the "Old" and "New" Dutch Americans

Contents

...

Preface and Acknowledgments

It was high time that two principal organizations devoted to the study of the Dutch in America got together to share their Dutch American past. For more than forty years, the New Netherland Research Center (NNRC, formerly New Netherland Project) and the Association for the Advancement of Dutch American Studies (AADAS) have been expanding our knowledge of Dutch America: the NNRC for the colonial Dutch and their legacy under British rule and in the early American Republic and AADAS for the Dutch immigration to the Midwest and beyond, beginning in the mid-nineteenth century and continuing to well after World War Two. AADAS in 2015 was marking its twentieth biennial conference, and a joint conference would provide an opportunity to learn from each other, to get to know scholars working in these different research areas, and to discover overlapping themes and connections. In short, the organizers hoped it would help build more solidarity in the field of Dutch American studies.

The logistical demands of joint conferences are particularly challenging. Once we decided on Albany, New York, home of the New Netherland Institute (NNI), the NNRC's support group, we realized that this would likely result in higher costs and lower participation from

AADAS members who are very much concentrated in the Midwest. For cost savings and convenience, AADAS chartered a bus to bring people from the Midwest to Albany, which certainly helped, but even so, attendance of AADAS members was half that of previous conferences. With the addition of NNI participants, however, total attendance exceeded that of a typical AADAS meeting.

With the venue in Albany, the logistics fell to local organizers from the NNI and the New York State Museum: many thanks are due to Marilyn Douglas, vice president of the New Netherland Institute, and her colleagues, Steve McErleane, Carole Otsu, and Bonnie Urso, for making all the arrangements for the facilities, hotel accommodations, the opening reception at the Fort Orange club, and the banquet, along with, very importantly, our guest speaker, Russell Shorto. The conference venue, the Huxley Theater at the New York State Museum in the Cultural Education Center of the Empire State Plaza, was outstanding. Russell Shorto deserves a large round of applause for his banquet address. The academic program of papers to be presented at the conference was put in place by Charles Gehring and Janny Venema, director and associate director of the New Netherland Research Center, and David Zwart and Henk Aay, AADAS president and vice president. Again, a vote of gratitude for all their work. Henk Aay organized the pre-conference field trip to Dutch American historical sites along the upper Hudson Valley, and thanks are due to Heleen Westerhuijs, co-editor of *Exploring Dutch New York* (Museum of the City of New York, 2011), for serving as tour guide on the bus.

Jack Nyenhuis, editor-in-chief of the Van Raalte Press, asked Henk Aay (senior research fellow, Van Raalte Institute), Janny Venema (NNRC), and Dennis Voskuil (director, Van Raalte Institute) to serve as editors for this volume of published papers that stem from the conference. JoHannah Smith, editorial associate of the Van Raalte Press, copy edited the final versions of the papers, and Russ Gasero, RCA Archivist, served as layout editor of the book. Special thanks are due to Nella Kennedy (senior research fellow, VRI) for designing the cover; it consists of a collage of images from the worlds of the "Old Dutch" and the "New Dutch." We are grateful for all the work these individuals have done to bring these papers to publication.

All in all, we are very thankful for this joint conference and this joint publication. We hope and trust that it will continue to bear fruit.

Henk Aay
Janny Venema
Dennis Voskuil

Introduction

Throughout their now four-centuries-long presence in America, Dutch Americans upheld a staunch commitment to education and inquiry that led to their establishing many grammar schools, academies, day schools, colleges, universities, and seminaries. Such places of learning and their graduates, especially those at the post-secondary level, created fertile ground for Dutch Americans to also enquire after their own history in their new home and the part it played in the larger American story. Beginning in the nineteenth century and finding its stride in the twentieth century, Dutch American history carved out its place and identity alongside other American ethnic histories. With only some one-and-a-half percent of the nation's population, the volume and breadth of the body of work in Dutch American history and culture is quite remarkable.

Although the results of research on Dutch America have been presented at any one of a number of national and regional disciplinary and interdisciplinary academic conferences and published in a wide variety of professional journals, a number of institutions have taken the lead and specialized in research, conferences, and publications on

Dutch America. Foremost are the New Netherland Research Center (NNRC) of the New York State Library in Albany, New York, supported by the New Netherland Institute (NNI), with its scholars, annual conference, educational programs, and publications; the Association for the Advancement of Dutch American Studies (AADAS), with its biennial conference and published papers; the Van Raalte Institute (VRI) at Hope College in Holland, Michigan, with its research fellows and publications; the Dutch immigration, education, CRC archives, and *Origins: The Historical Magazine of the Archives* at Calvin College in Grand Rapids; and the Joint Archives of Holland at Hope College in Holland, Michigan, with its *Joint Archives Quarterly*. Not to be overlooked is the American Association for Netherlandic Studies (AANS), with its biennial conference and its partnership with *Dutch Crossing: Journal of Low Countries Studies*. While focused more on Dutch language, literature, and art in the Dutch-speaking world, AANS has made room for Dutch American studies related to these primary interests. Similarly, the contribution to our knowledge of Dutch America from scholars in the Netherlands at universities and research institutes must be acknowledged. Of course, there are many other places and organizations that at times pay attention to and record their history as part of Dutch America—churches, communities, and educational institutions in which Dutch Americans and America form a significant legacy culture.

Throughout their relatively brief histories, these research institutions, together with the more local and regional attention to Dutch American history, have focused entirely either on colonial New Netherland and its enduring legacy in the Northeastern United States beginning in 1609 or on the Dutch immigration wave to the Midwest and beyond and its cultural impact beginning in 1847. The Van Raalte Institute and the Joint Archives of Holland are somewhat of an exception in that they also sponsor and publish research related to the history of the Reformed Church in America, which is found throughout both regions; although the emphasis here, too, falls more on the Midwest and West, rather than the Northeast. This geographic partition of research related to Dutch America has had a number of results. For one, scholars are not familiar with the researchers and the body of published history from the other region and time period. And this extends to people of Dutch American ancestry in general, as well as to the wider population. More knowledgeable Midwesterners perceive Dutch American history primarily as the founding and spread of Dutch settlements and the growth (and decline) of a distinctive Dutch

American subculture throughout the region and farther West. And if Easterners know anything about the Dutch in America, it is principally about those of New Netherland, the British colonies, and the early republic. One reason why AADAS and the NNRC/NNI decided for the first time to hold a joint conference was to give scholars working in each of these rather separate research entities a chance to interact and get to know each other and become more familiar with the content of each other's work. The results of this interaction were evident at the formal discussions and informal conversations during the coffee and lunch breaks of the conference. Easterners were amazed at and unfamiliar with the role of religious dynamic forces in the life of Dutch American communities of the Midwest; Midwesterners were equally taken by the influential political roles that Eastern Dutch Americans played. And this helps with the meaning of the title we have chosen for these published papers: *Sharing Pasts: Dutch Americans through Four Centuries.* NNI folks came to share their Dutch American pasts with AADAS folks and vice versa.

Another result of these rather separate research silos is that the connections between the "Old Dutch" of the Northeast and the "New Dutch" of the Midwest have not been carefully examined. The two regional groupings of Dutch Americans are regarded as quite shut off and independent from each other, with very little in common. This has made it more difficult to construct Dutch American history in some respects as a single and continuous story; even the landmark histories of Van Hinte and Lucas treat the "Old Dutch" as a prologue.[1] The organizers of the joint conference very much wished to attract research papers that explored the connections or the lack of connections between the two groups. The theme of the conference and the call for papers was advertised online and in the brochure as *The Dutch in America Across the Centuries: Connections and Comparisons.* If researchers were not able to document and present historical connections, they could at least focus on comparisons between the Old Dutch and the New Dutch. This objective of the conference met with only limited success. Several papers at the conference did deal with connections and comparisons, but most papers remained in their Old or New Dutch domains. This

[1]   Van Hinte, Jacob, *Netherlanders in America, A Study of Emigration and Settlement in the 19th and 20th Centuries in the United States of America,* ed. Robert P. Swierenga, trans. Adriaan de Wit (Grand Rapids, MI: Baker Book House, 1985); Lucas, Henry S., *Netherlanders in America: Dutch Immigration to the United States and Canada, 1789-1950* (Ann Arbor MI: University of Michigan Press, 1955. Reprinted, Grand Rapids, MI: Eerdmans, 1989).

underscores that few scholars are ready and equipped to step out of their familiar research area, something that would require delving into both periods and regions. Clearly, this remains an unexplored research direction. How might nineteenth century Midwestern Dutch American life have developed differently had the New Netherland colony never existed? Without the transfer of some of the wealth and human capital amassed over two centuries by eastern Dutch American economic, political, and educational elites and leaders, would pioneer Dutch American educational and religious institutions in the Midwest have been able to as readily foster a cohesive subculture?

As editors, where appropriate, we encouraged the writers to include New Netherland and colonial Dutch antecedents and connections in their papers but found that, lacking the opportunity to invest more research time, most were not in a position to do so. And so, with some exceptions, questions about connections and comparisons between Old and New Dutch were largely left on the table. The joint conference did, however, take a first step in bringing scholars from these largely separate research worlds together; they listened, reacted to, and discussed each other's presentations; they browsed the books on offer; and they made social and professional inroads. A longer-term agenda for the consideration of these connections and comparisons between Old and New Dutch might include attending one another's professional meetings more regularly, sharing bibliographies, sponsoring visiting research fellows at each other's institutions, and identifying a number of research projects for collaborative efforts and as projects for graduate students.

We grouped the topics of these twelve papers under five headings. The first group, *Immigration, Wilderness, and Cultural Persistence*, examines several hitherto unexplored aspects of the Dutch American experience. Hans Krabbendam, who has written extensively on Dutch immigration to America, tackles the topic of transnationalism among Dutch immigrants over time. Transnationalism looks at immigrants' relations to their homeland while they are fashioning a new life in their adopted country. Compared with other immigrant ethnic groups, the Dutch stand out with a very low level of interest and involvement in their home country. Krabbendam attributes this low level of transnationalism to a number of factors: low return migration to the Netherlands, positive attitudes to Dutch immigrants in America, a high gender balance and strong agricultural character among Dutch immigrants, and a stable Dutch political system.

The relations between Dutch immigrants and the natural environment is another neglected subject in Dutch American studies. Jan and Anthonia Boersema examined 129 general memoirs written by nineteenth-century Dutch immigrants who participated in pioneer life. It would be instructive to compare such nineteenth-century writings with those of seventeenth-century Dutch immigrants to New Netherland. A quantitative analysis of the topics taken up in these nineteenth-century memoirs reveals that, although church and livelihood dominate these writings, recollections about the natural environment (waters, landscape, wild animals, vegetation, weather, etc.) comprise a significant secondary topic. The authors discuss the significance, meaning, and regional variation of these environmental topics—especially the wild animals—in the light of pioneer settlement. Like other pioneer ethnic groups, Dutch immigrants regarded as progress the transformation and disappearance of the original natural environments and their wildlife (and native Americans) in exchange for farming, logging, and settlement landscapes.

The loss of distinctive cultural traits among Dutch Americans over time has been well documented. Some features associated with Dutch Reformed churches, however, have shown remarkable cultural tenacity over the centuries, even though they have accommodated themselves to a changing American context. Leon van den Broeke surveys a sample of the revisions to and challenges for the Dort Church Order of 1619, the body of laws that governed the Dutch Reformed churches in the Netherlands and overseas. This paper does show a continuity in Dutch American history from New Netherland to the present day. Throughout their history, Dutch Reformed churches in North America have had to seek an equilibrium between their heritage church order and changing conditions in the United States and Canada. Van den Broeke asserts that a Reformed church order has much less to do with Dutch heritage and more to do with Calvinist ecclesiology. In spite of all the revisions to the church orders of Reformed churches, he concludes that they remain fundamentally Dortian.

The second group of papers, *Dutch American Culture Moving West*, considers the geographic expansion of Dutch culture after the English took over New Netherland. The Dutch Reformed church, the only Dutch denomination in America, became the fulcrum for Dutch life and culture and, as such, its guardian and perpetuator. By mapping their spread, Henk Aay shows the expansion in two centuries from the original two churches (in today's New York City and Albany in 1650) to the Hudson River and its tributaries, followed by the Mohawk River and its tributaries to western New York State and, eventually, to dispersed locations in the Midwest during the 1840s. Ethnic mixing and assimilation took place at the same time, and by the mid-nineteenth century, Dutch American culture had lapsed into Dutch American memory. But just at that time, a new wave of immigrants brought an up-to-date Dutch subculture to the Midwest and beyond, also refreshing it in parts of what was once New Netherland. Once more, new Dutch Reformed churches preserved and fostered Dutch American life.

That A. C. Van Raalte, looking for a settlement area for his followers in the Midwest, sought out and was appreciably helped and directed by the descendants of the colonial Dutch, leaders in the Dutch Reformed churches and their acquaintances, is relatively well known. Less recognized are the financial support, advice, and professional manpower the Eastern Dutch Reformed churches and their wealthy and educated members continued to provide the fledgling Dutch colonies. Robert P. Swierenga thoroughly documents these forms of aid in his "Helping Hands: Old Dutch Aid Young Dutch," including money gifts, loans, and bonds to support the building of churches; Christian schools and academies, such as Holland Academy (later Hope college); the recovery effort from the devastating Holland Fire; and the improvement of the Holland harbor. Swierenga makes it clear that these helping hands were not motivated solely by benevolence; in return, the eastern Dutch Reformed church was able to organize and plant congregations throughout the Midwest and stave off union with other denominations that would have done away with its identity. Like that of Henk Aay, Swierenga's paper underscores that the history of the Dutch Reformed church is a connecting and unifying thread in the four-century-long history of Dutch America.

When the 1848 California Gold Rush began, very few new immigrants were interested in continuing farther west in quest of gold because they had just settled in the Midwest and were mainly interested in farming. Pieter Hovens found rather that Dutch immigrants profited from passing travelers en route to California by selling them produce, meat, and trade goods at high prices. Two centuries earlier, in New Netherland, and also later in the Upper Midwest and in the Dakotas between 1840 and 1877, Dutch colonists also looked for valuable metals, but the results were disappointing. Although this article is focused on the California Gold Rush, students of New Netherland will be interested in this paper because of the personal names discussed. For example, the experiences of Walter Van Dyke in California with local Indians shows remarkable similarities with those of the New Netherlander Hendrick van Dijck, who was deeply involved in two Indian wars: could these two be directly related? This article invites research into the connections between New Netherland and the California Gold Rush.

In the third group of papers, *Dutch and Indians under English Colonial Rule*, Erin Kramer and Andrew Stahlhut stress how unique and important the experiences with Indian relations, gained by the early Dutch around Albany and other settlers in parts of New England, proved to be for later generations. Kramer emphasizes that the descendants of the Dutch settlers maintained their friendship and alliances with the Iroquois during various wars between the English and French around 1700. They had earlier learned from their forebearers that trade (and reciprocity) was at the heart of alliances with the Indians. The financial resources from trade and smuggling were used for prisoner and information exchange. Also aware that a French-Iroquois alliance would threaten Albany and New England frontier towns, Dutch American leaders were able to cut off Montreal from cheap English goods and thus divert trade from Montreal to Albany. Contrary to earlier views, the interests of settlement and commerce did not work at odds but complemented each other.

Stahlhut stresses that the Commissioners of Indian Affairs, largely of Dutch ethnicity, should be recognized as notable actors shaping the British colonial world, locally as well as imperially. The basis for the institution was the early Dutch settlers' experience with Indian relations since the 1620s. Formally founded in 1696, the Commissioners of Indian Affairs consisted of a small core of highly active members who were overwhelmingly Dutch as well as tightly knit due to intermarriage. Trusted and relied on by the English government, they operated quite autonomously and were active on the local level in affairs of other British colonies and with issues related to the British rivalry with French Canada on the imperial level.

Americanization was and is, of course, a pervasive process of cultural change affecting all ethnic communities. We grouped two very different papers under the heading, *American Influence on Dutch Communities and Church*. The first paper by Earl Wm. Kennedy is a detailed examination of the views of the Reformed Protestant Dutch Church (RPDC), now the Reformed Church in America, on slavery as recorded in the debates and acts of its synods in 1855. Like other denominations transplanted from Europe, the RPDC, especially after its independence from the Dutch mother church in 1792-93, was more and more affected by American religious, political, and intellectual currents. The occasion for this extensive debate about slavery was the application for membership in the RPDC by the North Carolina Classis of the German Reformed Church. Some of its ministers and members were slaveholders. The RPDC ultimately rejected this application because of the issue of slavery. The debates on the floor of the synods reveal how divided also this Northern denomination was on this issue. Moreover, that the published minutes of synod about this decision say nothing about slavery as the bone of contention speaks volumes.

The second paper under this heading was made possible by a unique find: the Dutch-language minute book of a Holland, Michigan, debating society, established in 1872. Societies like these were part of a national trend during the latter half of the nineteenth century, one that focused on the self-improvement of the "common man." Participating in a debate on a resolution related to a weighty moral, political, biblical, or social issue, as well as voting on and discussing it afterward, would make for better informed and more responsible citizens. These and other like-minded organizations in Holland and throughout the nation were not part of the first generation's Dutch cultural habits. Rather, they reflect a rapid, although selective, Americanization. Nella Kennedy reviews the debate topics and votes and from them draws inferences about the mindset of the participants. That half of the debates were about biblical topics was unusual for an American debating society; this preponderance did reflect the centrality of the members' church life, something directly drawn from the Netherlands. This again underscores the complexity of Americanization: Dutch ways inhabit an American institution.

At a time when Dutch culture in America threatened to become forgotten, there were efforts to keep the importance of the Netherlands and New Netherland for the United States before the American public. The first paper in this group, *Rekindling Affection for the Netherlands*, is about Francis Adrian van der Kemp (1752-1822). Rather than remembering him for his poor translations of more than ten thousand Dutch documents, called the New Netherland Papers, Peter Van Cleave argues that this Dutchman's work should be understood as a great effort to promote the importance of Dutch and Dutch American history. Van der Kemp wanted to educate the Dutch, and later the Americans, about their shared history. As a patriot in the Netherlands during the Dutch Revolt against France in 1812-14, he demonstrated his support for the earlier American struggle for independence. Later, living in Barneveld, New York, he stressed that America should explore the Dutch past for lessons learned, since the Dutch recovered their liberty twice: first against Spain and then against France. By translating the New Netherland Papers, Van der Kemp wanted to show that New Netherland was a multicultural society based on the pursuit of religious and political liberty and as such was the bedrock for New York. There is a parallel here with Russell Shorto's *Island at the Center of the World*, based on the translated manuscript Dutch records of New Netherland.[2]

Non-Dutch people also contributed to the rekindling of affection for the Netherlands. Through Babs Boter's paper about travel writing, readers learn about two Americans who linked the history of Dutch America with the Netherlands. Living part of their lives in upstate New York, the businessman Elkanah Watson (1758-1842) and the teacher and minister William Elliot Griffis (1843-1928) both studied the history of the colonial Dutch; like Adrian van der Kemp, they both knew John Adams, the first American ambassador to the Netherlands and later the second president of the United States. Although these two men are usually placed in a historical and political context, Boter approaches them and their travel writing about the Netherlands via literary and semiotic analysis. These travel writers use different levels of ekphrasis or verbal (written) representation of visual imagery. They both try to find common ground in their writing with American readers by comparing Dutch sites with the home country and equating the Netherlands and America.

Henk Aay
Janny Venema

---

2   Russel Shorto, *The Island at the Center of the World: The Epic Story of Dutch Manhattan and the Forgotten Colony That Shaped America* (New York: Doubleday, 2004).

Part One

Immigration, Wilderness, and
Cultural Persistence

CHAPTER 1

They Came to Stay: The Weak Transnational Relations of the Dutch in America

Hans Krabbendam

Eritrean refugees in Europe are forced by their old government to pay a 2 percent tax on their earnings if they want any documents from their old country. Intimidation of citizens abroad by this so-called "diaspora tax," suspected of being used for military purposes, is an extreme example of the transnational grip of countries on emigrants who, in spite of having left their native country, are still forced to keep ties with it. There are also many positive examples of immigrants who voluntarily keep an active interest in their country of origin: Philippine housekeepers in the United States who support their families back home, successful immigrant entrepreneurs who finance political campaigns in their countries of origin, and hyphenated Americans who pressure the American government to accept certain policies that support their home countries. That this can be successful is illustrated by the Polish American demonstrations in Washington for American support for accepting Poland into NATO. This commitment stemmed from the large population of Polish Americans, the end of the Cold War, and the fact that two-thirds of Polish Americans have visited Poland.[1]

---

[1] Thaddeus C. Radzilowski and Dominik Stecula, *Polish Americans Today: A Survey of Modern Polonia Leadership* (Hamtramck: Piast Institute, 2010), 23-25.

Dutch immigrants and their descendants are hardly involved in the current affairs of their home country, and vice versa, the interest of Dutch authorities in an active role for their immigrants in the United States for transnational purposes is minimal. Apart from the standard consular care and a few import stores for Dutch staples and delicacies, such as VanderVeen's in Grand Rapids, Michigan,[2] the ethnic bonds per se seem to generate little commercial activity.

The financial, political, and commercial activities by immigrants are elements in the growing interest in immigrants' transnational relations. A transnational approach looks at immigrants as people who create a social space in at least two nations. It doesn't define immigrants exclusively by their presence in the United States but includes foreign relations. One may dismiss the usefulness of this approach for investigating the Dutch Americans because of their inconsiderable involvement in their home country. But it is exactly this quality that makes them a rewarding object for research, if only because of their long presence in North America. A long-term perspective that includes other parts of the Dutch colonial empire, contributes to a comparative analysis that explains the differences in transnational relations of Dutch immigrant groups.[3] Four centuries of transatlantic contact will reveal patterns in earlier migrations that stimulated or limited transnationalist contacts, even though this long period covers different phases of the Netherlands and the destination countries. This investigation contributes to fostering realistic expectations of keeping the descendants of Dutch immigrants and the Netherlands meaningfully connected.

Transnational immigrant relations transcend national borders because they function in a web of connections between public and private networks. These relationships don't stop when immigrants exchange one passport for another, because they can simultaneously participate in political and civic circles in the countries of residence and of origin. The source for these continued relationships is their almost universal, strong emotional attachment to the people and places left behind.

[2]   www.thedutchstore.com

[3]   Donna R. Gabaccia, *Foreign Relations: American Immigration in Global Perspective* (Princeton, NJ: Princeton University Press, 2012). See for a description of the decreasing interest of the Dutch in their home country, Michael J. Douma, *How Dutch Americans Stayed Dutch: An Historical Perspective on Ethnic Identities* (Amsterdam: Amsterdam University Press, 2014), 157-62.

Channels for communication and travel opportunities make transnational behavior possible. These technological means, however, provide the conditions, but not the core feature, of transnational contact. The clearest example of transnational immigrants are Mexicans who physically cross borders—legally or not—invest in their homeland economies, mobilize people for political or social change in their host country, or function as a transnational family across borders. Research on Mexican and Canadian immigrants reveals the strength of these transnational relations, but a home country much farther away does not block such relations.

There is not yet a more accurate quantitative standard to rank nations in order of the intensity of their transnational contacts in the North American context, but analyses of various immigration histories reveals at least five factors that advance these dynamics. First, the conditions for these contacts must be present, in the shape of open channels for communication and information exchange keeping dialogues and actions ongoing. Second, immigrants maintain or even intensify transnational contacts when they feel threatened or seriously marginalized by the host country. Third, transnationalism is stimulated by a situation of political instability, but with prospects for improvement, in the nation of origin. This often happened in times of war or attempts at revolution and includes the colonies of the home country. Fourth, a high level of international labor mobility that includes a considerable proportion of return is another strong pillar for transnationalism. Fifth, a cultural appreciation in the country of origin for those who return helps transnational exchange. Before we investigate these factors for Dutch Americans, we need to examine quantitative data of return migration and money transfers.[4]

Low Dutch return migration

Nothing strengthens the transnational networks as much as a high level of return migration or of recurring seasonal migration. A high level of mobility between two countries has a multiplier effect. Various sources confirm the low level of return migration of the Dutch, fluctuating between 10 and 15 percent, with a spike of 18 percent in the

---

[4] See references to various immigrant groups below.

years from 1908 to 1923.[5] This low percentage and the low visibility of those who returned are the key to explaining the limited transnational activity of Dutch immigrants. This trend confirms the widespread expectation (and reality) of permanent settlement. Return migration equaled failure in the mind of the public and of the immigrant. This might not be true for individual migrants for whom cogent decisions and needs of family members at home were often as important as homesickness, but still the home environment labeled them with some pity. *De Standaard*, a Christian weekly in the Netherlands, expressed these feelings in 1886: those who returned did so because their high hopes had been destroyed. Staying put was also a result of the immigrants' strong denouncement of the old country, as Klaas Niemeijer expressed forcefully in 1905: "The only thing that binds us to Holland is our dear family; otherwise we have no regard for Holland. We thank the God of providence that He has brought us here. . . . In Holland you can work yourself to death, but it is impossible to save anything if you have a family. And for that reason we wish that our family was all here."[6]

Marjory Harper has pointed out that all migrants freeze the idea of their homeland. She suggests that there is continuity in motives to return home, especially among young singles in American urban centers who realize that they had made a hasty decision to emigrate. When they find out that the difference in wages between the United States and their home country has narrowed, they use the regular international transport connections to return home.[7] Russian, Central European, Italian, and British Isles immigrants have exhibited relatively high return rates compared to Scandinavian and Irish immigrants. But even these were high compared to the Dutch. If the homeland offers opportunities to buy land or start a profitable business, there is a stronger inclination to return; this has added positive stories to the negative ones of loss and hardship. Moreover, the Irish have had a distinct narrative of exile and banishment explaining their involuntary exodus from their country and their reluctance to consider a return.[8]

---

[5] Hans Krabbendam, *Freedom on the Horizon: Dutch Immigration to America, 1840-1940* (Grand Rapids: Eerdmans, 2009), 263-65; Mark Wyman, *Round-Trip to America: The Immigrants Return to Europe, 1880-1930* (Ithaca: Cornell University Press, 1996), 11.

[6] Klaas Niemeijer to his relatives in Middelstum, Groningen, 4 June 1905. Herbert J., Brinks, ed., *Dutch American Voices: Letters from the United States, 1850-1930* (Ithaca: Cornell University Press, 1995), 314.

[7] Dennis Conway and Robert B. Potter, "Caribbean Transnational Return Migrants as Agents of Change," *Geography Compass* 1 (2007): 25-45; Marjory Harper and Stephen Constantine, *Migration and Empire* (Oxford: Oxford University Press, 2010), 306-37.

[8] Kevin Kenny, "Diaspora and Comparison: The Global Irish as a Case Study," *Journal of American History* 90 (June 2003): 134-62.

Mark Wyman, a specialist on return migration, has listed as the top reason for return, reaching the goal of earning enough money to buy property back home, second is failure in the host country, and homesickness and death in the family are the two remaining reasons. The dominant factor for return is important because it sets the tone for the public image of migration. When emigrants return with funds or skills their status rises, but when failed adventures dominate, returning is tainted with a negative image.[9]

The low level of Dutch interaction with their home country is confirmed by the low level of remittances (money sent back to the homeland). By 1887 Dutch Americans were sending more money to the Netherlands than they received, showing that they were financially solvent. In the fifty years between 1870 and 1920, they had sent six million dollars back to the Netherlands, while they collected two million from the Netherlands. More remarkable than this proportion was the small annual amount of these private transfers. In 1909, for instance, the total sum of money received from home was $100,000, whereas $275,000 was sent home to the Netherlands.

This low figure is not a result of poverty, because most Dutch immigrants were doing well, but from a lack of personal interest in the old country. In comparison with private transfers, the value of Dutch exports to the United States in 1910 was $34 million and imports from the United States were $118 million. The sum of $1.5 million sent back to the Netherlands between 1900 and 1909 may sound substantial, but it was only 3.5 percent of the $419 million, all the money sent back to Europe. Only Luxembourgers and Portuguese sent less money home, but these states also had much lower immigration rates than the Dutch. In comparison, in the same period, Belgians sent $4.3 million home, Danes $4 million, British $82 million, and Italians $98 million.[10] These

---

[9]   Mark Wyman, "Emigrants Returning: The Evolution of a Tradition," in *Emigrant Homecomings: The Return Movement of Emigrants, 1600-2000*, ed. Marjory Harper (Manchester: Manchester University Press, 2005), 16-31. The database with millions of Dutch newspapers (www.delpher.nl) listed no positive stories about a return migrant from the United States. Only one person, called "TT," was mentioned in *Nieuwsblad van het Noorden*; he had stolen lawn chairs (17 April 1929). He was partly identified as a forty-seven-year-old man who had just returned from the United States, where he had lived for twenty years.

[10] By 1910 the census reported 120,063 Dutch, 3,071 Luxembourgers, 59,360 Portuguese, 49,400 Belgians, 181,649 Danes, 1,221,283 British, and 1,343,125 Italians. See Campbell J. Gibson and Emily Lennon, "Historical Census Statistics on the Foreign-born Population of the United States, 1850-1990." https://www.census.gov/population/www/documentation/twps0029/twps0029.html;

figures indicate that for Dutch immigrants, maintaining financial ties with the homeland was not important.

Also, from the Dutch side, there was little organized or governmental encouragement to keep the contacts alive. Consuls were the connecting points in the United States for Dutch immigrants needing something from the old country. Dutch diplomats were late in showing interest in the immigrant communities in the Midwest, which they believed were well served by mostly honorary consuls who were part-time appointees. They tried either to advance trade or to assist immigrants in trouble, but they did not intentionally strengthen transnational ties.

The first Dutch envoy to visit West Michigan and Chicago was Reneke Marees van Swinderen in the winter of 1906.[11] He advised his successor, John Loudon, in 1911 that these visits should be limited to once a decade, since they were important primarily for the locals but lacked prestige for the mother country. Curiosity won out, and Van Swinderen's successor, Loudon, took the journey within a year of his arrival and was as warmly welcomed as his predecessor.[12] These experiences show the lack of the Dutch government's attention to Dutch settlements at the height of their ethnic life in the United States.

Conditions for transnational intensity

A maritime and urbanized nation, the Netherlands had no lack of transport, communication, and information facilities to connect with overseas migrants. Though the efficiency of the connections

---

Verslagen aan de Koning betrekkelijk den Dienst der Posterijen, der Rijks-Postspaarbank en der Telegrafen in Nederland (1878-92) . . . aan de Koningin-Weduwe/Koningin betrekkelijk den Dienst der Posterijen en der Telegraphie in Nederland (1893-1904), and Verslag aan de Koningin betrekkelijk den Dienst der Posterijen, der Telegrafie en der Telefonie in Nederland (1905-19). Reports of the Immigration Commission 37: 275-76, 280. Jeroen Touwen, "American Trade with the Netherlands and the Dutch East Indies," in *Four Centuries of Dutch American Relations*, ed. Hans Krabbendam, Cornelis A. Van Minnen, and Giles Scott-Smith (Albany: State University of New York Press, 2009), 274. In the first decade of the twentieth century, 30,479 immigrants from the Netherlands arrived in the United States.

11   *De Volksvriend*, 29 November 1906. *De Grondwet* reported about this visit on November 19 in its 27 November 1906 issue. Douma, *How Dutch Americans Stayed Dutch*, 87-100

12   National Archives, Den Haag, inv. 2.21.205.37. Collectie John Loudon, file 3: correspondentie met de Marees van Swinderen, letter 23 February 1911 to Dr. John Loudon.

between England and the United States was unparalleled, the frequency of shipping from Dutch ports, the professionalization of postal arrangements, the high literacy rate, and the more than fifty ethnic periodicals circulating in the United States provided all the infrastructure needed for transnational contacts.[13]

Reliable transport opportunities were a precondition for transnational contacts but not the cause of these contacts. Written communications were more important; regular mail service and news reports about events in the homeland could stir transnational interest. But again, these were a precondition, not a cause. Political or economic causes in the homeland made the press a transnational vehicle for immigrant Americans. For Germans the failed revolution of 1848 was such a cause, and of course, World War I.[14] The Great War functioned as a lightning rod for Belgian immigrants as well. They became deeply involved in supporting their homeland occupied by the Germans. Shortly after the German invasion, ten Belgians in Mishawaka, Indiana, volunteered for the Belgian army in order to defend the Fatherland, and after the armistice, many returned to find out what had happened to their relatives. This combination of war and humanitarian need greatly enhanced investment in transnational relations. The Dutch, remaining neutral, missed out on this incentive.[15]

Dutch immigrants were not systematically victimized. Though the journey across was no pleasure trip, they often received preferential treatment on board the Holland America Line steamers in comparison to eastern Europeans. Many Dutch emigrants could afford to travel second class or else were put in the quiet part of third class. Upon arrival in New York or other ports of entry, they might well encounter class bias but never racial discrimination. On the contrary, they were privileged. The Dillingham Commission that published a detailed examination of immigrants between 1907 and 1910, listed the Dutch in the top of the Anglo-Saxon hierarchy: "In social customs, the Dutch show greater affinity to the English than to the Germans. They have been called the Englishmen of the mainland. Like the English, the Dutch have been

---

[13] Krabbendam, *Freedom on the Horizon,* 270-79.

[14] Walter D. Kamphoefner, Wolfgang Helbich, and Ulrike Sommer, eds., *News from the Land of Freedom: German Immigrants Write Home* (Ithaca: Cornell University Press, 1993), 23-25. It seems that it was mostly the first generation who continued to support Germany in the Great War.

[15] Andreas Stynen, "Twee werelden? Banden met het oude Vaderland," in *Boer vindt land. Vlaamse migranten en Noord-Amerika,* red. Andreas Stynen (Leuven: Davidsfonds, 2014), 192-211.

great colonizers."[16] This positive attitude about Dutch immigrants continued until after World War II; in the words of Republican senator Alexander Wiley from Wisconsin: "They are a good breed; we can use them."[17]

Of course, many Dutch immigrants suffered the insults and denigrations that all newcomers encountered, but they suffered no structural discrimination, as did, for example, the Japanese and Chinese. Historians of these nationalities have noted that the more these groups suffered from exclusion, the more they strengthened their contacts with their relatives in China to reinforce their ethnic identity.[18]

International labor mobility

Immigration becomes a serious option when the perceived differences between the economically depressed area of origin and the promise in the area of possible settlement is large. Mass movement can happen as a result of a strong tradition of emigration, but the Netherlands had the opposite experience. In the seventeenth and eighteenth centuries, the western parts of the Dutch Republic were the destination of immigrants from its North Sea neighbors, thanks to higher wage levels and comparatively high urbanization, but with its high death rates, this area needed and could well accommodate additional migrants from outside the country. The opportunities at home were simply too good for a transatlantic exodus of Dutch citizens. Since free enterprise was restricted until the 1640s, immigration could take off only in the next decade in New Netherland, the number of immigrants that were officials, traders, and soldiers was high compared to the number of artisans and farmers. This resulted in a population too small for genuine independent development. In general, Dutch migration within Europe outnumbered the movement to the Americas at a rate of three to one (160,000 vs. 50,000). Amsterdam shared its position as the transit center of these transatlantic migration flows in the seventeenth and eighteenth centuries with London, even though

---

[16] *Reports of the Immigration Commission, Summary* (Washington, D.: Government Printing Office, 1911), 1:232. See also the positive reception of a model Dutch family (De Jong from Baarn, wealthy and healthy), as reported in *Onze Toekomst*, 23 July 1920.

[17] Senator Alexander Wiley (Republican from Wisconsin) in *Hearings Before a Subcommittee of the Committee on Foreign Relations United States Senate, Eighty-Second Congress, First Session on United States Economic and Military Assistance to Free Europe* (Washington, DC: Government Printing Office, 1951), 249.

[18] Gabaccia, *Foreign Relations,* 114-17.

the actual number of citizens of the Dutch Republic living abroad was low.[19]

The European citizens of the American colonies maintained close contacts with their mother countries because they were dependent on their legal, political, commercial, and religious services. The development of larger populations and toward greater autonomy gradually reduced the grip of the home countries. The volume of the British and Dutch transatlantic migration during the seventeenth and nineteenth centuries was high in comparison to the size of their population. Other areas like Scotland and Scandinavia occasionally experienced migration waves, but these fluctuated much more and lost momentum. As long as the sending nation exerted authority over its colonies, transnational contacts were necessary, particularly for the elite. Scotland had a high proportion of citizens living outside the nation, and Sweden and Norway reached similar levels around 1900.[20]

Labor migrants circulating between two countries kept the transnational project alive. Their migration brought them into contact with new skills and modern ways of organization which enabled them to create international networks. Unlike the Dutch, the Poles spread out in Europe before they arrived in the United States. This resulted in an impressive 10 percent of the Poles working in western Europe and the United States from 1870 to 1924. The immigrants' new experiences were empowering. Lower class Poles underwent a modernization process when they (temporarily) migrated for work and returned with ideas to change their homeland. Paradoxically, their efforts to organize and find protection in solidarity integrated Poles into the American cultural scene. It was easier for a Pole to be (culturally) accepted by America than by Germany. Historian Brian McCook concludes that, although the short-term plan of migrant Poles to change their home country failed, they did succeed in introducing a more pluralistic attitude. This was not necessary in the Netherlands, since it already had a very well maintained system of pluralism in its pillarized society which granted religious and nonreligious subcultures the right to organize in civic and political organizations and share national power.[21]

---

[19] Jelle van Lottum, *Across the North Sea: The Impact of the Dutch Republic on Labour Migration, c. 1550-1850* (Amsterdam: Aksant, 2007), 161-80. It would be interesting to investigate the volume and character of personal connections across the Atlantic that tied the colony to the motherland.

[20] Ibid.

[21] Brian McCook, "Becoming Transnational: Continental and Transatlantic Polish Migration and Return Migration, 1870-1924," in *European Mobility: Internal,*

Greek and Italian immigrants had return rates from 40 to 50 percent.[22] The return pattern among Scandinavian immigrants shows an initial low return rate of about 5 percent during the wave of the 1880s, but Swedes responded quickly to the economic depression in the United States during the mid-1890s, and 23.5 percent of the newly arrived returned. This behavior suggests that Swedes were a more integral part of international labor migration than were the Dutch. The peaks in departure were followed by peaks of return. In comparison, the Dutch looked at immigration as much more permanent. This attitude corresponds with the more modest rate and relatively steady Dutch emigration pattern, one with a high level of gender balance. Gender imbalance stimulated return migration, if only to find a partner.

Many single men returned from America after working for a few years in manual jobs such as mining, logging, or construction. As crews often were of the same nationality, their situation offered few chances and little encouragement for integration. No wonder that 75 percent of European return migrants were male. The Swedish return migrants often bought a business in their home country and were quite innovative. Those who returned to farm, did so in their area of origin.[23] The sudden and massive exodus of Scandinavian immigrants to America suggests a higher level of transnationalism, as many had decided to emigrate on the spur of the moment, something which made returning home a serious option when adverse conditions arrived. This trend caused immigrants to have a personal interest in the development of their homeland. The slow pace of industrialization and the strong agricultural character of the Netherlands strengthened the permanency of immigrants and suggested that the best prospects for improvement of the family were in the United States. A relatively high percentage of the Dutch emigrated as families, although some moved in stages; children left behind often joined their families later on. No evidence exists of Dutch immigrants

International, and Transatlantic Moves in the 19th and Early 20th Centuries, ed. Annemarie Steidl, Josef Ehmer, Stan Nadel, and Hermann Zeitlhofer (Göttingen: Vandenhoeck & Ruprecht Unipress, 2009), 151-74.

[22] Anastasia Christou, "Greek American Return Migration: Constructions of Identity and Reconstructions of Place," *Studi Emigrazione* 145 (2002): 201-29; Dino Cinel, *The National Integration of Italian Return Migration 1870-1929* (Cambridge: Cambridge University Press, 1991).

[23] Hans Norman and Harald Runblom, *Transatlantic Connections: Nordic Migration to the New World after 1800* (Norwegian University Press, 1988), 107-11; Harald Runblom and Hans Norman, eds., *From Sweden to America: A History of the Migration* (Minneapolis: University of Minnesota Press, 1976), 201-27.

returning home to buy farms or start businesses with money earned in the United States. They came to stay.[24]

Political incentives for transnational activities

In sum, the labor market, economic prospects, and past experience discouraged transnational behavior. If anything, it was the political opportunities created by wars and revolutions which gave immigrants an incentive to activate transnational contacts through political mobilization in the homeland. Irish Americans, for example, intervened on behalf of their old country time and again. For instance, some of the 125,000 Irish American veterans of the American Civil War attempted to use their military experience to expel the British from their homeland by sending weapons and offering training. When this proved impractical, Fenians, members of the Irish republican organization founded in the United States in 1858, planned raids on Canada to hurt the British Empire during the late 1860s; this sabre rattling was tolerated by American authorities. Chinese immigrants joining an effort to boycott American goods as an act of transnational solidarity against American bullying of the Chinese is another example. Such transnational acts, in fact, did more harm than good because they associated immigrants with radicalism and violence.[25]

Compared to many other nations, the Netherlands had a stable political system that was slowly, but steadily reforming itself toward a constitutional democracy with universal suffrage (in 1917 for men, in 1922 for women). The Netherlands marked its political distress with periods of nonviolent transition. The most likely period during which the country was open to a new political order was at the end of the eighteenth century with the Dutch Republic under siege from within and without. A civil war might have erupted between the Orangists and the Patriots. Some intellectuals pointed to the American Constitution as a model, and some young Dutch regents traveled to the United States to observe its workings. But no immigrants returned to the newly formed kingdom to advance an American model.[26]

---

[24] There were no reports in *De Volksvriend, Het Oosten, De Grondwet, Onze Toekomst, De Sheboygan Nieuwsbode,* and the *Volksstem,* about any successful returnees, and there were more reports about agricultural hardships in the Netherlands than about successes.

[25] Gabaccia, *Foreign Relations,* 108-11.

[26] Edwin van Meerkerk, "Gijsbert Karel van Hogendorp: de man van 1813," in *Een nieuwe staat. Het begin van het Koninkrijk der Nederlanden,* ed. Ido de Haan, Paul den Hoed, Henk te Velde (Amsterdam: Prometheus Bert Bakker, 2013), 35-41.

With the exception of the German occupation in World War II, the danger of imminent destabilization of the nation, something that would encourage intervention, was low. Few immigrants felt the call to change the political system. The revolutionary years of 1848 and 1868 resulted in constitutional changes that promised a gradual extension of democratic participation.

Visionary immigrants can use their transnational social space when their home countries experience upheaval. This happened especially in the international labor movement, but the example of labor organizer Louis van Koert shows the limitations of the Dutch-American connection.[27] Van Koert had left The Hague to find a job in Chicago and escape both the domestic problems of a pregnant mistress and an angry wife, as well as internal conflicts in the Dutch labor movement that had marginalized him. Van Koert was a typical temporary migrant, who had created a transnational family and hoped to rehabilitate himself. He faced labor leader Ferdinand Domela Nieuwenhuis, whom he challenged in Dutch newspapers. Moreover, labor protests in the Netherlands prodded him to report the victories of American labor unions, which he felt were misrepresented in the Dutch labor press and the hostile Dutch-American press. This is how Van Koert used his transnational social space. Despite the insecurity of his existence, Louis felt empowered as an independent worker in Chicago because he could speak up freely, something impossible to do in the Netherlands.[28]

Van Koert's failure to make the best use of his transnational space was caused by the ineffective operations of the American unions, whose members were more interested in a quick win than in structural change. On top of that, he noticed that the Socialists were as corrupt as the boss system in American politics. He was forced to strengthen his contacts with other European immigrants because the critical mass of Dutch American workers was insufficient, even in Grand Rapids. He sought affiliation with Germans, but had to conclude that ethnic divisions weakened the power of the unions.[29] In fact, he concluded that workers

[27] Pieter Stokvis, "Socialist Immigrants and the American Dream," in *The Dutch American Experience: Essays in Honor of Robert P. Swierenga*, ed. Hans Krabbendam and Larry Wagenaar (Amsterdam: VU University Press, 2000), 91-101. Stokvis focusses on the experiences in the United States, while his contacts at home are at least as relevant for transnational research. Van Koert served as vice treasurer the Central Board of the Social Democratic Association that was torn by financial quarrels.

[28] Archief Ferdinand Domela Nieuwenhuis. Internationaal Instituut voor Sociale Geschiedenis, Amsterdam. Algemeen, Correspondentie, 127, Koert, L. W. van. 1893-94, 3 May, 20 June, and 10 October 1893.

[29] 10 October 1893 and 26 September 1894.

in the United States were even more enslaved by factory owners than in Europe.[30] This example shows that transnational hopes were certainly present among some Dutch workers, but they missed a large enough support group for engagement with the Netherlands and an inspiring example in the United States.

The same handicap prevented transnational exchange during the one revolutionary moment in the Netherlands, the Troelstra Revolution in 1918. This event happened at a time of reduced accessibility to the Netherlands for immigrants due to World War I but was concluded with an acceptable compromise. Pieter Jelle Troelstra, the leader of the Social Democratic Labor Party in the Dutch Lower House, hoped that the apparent success of the Social Democrats in Berlin would spill over into the Netherlands and voiced his claim that the proletariat was ready for a nonviolent takeover of the government on Armistice Day, November 11. Division in his own ranks, rapid consent for practical reforms, military precautions, and a public demonstration for the monarchy, stopped the movement in its tracks. Troelstra had misjudged the situation. Even if the revolution had succeeded, there was no labor organization among Dutch immigrants in the United States that could support the revolutionary effort. There was no organized back-up group in the United States.[31]

Political developments in the Netherlands did not invite transnational involvement, but events outside the kingdom, such as the Boer wars in South Africa and conflicts in the colonies of the Dutch East Indies, did. Dutch Americans identified these situations as chances to help their "tribe," with whom they could identify. The Dutch American sympathy for the Boers drew from a historical lineage of competition with the British, a romanticized frontier tradition, similarities in religious beliefs, and work ethic, even though the Boers were much less advanced than Dutch American immigrants.[32] Dutch Americans collected thousands of dollars for the Boers using Dutch channels

---

[30] 17 December 1894.

[31] Hans Krabbendam, "Waarom een christelijke vakbeweging onder de Nederlandse immigranten in Amerika niet aansloeg," *Cahier over de Geschiedenis van de Christelijk-Sociale Beweging* (2009), 132-50. The Dutch American press reported via British sources about the threat of a workers' revolution in the Netherlands, and a week later, it related that the attempt at revolution had failed. See also *De Grondwet*, 19 and 26 November 1918, *De Volksvriend*, 21 November 1918, *Het Oosten*, 22 and 29 November 1918.

[32] Michael J. Douma, "Ethnic Identities in a Transnational Context: The Dutch American Reaction to the Anglo-Boer War, 1899-1902," *South African Historical Journal* 65, no. 4 (2013): 481-503.

and used the Boers' struggle to confirm their own independence from a British-dominated culture. Only a few, however, volunteered as soldiers; Dutch Americans hoped for diplomatic solutions. When news reports became less frequent and Boer defeats accumulated, attention waned. Real transnational contact proved difficult. Mentally, Dutch Americans had reinforced that their ethnic awareness was not restricted to transatlantic relations with Europe.

This ethnic awareness, however, did not lead to transnational action, not even as the sky darkened above Europe in the 1930s. A series of interviews with Dutch Americans in North Dakota in 1939 conducted under the auspices of the Works Progress Administration illustrated this attitude. Only an occasional respondent, usually a pensioner or an elderly woman, admitted to being worried about the tense situation in Europe and the threats to Holland, but most of their neighbors did not support a military intervention, nor did they express any ideas for reshaping the country after the war.[33]

The best moment for substantial change in the Dutch political system came right after World War II, but in order to have any impact on the debate, one needed to have been active in the resistance to the German occupation. No immigrants qualified, nor were they asked for advice. In the intellectual and political debate about constitutional reform, Dutch Americans were silent. The only example of extending influence overseas was the shipping of relief goods by Dutch Americans to their kindred church organizations in the Netherlands. This went against the wishes of American and Dutch relief organizations that advocated a nonsectarian approach to relief. But this effort lasted only two years, until Marshall Aid took over.[34]

The Dutch empire and transnational relations

Again, a situation outside the homeland triggered a Dutch American response. When Indonesia pressed for its independence between 1945 and 1948, most Dutch Americans supported the territorial integrity of the Dutch state, and the Midwest became the hub

---

[33]   State Historical Society of North Dakota, roll 16186 WPA project. Ethnic Group Files, Dutch.

[34]   Robert P. Swierenga, Nella Kennedy, Lisa Zylstra, eds., *Dutch Americans and War: United States and Abroad* (Holland, MI: VRI Press, 2014) chaps. 10 and 11. Bert Hofman, "Democracy or Dictatorship: An American Reaction to the Developments in the Netherlands between 1935 and 1945," *Pro Rege* (June 1991): 12-16; Harry A. Van Belle, "The Impact of WWII on the Reformed Dutch in the Netherlands and Canada: A Comparison," *Pro Rege* (June 1991): 27-33.

of resistance toward American pressure for Indonesian independence. Dutch diplomats had courted leading immigrants to defend and explain Dutch policies to the American public in World War I. These propagandists highly appreciated this attention from the homeland since it raised their status in the Dutch immigrant community. This need for cooperation resurfaced during and after World War II, as David Snyder has shown.[35]

Scholars of the cultural diplomatic relationship, such as David Zwart and Henk Aay, point to the tension in Dutch American communities in the Midwest between a nostalgic, old-fashioned image of the Low Countries and the modern Netherlands. A related tension existed between the outsiders' image of the Netherlands as "vulnerable little Holland," during World War II, in contrast to big and aggressive Germany, and the self-perception of the Netherlands as a midsized empire, a favored pronouncement of Queen Wilhelmina.[36] Dutch greatness as a cultural-historical asset, also in the United States, clearly resided in the past. The decolonization struggle threatened to reverse this positive imagery into one of a country violently crushing Indonesia's right to self-determination. The lack of transnational contacts between Dutch Americans and Indonesia made them take a conservative stand in the decolonization debate, and their lack of direct interest in the Dutch East Indies removed them from active engagement in the political debate in the Netherlands.[37] Some Dutch American publications advocated the importance of restoring the colonies for the future of Dutch international trade.[38] Shortly after the Dutch military interventions in 1947, American foreign policy and public opinion completely shifted to favor Indonesia, and the issue disappeared from the Dutch American agenda.

[35] National Archives, Den Haag, inv. 2.05.13 Gezantschap VS, 1117 dienstreis Michigan, "Losse aanteekeningen over Nederlanders en oud-Nederlanders in Michigan," April 1919. The *Banner*, 29 July 1920.

[36] David Zwart, "Constructing the Homeland: Dutch Americans and the Netherlands Information Bureau during the 1940s," *Michigan Historical Review* 33, no. 2 (2007): 98-100; Henk Aay, "Dutch Propaganda Films in America: Documentaries from the Netherlands Information Bureau in the 1940s," in *Dutch Americans and War*, 221-49.

[37] See for instance the reprint of a *Grand Rapids Press* editorial defending the Dutch for taking time to arrange Indonesian independence in the *Missionary Monthly* (September 1947): 239.

[38] Charlotte Kok, "*The Knickerbocker Weekly* and the Netherlands Information Bureau: A Public Diplomacy Cooperation During the 1941-1947 Era," (MA thesis Utrecht University, 2011), 61.

The volume of migration within the Dutch empire to the Dutch East Indies was equal to the Dutch emigration to the United States in the period between 1900, and apart from the language position, the intranational migration led to a crucial difference in education; while many Dutch migrants to the Indies sent their children to secondary schools in the Netherlands, Dutch Americans sent their children to schools in the United States. These choices tied the migrants to the Indies to the Netherlands, where many of them retired. The real boost for transnational relations came about with decolonization during the late 1940s and 1950s; three hundred thousand Indonesians and Dutch decided to return. To this day, cultural exchanges and political engagement with Indonesia remain strong, and enduring transnational relationships have been built.[39]

This comparison shows how the perspective of the future influenced behavior of the migrants. The temporary character of the migration to Indonesia kept contacts with the home land intact, visible especially in the education of the next generation. The presence of Dutch migrant communities in other parts of the world fostered the formation of a new kind of transnational contact, one that included multiple migrations, for example, from Holland via South Africa or Brazil to the Dutch settlements in the Midwest or via the Dutch East Indies to California. A systematic overview of such interconnections might enrich the knowledge of the dynamics of transnational behavior of Dutch and other Western migrants.[40]

High geographical mobility of the labor force created a pattern of return migration that promoted transnational contacts. A strong tradition of seasonal labor migration has made return migration acceptable, even at a great distance. But not very many Dutch laborers strayed far away from home in Europe. By comparison, central and eastern Europeans, as historian Adam Walaszek reminds us, were used to moving around.[41]

---

[39] Gert Oostindie en Jeannette Schoorl, "Migratie tussen Indonesië en Nederland," *Demos* 26.9 (2010): 12-14.

[40] Suzanne M. Sinke, "Crossing National Borders: Locating the United States in Migration History," *OAH Magazine* 19, no. 3 (May 2005): 58-63, describes the moves in the Enserink van der Vliet family among the Netherlands, the United States, Canada, and South Africa. Other examples are in the Polder family annals.

[41] Adam Walaszek, "Central Eastern Europeans in the Euro-Atlantic Migration System Before the First World War," in *Tales of Transit: Narrative Migrant Spaces in Atlantic Perspective, 1850-1950*, ed. Michael Boyden, Hans Krabbendam, Liselotte Vandenbussche (Amsterdam: Amsterdam University Press, 2013), 29-44.

Cultural factors in transnational relations

In the early 1800s, the diplomatic relations between the young American Republic and the Netherlands were at a low, which was symbolized by the absence of diplomatic exchanges. During the late eighteenth and early nineteenth century, the Dutch and American political structures moved in opposite directions: the Americans threw out their king, while the Dutch welcomed one. Despite the excitement about American independence, some Dutch observers had serious concerns about the chances for survival of the new republic due to their doubts about a stable social and political order. But there were other ties that would bind these two peoples together: religion and especially the narrative of the mass migration.[42]

Shortly before American independence, the last bastion of Dutchness, the Dutch Reformed Church, had cut itself loose from its subordination to a transnational authority, the ecclesiastical rule of Classis Amsterdam. The church began to educate its ministers on American soil, something that would eventually inspire many other educational initiatives for the new wave of immigrants beginning in the 1840s, including colleges, seminaries, and Christian day schools.[43]

Meanwhile during the 1830s and 1840s, the new Dutch kingdom encountered a series of constitutional, territorial, economic, religious, and financial crises that made mass emigration an attractive option for those who became victims of these troubles. The economic conditions in the United States, the availability of cheap land, and demand for labor made a transatlantic move attractive. The slow rate of industrialization in the Netherlands meant that agricultural and rural areas had the highest departure rates. Acquiring land anchored immigrants and made their settlement more permanent. Due to the absence of an international seasonal labor tradition and accusations that mass migration was an act of disloyalty to the nation, emigrant leaders had to create a plausible narrative for their departure. The religious migrant groups drew most attention due their size and

---

[42] J. W. Schulte Nordholt, *The Dutch Republic and American Independence* (Chapel Hill, University of North Carolina Press, 1982), 17.

[43] John W. Coakley, "John Henry Livingston (1746-1825): Interpreter of the Dutch Reformed Tradition in the Early American Republic," in *Transatlantic Pieties: Dutch Clergy in Colonial America*, ed. Leon van den Broeke, Hans Krabbendam, and Dirk Mouw (Grand Rapids, MI: Eerdmans, 2012), 295-314; Wim van den Doel, "From Distant Images to Closer Relations: The Netherlands and the United States during the Nineteenth Century," in Krabbendam, *Four Centuries*, 219-37.

publicity; they legitimized their emigration with strong moral arguments about the lack of religious freedom and unfair taxation. Both arguments discouraged later transnational investments because the emigrants envisioned a depressing future for the Dutch nation in contrast to the bright encouraging future for the United States. The feelings of the Dutch immigrants about the Netherlands were anchored in the past, not in the future. A decision to settle permanently meant a loss of citizens' rights in the Netherlands, but few seemed to regret that.[44] Their master narratives emphasize the hardships and injustices they had experienced at home. As these religious communities founded new settlements, in time, these stories of liberation from a gloomy past were commemorated with the result that this negative perspective of the homeland dominated the emigration tradition.[45]

Many immigrants of other nations became engaged in modernizing their own country, such as Chinese immigrants in the United States who returned to assist in building schools and hospitals. Dutch emigrants, however, were hardly involved in such modernization of their home country. They preferred to take their chances in the United States.[46] They gained necessary expertise from their immigrant European neighbors and not from return migrants. Dutch immigrants built religious and educational institutions in the United States that helped them connect to and participate in their new environment; these were inspired by Dutch examples but quickly became independent. Only a handful of Dutch immigrant students, mostly theologians, came to the Netherlands to get advanced degrees. After World War II, the Marshall Plan and educational exchanges such as the Fulbright program, created a web of transnational information contacts, but those then took place mostly outside Dutch American educational institutions.

Remigration was a crucial pillar of transnational contact. All over Europe, return migrants maintained contacts with the United States, but the Dutch had a low level of return migration. The low percentage of 10 to 15 percent confirmed the expectation of permanent settlement. Also the number of return trips was modest. After 1900 return trips

---

[44] Marlou Schrover, "Burgers, ingezetenen en vreemdelingen," in De Haan, *Een nieuwe staat*, 242-49.

[45] David Zwart, "For the Next Generation: Commemorating the Immigration Experience in the United States and Canada," *Tijdschrift voor Sociale en Econonmische Geschiedenis* 7 (2010): 126-50.

[46] See Krabbendam, *The Model Man: A Life of Edward W. Bok, 1863-1930* (Amsterdam: Rodopi, 2001).

became more common. A survey in 1909 reported that 40 of the 578 Dutch workers in the furniture industry in Grand Rapids had been back to the Netherlands either once or several times. Those who had lived in America between five and nine years had a return rate that was twice as high as among those who had been in the United States either less than five or more than ten years. Starters did not have enough money for travel, and heads of families had more pressing responsibilities. Other European immigrants in the Grand Rapids area visited their home countries at twice the frequency of the Dutch.[47] These visitors to the old country exchanged information and urged others to emigrate but did not seek to bring about change in the Netherlands.

A telling counter example of this phenomenon was the Association of Former Americans that organized activities in Eeklo, seven miles south of the Dutch-Belgian border in between Ghent and Bruges. In the 1930s, this club staged reunions on July 4 and Labor Day with picnics, American patriotic songs, and opportunities to exchange stories.[48] This Flemish example confirms three factors that reinforced their transnational contacts. First, emigration to the United States was a variation of seasonal labor in Northern Belgium and was therefore expected to be temporary. Second, the slow emancipation of the Flemish from the dominant French-speaking culture led to celebrating and idealizing Flemish culture. This feeling strongly appealed to those who had left: the true fatherland was Flanders. A third distinctive element in comparison with the Netherlands was Belgium's overwhelmingly Catholic affiliation, something that made departure for the predominantly Protestant United States more risky. Bishops saw emigration as temporary as well, and, not until after World War I, did they realize that their former parishioners were there to stay. These features illustrate that the transnational incentive was stronger in Belgium than in the Netherlands.

Among the examples of transnational "successes," the factor of religion is common. First of all, many ministers in two Reformed immigrant church denominations had been educated in the Netherlands, but since their new communities quickly gave priority to founding their own seminaries, the need for continued exchange was much reduced. In the Christian Reformed Church, the clergy's return rate was 14 percent, similar to the rate for all Dutch remigrants. The number of Dutch Catholic parishes was small, and the American

---

[47]   Krabbendam, *Freedom*, 264.
[48]   Stynen, *Boer vindt land*, 197-98.

Catholic Church leadership was more concerned with providing services for new immigrants and strengthening the ties to Rome than with building churches based on nationality.[49] Immigrant churches were important mediators between the cultures of origin and settlement. But beneath the practical advantages of churches smoothening the immigrants' transition, resided a framework of meaning that tied immigrants together. This shared vision also connected sending and receiving countries.[50]

The quick decline of church membership in the Netherlands since the 1960s has created a widening gap with the more thriving and visible religious landscapes in the United States; this has further alienated the religious Dutch American community from the secular Dutch.[51]

Conclusion

Transportation and communication networks prepared an excellent and expanding groundwork for transnational relations of Dutch immigrants in the United States. These preconditions could not have been the reason for the low level of transnational contacts between Dutch immigrants and their home country. A rough longitudinal and comparative pattern shows a low level of seasonal labor migration of the Dutch outside their borders, a stable society, and a steady stream of mostly rural migrants who made calculated optimizing decisions. As a result, emigration from the Netherlands to North America was considered a permanent move by families. Returning was considered a defeat: the few that did come back carried the burden of failure.[52] In addition, the few political crises in the Netherlands did not inspire

[49]   Since 1857, seventy-three ministers had come from the Netherlands to serve in the Christian Reformed Churches in North America. Three returned upon retirement, and ten had taken calls from churches in the Netherlands. That is about 14 percent. Databases, courtesy of Dick Harms, Heritage Hall, Calvin College, Grand Rapids. Krabbendam, *Freedom on the Horizon*, 138-46.

[50]   Alejandro Portes and Rubén G. Rumbaut, *Immigrant America. A Portrait* (Berkeley: University of California Press, 2006), 299-342.

[51]   Peter van Rooden, "The Strange Death of Dutch Christendom," in *Secularisation in the Christian World*, ed. Callum G. Brown and Michael Snape (Burlington, VT: Ashgate, 2010), 175-96.

[52]   *Rotterdamsch Nieuwsblad* (31 August 1882) reported that each week from sixty to ninety German migrants arrived in Amsterdam back from New York. Occasionally a returning migrant advertised his skills in a newspaper ad for salesmen: *Nieuws van den Dag* (28 December 1905). See also *Rotterdamsch Nieuwsblad* (9 October 1907), reporting hundreds of Germans returning. *Limburgsch Dagblad* (28 September 1932) reported on Polish remigrants who had used their American savings to buy farms in Poland.

immigrants to call for political change, except for several exigencies that threatened the Dutch colonial empire.

As positive transnational factors advance and multiply exchange, the reverse is also true. The lack of transnational activities makes the Dutch an interesting counter example in the debate about the importance of immigrants' relations with their home country. This paper has not exhausted all aspects of Dutch immigrants' transnational behavior. We need to examine immigrant newspapers in more detail to see whether these conclusions need qualifications for different social classes, denominations, and regions. More evidence from immigrant correspondence is also needed to confirm or correct the impression of negative reports about the home country discouraging investment in the Netherlands and to document the damaged reputation of those who returned. And the time frame can be expanded to include the more recent waves of emigrants. In any event, the Dutch case shows how important the framework of the nation-state and its economic, political, and religious conditions was for the level of transnational relations. Even high-speed Internet connections will not be able to change that.

CHAPTER 2

"The wilderness has been made to blossom": Nineteenth-Century Dutch Immigrants and the Natural World

Jan J. Boersema and Anthonia Boersema-Bremmer

In the 1880s, Holland, Michigan, postmaster Gerrit Van Schelven conceived the idea of asking pioneer immigrants to write an account of their early years of settling. He realized that the world was rapidly changing and was convinced that it was important to document the history of these very trying times. Van Schelven was also one of the editors of *De Grondwet*, a newspaper started in 1860 for Dutch immigrants in West Michigan who had come to the area since around the 1850s. The Dutch were mostly orthodox Calvinists, and in the United States, they joined either the Reformed Church of America (RCA) or the Christian Reformed Church (CRC). In the Netherlands many of these immigrants had either joined or supported the Afscheiding (Secession). This movement began when Hendrik de Cock, minister of the church of Ulrum, seceded from the national church, the Nederlandse Hervormde Kerk.

Dozens of people responded to Van Schelven's invitation and sent him their memoirs, the publication of which encouraged new contributions. This process was furthered by Van Schelven, who attended festive meetings in order to make his project more widely known and thereby collect more memoirs. In 1955 historian Henry S.

Lucas published a substantial selection of these memoirs.[1] The extant contributions received by Van Schelven are held in the Holland Museum Archives (HMA). These memoirs, reminiscences, and life sketches, together with thousands of letters written during the same period, are the singular most important sources from which we can piece together a picture of life in those early years.

In this article, the memoirs have pride of place; other sources will be adduced where they help interpret the data. This article will highlight the information the sources provide on the relationship between the settlers and their natural environment. How did the settlers look back on this issue, and how are we to interpret it contextually? Do the views expressed by the Dutch immigrants concur with patterns and attitudes held more generally?

The following section will touch on a number of significant developments in the nineteenth century and single out some biblical notions that might have had some bearing on the way the Dutch settlers perceived their new environment. Together they will produce the larger frame in which the picture painted by the documents can be interpreted.

The general framework

The nineteenth century was an era of immense territorial expansion for the United States, with radical consequences for its plant and animal life and for its landscape.[2] This expansion had an East-West character and was justified with moral overtones.[3] Many Americans believed that this "conquest" of the land was their destiny, their vocation, indeed their "manifest destiny."[4]

The arrival of the railways, the plough, and the stagecoach, along with the new settlers, meant the arrival of civilization. This markedly

---

[1]   Henry S. Lucas, ed., *Dutch Immigrant Memoirs and Related Writings. Selected and Arranged for Publication by Henry S. Lucas*, rev. ed., reprint of the original, 2-vol., 1955 ed. (Grand Rapids, MI: Eerdmans, 1997). The two volumes in this one-volume reprint hereafter are Lucas, *Memoirs*, 1 and Lucas, *Memoirs*, 2. Lucas included and translated memoirs written in Dutch and sometimes edited the memoirs that were written in English.

[2]   Anne F. Hyde, *Empires, Nations, and Families: A New History of the North American West, 1800-1860* (NY: Ecco/Harper Collins, 2012).

[3]   Jan W. Schulte Nordholt, *The Myth of the West: America as the Last Empire*, trans., Herbert H. Rowen (Grand Rapids, MI: Eerdmans, 1995).

[4]   Anders Stephanson, *Manifest Destiny. American Expansion and the Empire of Right* (NY: Hill and Wang, 1995); Robert J. Miller, *Native America, Discovered and Conquered: Thomas Jefferson, Lewis and Clark, and Manifest Destiny* (Lincoln: University of Nebraska Press, 2008).

American Progress, John Gast, 1872

strong movement was a one-way route. The light from the East was to dispel the prevailing darkness of the West. Once science and technology entered the scene, together with the rifle, of course, the untamed animal had to flee, and the uncouth native had to make way: this is the scene depicted in "American Progress," the well-known painting by John Gast in 1872. This piece is typical for the long tradition that Schulte Nordholt expounds so convincingly in *Myth of the West*.

Nowhere in the world had the face of the earth been changed so radically, on such an enormous scale, and in such a short period of time. Forests were cleared, endless prairies gradually ploughed under, railway tracks and roads built, and villages and towns established. The changes in and disappearance of biotopes, as well as active hunting, took its toll on the existing flora and fauna.[5] There was no escape, not even for the bison, which were counted in the millions. Around the year 1900, hunting and farming had disposed of prairie life, and a mere one thousand bison remained in the Rockies, mainly in reserves.[6]

The Louisiana Purchase added an immense territory west of the Mississippi, roughly the Missouri and the Arkansas Red-White River

[5] Frederick W. Turner, *Beyond Geography: The Western Spirit against the Wilderness* (New Brunswick: Rutgers University Press, 1994); Michael Lewis, ed., *American Wilderness: A New History* (Oxford: Oxford University Press, 2007).

[6] Andrew C. Isenberg, *The Destruction of the Bison: An Environmental History, 1750-1920* (Cambridge: Cambridge University Press, 2000).

Newhouse traps
Nineteenth-century animal traps
made by the Oneida community in
upstate New York (*Project Gutenberg,
http://www.nybooks.com/wp-content/
uploads/2013/01/Gutenberg-Wolves.jpg*)

watersheds. After the Corps of Discovery expedition, led by Meriwether Lewis and William Clark (1804-6), the wholesale trek westward began a human migration that was to continue for the entire century. The federal government practically forced the First Nations peoples to yield their territories and surveyed and platted the new land, land that was then made available to the settlers.[7] The larger proportion of these settlers were European immigrants hoping to better their lives, and many of them wanted to farm the land.

The growth of industrialization in the latter half of the century caused great optimism among the persistent stream of immigrants; they were great believers in social and technological progress.[8] There was also a certain order in this progress, as can be seen in an advertisement for the Newhouse traps, animal traps designed by Samuel Newhouse. These traps were produced at Oneida, New York, beginning in the 1850s and soon dominated the market. They were widely used across the country. The Newhouse trap, "going before the axe and the plow," according to the advertisement, "forms the prow with which iron-clad civilization is pushing back barbaric solitude, causing the bear and beaver to give way to the wheatfield, the library, and the piano."[9]

Crop failures, a bleak economic future, and a lack of religious freedom stimulated the mass emigration from Europe beginning in the 1830s, and about ten million people sought opportunity in the New World. The greatest number of people left from Ireland and Italy, and in the Netherlands, many people also read and spoke about *landverhuizen* (emigration). The number of people who left from the Netherlands

---

[7]   Stephen J. Rockwell, *Indian Affairs and the Administrative State in the Nineteenth Century* (Cambridge: Cambridge University Press, 2010).

[8]   Michael Adas, *Dominance by Design: Technological Imperatives and America's Civilizing Mission* (Cambridge: Harvard University Press, 2006).

[9]   The story of the Newhouse trap and the citation can be found in Christopher Benfey's article, "The Lost Wolves of New England," *New York Review of Books* (22 January 2013), http://www.nybooks.com. The source of the citation is: Samuel Newhouse, *The Newhouse Trapper's Guide* (Oneida Community, Ltd., 1914), 155. We are grateful to Christopher Benfey who related to us the details.

and landed in North America between 1835 and 1880 is estimated to be close to one hundred thousand.[10] A sizable number of these were members of the newly organized, nonconformist Afscheiding. The nonconformist ministers, Albertus C. Van Raalte and Hendrik Scholte, emigrated to the New World in 1847, both with a few hundred followers. For a number of years, this influx of *volksplanters*, a nineteenth-century Dutch term for the colonists, continued.[11] Van Raalte settled in the forests of West Michigan and founded a fast growing colony named Holland. Scholte moved to Iowa and named his colony Pella. After a few decades, a group of colonists moved from Pella to Northwest Iowa, where they founded Orange City and Sioux Center. In all of these places, Dutch Reformed churches were established, Dutch-language periodicals appeared, and university-level educational institutions were founded. Partly as a result of this development, these places have remained the nuclei of Dutch American culture, in spite of the fact that the immigrants subsequently moved to numerous other places in the nation. The original concentrations, however, also explain why so much material about these immigrants was collected and preserved there.

The views held in the western Christian world on the relationship between humans and nature were largely shaped by the Old Testament and, more specifically, by the Creation account. The second Creation story (Genesis 2 and 3), for instance, tells us that harmony in all of creation was lost; man was banned from the Garden, and that he was doomed to toil and till the land "by the sweat of his brow." The Bible paints a realistic picture of preindustrial, agricultural life. But many Christians read these passages prescriptively. It was humanity's task to cultivate the unmanageable and "uncharitable" world, which means: tame it and then till the land. The history of the people of Israel shows exactly this pattern. It gave nature its ambiguous character. There are, on the one hand, domesticated cultivated elements such as the fields yielding crops, orchards, and fig trees. But there is wildlife too, undomesticated nature, which inspires admiration for its beauty, the "lilies of the field," and respect for and fear of its inherent chaos and harshness. The latter face of nature—the depths of the sea, droughts

10 Robert P. Swierenga, *Faith and Family: Dutch Immigration and Settlement in the United States, 1820-1920* (New York: Holmes and Meier, 2000), 313.
11 Jacob Van Hinte, *Netherlanders in America: A Study of Emigration and Settlement in the 19th and 20th Centuries in the United States of America,* ed. Robert P. Swierenga, trans. Adriaan de Wit (Grand Rapids, MI: Baker Book House, 1985); Hans Krabbendam, *Freedom on the Horizon: Dutch Immigration to America, 1840-1940* (Grand Rapids, MI: Eerdmans, 2009).

and deserts, locusts, and wild animals—can be experienced as the wages of sin, when God's ordinances are not observed.[12]

The memoirs show that the Dutch settlers were familiar with the Bible, and, as their language reveals, especially the Old Testament. In their perception, their exodus to the new and unfamiliar world ran parallel to the Israelites' wanderings to the Promised Land, and their leader was much like a latter-day Moses. They had memorized many Psalms, and they sang the old Genevan tunes while working in the woods. These permanent religious resources stayed with them and afforded solace.

Sources and methods

Research began by systematically sifting through the fourteen boxes that contained all the Van Schelven documents in the Holland Museum Archives. Lucas had chosen from this material the memoirs that he saw fit for inclusion in his "balanced" anthology, and we were looking for additions. This investigative exercise produced a harvest of 129 useful memoirs.

For the purposes of this study, the most useful memoirs were those that were written by persons who had witnessed all or part of the period described, roughly the first twenty years of the colonies, and which were of a general nature, so that—in theory—they could deal with any subject. More or less thematic accounts, for instance, about transport or leaders of the colony, were not included.

It is useful to categorize the memoirs into three different geographical groups, so that differences will come to light with respect to distinctive natural environments. Some writers moved on when older, but since Van Schelven had asked for reminiscences of pioneering times, the memoirs still fit neatly into these three different areas. They are not evenly balanced, probably because the initiative for the memoirs originated in Michigan.

Number of Memoirs Per Area	
West Michigan Holland forests	92
Iowa/South Dakota prairie	18
Wisconsin/Illinois/Minnesota forests, grasslands	19
Total	129

---

[12]   Jan J. Boersema, *The Torah and the Stoics on Humankind and Nature* (Leiden: Brill, 2001), 215-17.

The next two steps were the quantitative and qualitative analyses of these 129 general memoirs.

After perusal of the memoirs, a list was drawn up of all the subjects mentioned by the authors, however summarily. This list includes twenty-four topics, depending of course on decisions taken in itemizing them. After that, each memoir was check listed, first for whether or not the topic was mentioned and second for how it was treated. This produced topical profiles for the memoirs, making it possible to assess specific topics for the natural environment against the background of the full memoir. For cases of wild animals and trees, we listed each species. Where authors made striking comments on nature or progress, we added these passages at the bottom of the checklist.

Fig. 1a. Example of a memoir checklist

HMA Box 8 Number T88-0234 Herinneringen van C. Zwalu-wenberg	M/D/Y 1/19/1915	Writer C. Zwalu-wenberg	Gender Staus M.	Place (s) Holland, MI

	X	Comments (with X)
1. Occupation	X	Farmer. Gekomen als jong mens om land te kopen en zelf boer te worden.
2. Family Life	X	Hoe de kinderen op te voeden?
3. Community & or friends		
4. House / Barn	X	Blokhuis, kosten $50.
5. Church & or Rel. Life		
6. School		
7. Language		
8. Farming / soil	X	Corn en aardappelen geplant tussen de stompen, varkens, kippen, cornstalks voor de koeien,
9. Econ. & Business		

10. Prices goods Serv.	X	Landprijzen: 80 acres voor 1.25 per acre. Toen ik trouwde 4 tot 10 dollars per acre.
11. Health		
12. Food Beverages		
13. Clothing		
14. Customs		
15. Adm. & or Politics		
16. Climate Weather		
17. Logging lumber		
18. Initial Clearing & Draining	X	"we kapten wat bomen om en bouwden een blokhuis" In de zomer brandden wij het hout op
19. Natives		
20. Wild Animals		
21. Vegetation		
22. Landscape & Waters		
23.Travel & Infrastr.		
24. Culture 24a. Motivation	X	Een orgel voor de kinderen: "Wij kochten een orgel en betaalden het onderhands." Gospel hymn van Moody en Sankey. Het hield de kinderen van de straat!. Later ook piano's Motivation: land kopen en zelf boer worden.
25. Miscellaneous	x	Zie ook citaat hierboven. "In den winter kapten wij boomen om; in den zomer brandden wij het hout op."

Fig. 1b. Example of a memoir checklist

Archive Pella's weekblad May 26, 1922 Number pp. 41, Lucas II	M/D/Y	Writer Mrs. G. van Horsen	Gender Status F	Place (s) Pella
	X	Comments (with X)		
1. Occupation	X	farmer		
2. Family Life	X	42, 43		
3. Community & or friends	X			
4. House / Barn	X	43 strooien stad, hutten met loof takken en stro		
5. Church & or Rel. Life	X			
6. School				
7. Language	X			
8. Farming / soil	X	42 paarden		
9. Econ. & Business				
10. Prices goods Serv.				
11. Health				
12. Food Beverages	X	42 tarwe, corn, stroop, cornbrood		
13. Clothing				
14. Customs				
15. Adm. & or Politics				
16. Climate Weather	X	44 storm		
17. Logging lumber				
18. Initial Clearing & Draining				
19. Natives	X	43, 44		
20. Wild Animals	X	44 wolven , slangen		

21. Vegetation		
22. Landscape & Waters	X	42 Kreken en bergen; 41, Pella: een plaats in de wilderness
23.Travel & Infrastr.	X	42 Ongebaande wegen
24. Culture		
24a. Motivation	X	Godsdienstvrijheid
25. Miscellaneous		

Results

Quantitative: general

Figures 2 to 4 give the quantitative results for the three different regions separately, and fig. 5 shows the results for all the areas together. The histograms give the counts (y-axis) of the topics (x-axis) that are mentioned at least once in the memoirs. The counts do not include the frequency or contents of the comments. For the sake of comparison, the data from the other areas have been made proportional to the number of the West Michigan memoirs. Frequencies are shown from high to low: as a result, the sequence of topics may change from figure to figure. In order to show the differences among the three areas, they are presented together by topic in fig. 6.

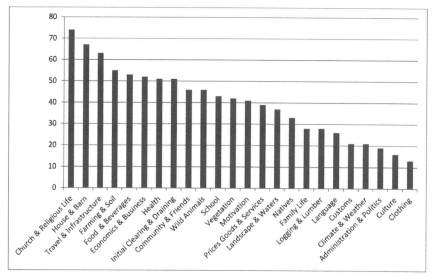

Fig. 2. Topic frequencies in the ninety-two memoirs from West Michigan

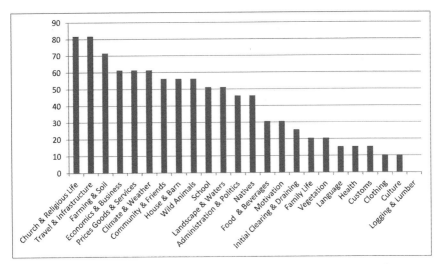

Fig. 3. Topic frequencies in the eighteen memoirs from Pella, Sioux Center, and Orange City, Iowa, and Harrison, South Dakota. Data adjusted to the ninety-two West Michigan memoirs

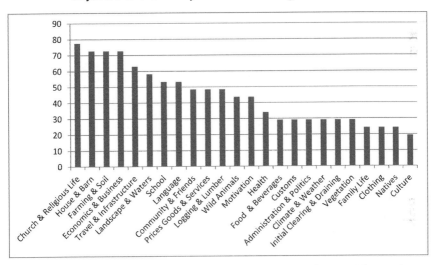

Fig. 4. Topic frequencies in the nineteen memoirs from settlements in Wisconsin, Illinois, and Minnesota. Data adjusted to the ninety-two West Michigan Memoirs

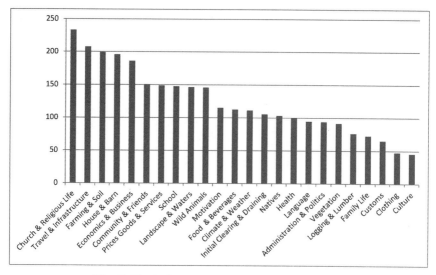

Fig. 5. Topic frequencies in all 129 memoirs

In nearly 90 percent of the memoirs, church and religious life figure most prominently, whereas subjects such as clothing and culture are least prominent. The relative topic frequencies in the memoirs show a picture of the familiar matters with which our pioneers were primarily concerned. From the outset, religious life and the church were the focal

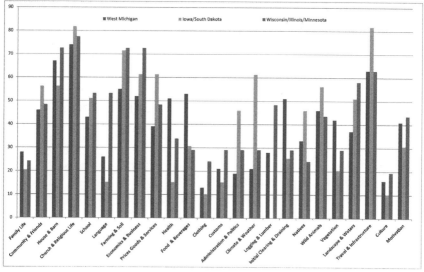

Fig. 6. Comparative topic frequencies in the memoirs from each area. Data adjusted to the West Michigan memoirs

point of the community. In fig. 1, we can see four topics of the second rank, each related to economic life, which in this case was everyday life on the farm. In a third group, present in a considerable majority of the memoirs, we find the subjects of landscape and waters and wild animals. For the colonists these were clearly essential matters and occurred more frequently than, for instance, food and beverages, climate and weather, or health.

The differences among the three regions can be seen in fig. 6. Let us look at the more striking differences (50-100 percent difference). In the memoirs from Wisconsin, Illinois, and Minnesota, more text is devoted to language, clothing, and logging and lumber. In these states, the groups of Dutch immigrants were smaller, and they had settled in culturally more heterogeneous areas where cultivation was well on its way and with much building activity, especially around Chicago. Those sorts of areas gave rise to deliberations about language and dress and offered opportunities for the lumber trade.

In Iowa, where there were no forests, there is obviously no mention of logging and lumber. In these memoirs, we find lots of observations about politics and administration. One reason for this may be the activism of their leader, the Reverend Hendrik Scholte. Like Albertus Van Raalte, he encouraged his flock, for instance, to apply for citizenship as soon as possible, so that they might have a say in relevant matters. There is also much more written about weather and climate, which is not at all surprising in view of the inclement winters the immigrants had to endure. Blizzards were so fierce that people tied ropes between house and barn lest they lose their way. Attention is also paid to travelling and infrastructure in the Iowa memoirs, because some settlers did not stay in Pella, but moved farther westward after some decades and founded new communities. Health and food and drink figure most prominently in the memoirs from West Michigan because there was considerable hardship on this score. The land was not cultivated, but forested and swampy, which brought much ill health.[13] It was only after much laborious initial clearing and draining that crops could be grown.

For all regions the overall picture is one of communities of devout pioneers who were determined to build their lives and religious communities in the face of natural surroundings that were harsh and completely new to them.

---

[13] Jan P. Verhave, *Disease and Death Among the Early Settlers in Holland, Michigan* (Holland, MI: Van Raalte Institute, Hope College, 2007).

Quantitative: wild animals

What did the pioneers write about nature? In this context, it is interesting to study the data in the category of wild animals, those animals that were not kept domestically. Whenever farm animals are mentioned, they are counted as belonging to either farming and soil or house and barn, respectively. It must be noted that pets are not mentioned in the memoirs. This seems significant; they most likely had pets on the farm in the Netherlands.

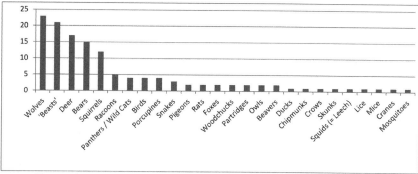

Fig. 7. Wild animals mentioned in the West Michigan memoirs

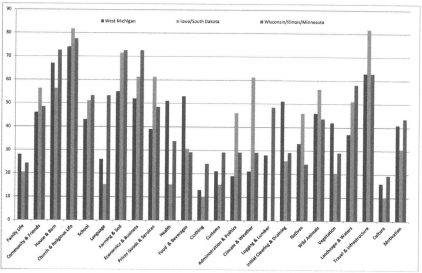

Fig. 8. Wild animals mentioned in the Iowa, South Dakota, memoirs

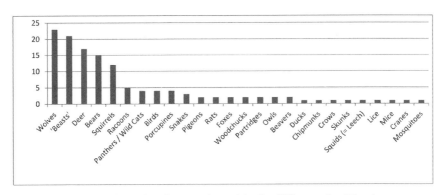

Fig. 9. Wild animals mentioned in the Wisconsin, Illinois, and Minnesota memoirs

The lists of wild animals reflect the differences in the natural environment. We meet the grasshoppers and the gophers on the prairies and the owls and beavers in the swampy forests. They are also related to differences in the settlers' activities. In Wisconsin one settler soon adopted the American leisure activities of hunting and fishing, so that we find some writing about small game. From the West Michigan memoirs, it appears that, there too, animals were indeed killed but for reasons of disinfestation. In the early years, settlers bought from or bartered with the natives for venison and "big fish," but given the enormous quantities of game and fish available at the time, the accounts of hunting and consumption of game are very sparse indeed. Working with firearms was a skill to be learned of course, and if there were any reports of stalking game, it was practically always deer.

The descriptive words used—especially in Dutch—tell us a great deal about how wildlife was perceived by the Dutch immigrants. Untamed nature must have inspired great awe among the immigrants, especially in the forests. Unfamiliar animals stole crops; there were encounters with predators, and during the night, there was the eerie hooting of owls and many other unfamiliar wildlife noises. For many, many years, this great variety of strange and generally unwelcome animals was therefore grouped together under the Old Testament heading of beasts (*wild gedierte*). We come across "evil beast" (*on-gedierte*), "harmful beast" (*schadelijk-gedierte*), and "gnawing beast" (*knaag-gedierte*). There was not a trace of tender feelings for them; they were unwanted; they devoured the crops and were regarded as a nuisance.

Memoirs are personal reminiscences; they were never intended to serve as early surveys of wildlife. In the West Michigan lists, there

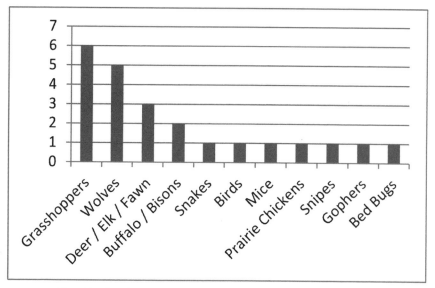

Fig. 10. Top five animals listed in memoirs from all areas

is no mention of fish, in spite of the fact that fish were abundant and were surely caught and eaten. But the Dutch did not traditionally fish for food; they had purchased their fish in the market in the Netherlands. Apparently, what the authors mention is what they had remembered after so many years and regarded as worth relating. The greater predators, however, must have inspired awe and terror in the hearts of the settlers, though there was little chance of meeting them face to face. Even the panther is mentioned, although in those days, this animal made only an extremely rare appearance in West Michigan. This applies to the bear also—but especially to the wolf. The wolf heads the list of the five animals mentioned most often. This legendary beast of prey appeals very strongly to the imagination; it is mentioned in memoirs from all three areas. Their presence and the tales about their appearance must have made a much deeper impression than the much greater number of deer or the numerous species of birds. Wolves tend to stir deep emotional responses that are hard to explain in terms of the actual very limited danger they pose to human life. In religion and literature, the wolf often serves as the symbol of evil.[14]

[14]   Some of the immigrants may have associated the animal with a defensive pamphlet written by the seceding minister Hendrik de Cock, saying "the sheepfold of Christ attacked by two wolves," referring to Matthew 7: "They come to you in sheep's clothes, but inwardly they are ravenous wolves." This pamphlet was, in fact, the overture to the 1834 Secession.

Qualitative

The memoirs are mostly unpolished texts with an authentic feel. In the translations of the quotations into English, some of this authenticity and idiosyncratic use of language is inevitably lost. There are traces of Old Testament idioms, and the style owes very much to the language of the seventeenth-century, Dutch Statenvertaling of the Bible. In addition to the use of quantitative analysis, it is important to listen to the pioneers themselves in their own words. Following are quotations from the memoirs. Some of these are in a translation that differs from Lucas's translation.[15] How did the authors write about wildlife, wilderness, and progress? What images did they use, and what implicit or explicit analogies did they employ?

Qualitative: wild animals

Coming from a country virtually devoid of woods and wildlife, the Dutch immigrants initially must have had considerable misgivings and fear in the dense and dark forests of West Michigan.[16] They were real pioneers, arriving in old growth forests. The towering trunks inspired great awe, and the settlers referred to these woodland giants in an Old Testament metaphor as "the children of Anak."[17]

In their description of wild animals, three things stand out. First, as has already been mentioned, the frequent use of "beasts" (*wild gedierte*) in various forms. Second, there are numerous passages describing the damage done to crops by animals. Third, the noises frightening the immigrants—howling wolves, for example, usually heard in the night and perceived as a besieging army. Hooting owls, often mentioned together with wolves, were also unnerving.

Engbertus van der Veen from Holland wrote about the sense of alienation experienced in the first few years of life in the woods:

---

[15]   The memoirs were written in either Dutch or English. If a quotation is given in English and Dutch, the Dutch is the original. We indicate in the note if the translation is our own.

[16]   Between 1750 and 1850, the percentage of forested area in the Netherlands was at an all-time low, between 2 and 3 percent.

[17]   See Van Schelven, Gerrit (1842-1927), papers, 1836-1958, 14 boxes, T88-0234, HMA, box 6, no. 100, Rev. Jac. Van der Meulen. In his account, Van der Meulen wrote: "wat men nog al eens noemde de Enachs kinderen" (what was frequently referred to as the children of Enak). "The children of Enak" are first mentioned in Numbers 13, where the twelve spies sent out by Moses report that the men of Canaan were taller and stronger than the Israelites, the sons of Anak dwelt in the land, and they felt like grasshoppers in their presence.

We could not see how dismal and fearful our surroundings were. The moaning sounds of the western pine, the night birds squawking and shrilly breaking into weird cries, the hooting of owls, and the croaking of a multitude of strange creatures made a painful impression on our family just arrived from Amsterdam and filled our hearts with dismay.[18]

Soon enough the settlers learned that bears should not be treated with indifference. Hendrik Freriks from Vriesland, Michigan, wrote:

The beasts have more than once destroyed almost all of our crops. Bears have often carried off our pigs out of the sty, and we have often helped one another in chasing off the bears.[19]

Bears stealing pigs from the sty is a recurring topic in the memoirs; it must have happened regularly. But toward humans, the bears seem to be more or less harmless. Engbertus van der Veen wrote: "On another occasion, when people who had been frightened met a bear, the latter quietly ambled away."[20] In many accounts, fear of wolves is more evident. Listen, for instance, to Henry Utterwick from Holland, who wrote about "the wives and the mothers in the often rude huts of those first settlements": "What fears would lay hold of them, when, alone with their little ones, they heard the wolves actually howling about their doors."[21]

Not surprisingly, there was no love lost for wolves. There was a bounty for every dead wolf. Mrs. H. Kleinheksel–Kronemeyer, who grew up in Fillmore, recalled this occasion:

One day my father and brothers went into the woods, and they found a litter of seven young wolves; they killed them, and took the heads to Isaac Fairbanks, Justice of the Peace, and there they were given a bounty of $18 a head.[22]

---

[18] Lucas, *Memoirs*, 1:490. Van der Veen's *Life Reminiscenses*. These reminiscences were published in pamphlet form. Lucas corrected the spelling.

[19] "Het wild gedierte heeft ons meer dan eens den oogst bijna geheel vernield. De beeren hebben ons dikwijls de varkens uit het hok gehaald en vaak hebben wij elkaar geholpen om de beeren te verdrijven." Lucas, *Memoirs*, 1:290; Boersema translation.

[20] Lucas, *Memoirs*, 1:494.

[21] Van Schelven Papers, box 4, no. 6, Rev. Henry Utterwick.

[22] "Op zekeren dag gingen vader en mijn broers het bosch in, en vonden daar een nest met zeven jonge wolven; die maakten zij dood, en de koppen brachten zij naar Isaac Fairbanks, Justice of the Peace, en daar kregen zij een bounty voor van $18 per stuk." Van Schelven Papers, box 5, no. 45, Mrs. H. Kleinheksel-Kronemeyer; Boersema translation.

Many species were after the pioneers' crops: deer, racoons, porcupines, and squirrels, among others. In some years, especially those with mild winters, the animals came in enormous numbers. Adriaan Keizer from Drenthe described a plague:

> In the summer and the fall of 1851, squirrels destroyed all the corn and potatoes. So great was the multitude of these destructive creatures [caused by the exceptionally mild winter which had preceded] that they invaded the houses and at times actually made away with the food placed on the tables. This again happened in 1854, with the result that some left the settlement.[23]

Reverend Jac. van der Meulen from Holland, describing the "first wrestling's" (*eerste worstelingen*) of the settlers, told us how in a log church in Zeeland, Psalm 68:31 was quoted in a prayer: "Lord, rebuke the beast."[24] Van der Meulen qualifies the use of that biblical phrase as very remarkable (*opzienbarend*), but according to him: "The timeliness of the prayer could not be denied."[25]

There are fewer memoirs from Wisconsin, Illinois, and Minnesota, but they cover a more extensive area. In most cases, Dutch immigrants were not the first white settlers. They followed the tracks of earlier pioneers and settled where trees had been felled and there was some cultivation, notably around Chicago and Milwaukee, Wisconsin. In the memoirs from these areas, we find a few animal species that were not mentioned in the memoirs in West Michigan, such as the prairie chicken, geese, and bison (which, according to the author, had already been "exterminated").[26]

The abundance of wildlife must have been overwhelming. According to Harry Eenigenburg from Roseland and South Holland, "This area was frequently referred to as the "Garden of Eden" because of its abundance of wild animals and birds."[27] It is no wonder that settlers soon turned to hunting and fishing, the more so because, as Arnold Verstegen from Little Chute, Wisconsin, noted: "There are no game

---

[23]   Lucas, *Memoirs*, 1:261.
[24]   "Heere, scheld het wild gedierte." Van Schelven Papers, box 6, no. 100, Rev. J. van der Meulen; Boersema translation; in Psalm 68:31 (Staten Vertaling), we read: "Scheld het wild gedierte des riets" (KJV: "Rebuke the beasts of the reeds").
[25]   Van Schelven Papers, box 6, no. 100, Rev. J. van der Meulen; Boersema translation.
[26]   C. A. Verwijst from Hollandtown, Wisconsin, in his "Reminiscenses of a Pioneer Missionary," Lucas, *Memoirs*, 2:179.
[27]   Lucas, *Memoirs*, 2:50.

laws; you can go fishing and hunting whenever you please. There is plenty of game, big and small, in the woods; the rivers are full of fish."[28]

In spite of bears stealing pigs from sties and wolves assaulting cattle, there seems to have been some peace and quiet at night. These are Henry Harmeling's words, written in Cedar Grove, Wisconsin: "All had a good night's rest—notwithstanding the occasional yelp of wolves, which infested the forests of those early days, and the terrifying and fearsome hoot of screech owls."[29]

Landscapes in Iowa were a more pleasant experience. The Dutch appreciated the endless, seemingly infinite rolling prairies, even though the grass was shoulder high, and it was easy to completely lose one's way. Most thoughts on nature came from memoirs in the more westerly colonies. The immigrants came across the typical prairie animals: prairie wolves, snakes, gophers, and prairie chickens. In D. Gleysteen's reminiscences from Sioux Center, Iowa, we read: "Wolves were quite common, and though I never heard of any damage done by them, they were soon exterminated."[30]

Iowa's climate is that of very hot summers and severe winters with heavy blizzards. In the dry periods of the year, fierce prairie blazes would spread far and wide, and houses and human lives were lost. Snowstorms sometimes went on for days on end and also took human lives. The greatest enemy in the early days was undoubtedly the plague of locusts. They were frequent and unwelcome visitors as A. J. Betten reports in his history of Sioux County: "But this month a winged army of eaters descended on the fields. They were grasshoppers . . . Mere Man is powerless against these hosts."[31]

Joe Rexwinkel portraying pioneer days in Nassau Township, Sioux County, Iowa, noted:

> Experiences of the early settlers were varied, although they had one thing in common, they were all poor, poor in money when we came and poorer still when the grasshoppers came; for a few years, it surely was a trying time, especially the years 1874 to 1878.[32]

---

[28]   Ibid., 158.
[29]   Ibid., 110.
[30]   Ibid., 247.
[31]   "Doch in deze maand daalt er een gevleugeld leger opeters op den akker neder. Het zijn sprinkhanen . . . De mensch vermag niets tegen dit heir." Ibid., 210; Boersema translation.
[32]   Ibid., 251.

Locusts had struck terror into the hearts of the immigrants. Many years later, when descendants of the Orange City immigrants performed a pageant about the pioneer years, the actor playing the role of the real pioneer Jelle Pelmulder addressed the hopping locusts:

> You fright us, Spirit of the Wilderness,
> But show us naught we knew not of before.
> We are not strangers to thy power to hurt.
> By Faith and industry, we'll thwart thee still.[33]

Qualitative: on progress

The Dutch immigrants witnessed the major changes that took place in North America during the nineteenth century. They also contributed to them and experienced the rapid transformation of their own environment. Their memoirs commonly reflect on these changes, usually in a favourable way. The introduction of machinery in agriculture and the reclamation of waste land were welcome and so were modern means of transportation and a new infrastructure. There was great gratitude for increased wealth and education, which led to social emancipation. At the same time, some authors expressed concern about the loss of sobriety and strictness in religious observation. The growing popularity of the saloon was seen as a negative development, bringing anything but progress.

Progress was closely connected with the protestant worldview. In the words of Reverend Henry Utterwick from Holland: "Calvinism, freedom, progress—these three words were read on many a page of modern history."[34] The products of technological change were very succinctly summarized by Harrie Eenigenburg of Calumet, Wisconsin, and Roseland, Illinois. Change had accelerated and become commonplace:

> I have lived through the above-mentioned pioneer days, have seen all the new inventions such as telegraph, locomotive, harvesting selfbinder, moving picture, telephone, bicycle, automobile, airplane, potato digger, cornhusker, haybailer, grain thrasher, linotype, printing, and a thousand others. We see something new every day and without any surprise.[35]

33　Andrew J. Kolyn, *Golden Jubilee Pageant*, held at Orange City, Iowa, 30 September 1920, 3rd act, Jelle Pelmulder.

34　Van Schelven Papers, box 4, no. 6., Rev. Henry Utterwick.

35　Lucas, *Memoirs*, 2:60.

Although these technological innovations were welcomed by the settlers, there was certainly much discussion about their consequences for farm life and the community, but on balance, there was appreciation and thankfulness for material progress. It was perceived as a blessing of the Most High. This comes across in a number of ways. Anna C. Post from Holland wrote "And now, the wilderness has been made to blossom like the rose and a change has been wrought which at first seemed impossible."[36] And from D. Broek from Holland: "We have grown ever since, in numbers and material wealth, as well as in knowledge, science, and development; in nearly all fields, we have seen progress."[37]

In the writings of C. A. Verwijst, from Hollandtown, Wisconsin, we can hear wholesale rejection of the wilderness and wildlife:

> Thus primitive Wisconsin developed into one of the most prosperous states of the Union. . . . The German, Dutch, and Irish immigrants dug our canals, built our railroads, cleared our forests, and made a paradise of what was but a few years before a dreary wilderness, the habitation of uncivilized Indians and of wild animals.[38]

Were the Dutch settlers aware of the gradual disappearance of this unique landscape? Just witness the outpouring of Stephen J. Harmeling, from Marion, South Dakota:

> In 1879 the great railroad systems began to push their lines westwards into the Great Western Desert, as that region was named in our early geographies. It was discovered that this region was no desert at all, but a fertile rolling prairie on which millions of bison grazed throughout the year.[39]

But the predominant feeling and belief was that the changes should be viewed as a good thing not only because they had created more wealth but also because the wilderness had been converted into fertile land and the desert into a blossoming garden. This was a blessing, a fulfilment of the Old Testament prophesy that the desert shall blossom as the rose.[40] James De Pree, from West Branch Township, Iowa, wrote:

---

[36] Ibid., 1:404.
[37] "Wij zijn sedert dien gegroeid in getallen en stoffelijke welvaart, in kennis, wetenschap en ontwikkeling; bijna op elk gebied zijn wij vooruitgegaan." Van Schelven Papers, box 6, no. 82, Rev. D. Broek; Boersema translation.
[38] Lucas, *Memoirs*, 2:184.
[39] Ibid., 339.
[40] Isaiah 35:1.

And in His own good time [God] bestowed upon them His richest blessings . . . these once bleak praries [*sic*] have been converted into a veritable garden spot and from the abode and haunts of wild animals into the heritage of thrifty and prosperous tillers of the soil.[41]

Rev. A. A. Pfanstiehl from Chicago described the character of church members in his address, "Lessons from Colonial Life and Times," held at the semicentennial celebration, September 1897:

Their staunch religious character . . . was the great motive power in their indefatigable labors that have made this wilderness to blossom as a rose, has transformed these wild forests into fertile fields, has caused the sound of factory whistle to take the place of fierce shrieks of wild beasts, and has turned their haunts into beautiful human habitations.[42]

In the poetical memoirs of Diekema and Borgers, we can recognize the same thrust as the Newhouse trap advertisement but now with Biblical phrasings, in which the piano is replaced by the Psalms. G. J. Diekema from Holland wrote:

What mighty changes our eyes behold—forests and swamps have given way to fields and gardens, to the flowers of summer and the waving and golden harvests of autumn, the log cabin to the palatial dwelling, the little corner store to the stone front business block, and the small mill by the side of the stream to the great factories teeming with human life and humming with human industry.

The wild deer, the wolf, and the bear have made room for herds and flocks that graze over a thousand hills along a thousand valleys.[43]

And Herman Borgers from Greenleafton, Minnesota, wrote:

The desert blossoms like a rose, the wild grasses and heavy sod have vanished, made room for beautiful gardens and golden grain, where a few years ago, the buffalo, fox, wild cat, skunk, and other animals roamed freely. The psalm of praise [he cited Psalm 84:1 in Dutch] has supplanted the call of wild beasts.[44]

---

[41]   Lucas, *Memoirs*, 2:243.
[42]   Van Schelven Papers, box 6, no. 81, Rev. A. A. Pfanstiehl.
[43]   Ibid., no. 86, Hon. G. J. Diekema.
[44]   Lucas, *Memoirs*, 2:200.

These pioneers were earnest, energetic souls. With a determined will and fixed purpose they came, with God's help, to build homes for themselves and their families, to induce the wild, naked prairie to bring forth its hidden treasures in response to diligent and intelligent farming.[45]

It is in this spirit that both these immigrants had fulfilled their aspirations, and the land had come to full fruition.

Discussion

The overall picture of the Dutch immigrants and their environmental surroundings that emerges from the above quantitative tables and from the quotations looks familiar and is recognizable and consistent. The immigrants were "earnest, energetic souls" who worked hard and skilfully; they broke new land and embraced new technologies and science. They believed they were blessed because the wilderness was either gradually tamed or completely replaced by waving wheat, colourful flower beds, and bustling towns. We may therefore assume that the picture painted here is a representative one, although the memoirs were written by a relatively limited number of people. They were farmers who saw nature primarily through the pragmatic glasses of tiller of the soil and entrepreneur. Some letters written on the way to America already speculated about the fertility of the soil and its suitability for agriculture.

There are no indications that, in the first few decades, the immigrants felt inspired by discussions in American public life on subjects like "manifest destiny." Neither is there any indication from the memoirs that the Dutch were familiar with John Gast's painting or whether they identified with that particular philosophy of American progress. It is not inconceivable that the magazines they read discussed these views. But it is quite clear from the quotations that in their comings and goings the Dutch immigrants fit into the general framework briefly described up front. Interestingly, the memoirs prove that, in many respects, this was also the way they felt about it themselves.

Rolling back the wilderness was not only a necessary condition for carving out an existence, the process itself was also a symptom of progress and civilization per se. This view was widely held in the western world shaped by Christianity, and it thrived on both Old Testament and Greek philosophical traditions.[46] The rise of industrialization in the

---

[45]   Ibid., 198.
[46]   Boersema, *The Torah and the Stoics*, chs. 4 and 5.

nineteenth century created new means and necessities for embarking on an energetic process of "rolling back and civilizing the wilderness" not only in the Old World, first of all in England[47] and in Germany[48] but also, after Lewis and Clark, in the New World: the virgin territories of North America.[49]

The fight against the wilderness also meant a fight against the "savages" (see C. A. Verwijst's quote). In the memoirs, this causal connection is implied, but the writers rarely mention any serious clashes with the natives. It is clear, however, that the natives were to leave; their way of life could not be maintained since their biotope was vanishing. And the authors did not really question this development. Initially, they may have imagined that there was Lebensraum farther west, but later some justification had to be used.

In the Orange City pageant of 1920 mentioned above, the descendents of Dutch pioneers found an "elegant" solution. In their play, a wise Sioux medicine man is given the following passage with which he addresses the belligerent chief Okoboji:

> While ye bravely fought to westward
> I a journey took to eastward—
> There I saw a covered wagon
> Carrying four paleface strangers.
> Coming slowly westward, westward.
> Over hills and through the rivers.
> Gitchie Manitou the Mighty
> In a vision bade me greet them,
> And he bade me treat them kindly.
> All these rolling hills and valleys
> Which your eyes delight to feast on
> Are decreed to be their portion.
> They will plow and they will till it.
> All these lands will feed the hungry
> Of all nations, climes and peoples.
> We must follow the Dakotahs,
> We must westward take our journey.[50]

[47] Jeremy Pursglove, *Taming the Flood. A History and Natural History of Rivers and Wetlands* (Oxford: Oxford University Press, 1989).

[48] David Blackbourn, *The Conquest of Nature: Water, Landscape, and the Making of Modern Germany* (London: Jonathan Cape, 2006).

[49] Daniel W. Howe, *What Hath God Wrought? The Transformation of America, 1815-1848* (Oxford: Oxford University Press, 2007).

[50] Kolyn, *Golden Jubilee Pageant*, Act Two, *Medicine Man*.

CHAPTER 3

Flexibility or Fixed Idea: The Dort Church Order of 1619 as a Cultural Import in America

Leon van den Broeke

Introduction

After the death of Willem Lupardus (1669-1702), the members of four congregations on Long Island began looking for a new pastor.[1] The appointment of Lupardus' successor, Bernardus Freeman (1662-1743), became a legal issue from a church polity point of view.

The case is complicated and deserves more attention than can be provided here. My focus is the use of and the references to the church order in a letter of protest of 15 February, 1706. Herein, the elders of three consistories on Long Island opposed Freeman's ministry on Long Island. Freeman had secured this ministry with the consent of the English governor but without that of the Classis of Amsterdam.[2] Wanting to teach Freeman a lesson in church polity, the elders referred

[1]   I would like to express my gratitude to my friend and colleague, Allan J. Janssen, for his help with my English.
[2]   Sage Library, New Brunswick, NJ, Amsterdam Correspondence (SLAC), letter of the consistory of the joint congregations of Vlakbosch, Breukelen, and Nieuw Amersfoort to Freeman, 15 February 1706, 345-48; Huge Hastings, ed., *Ecclesiastical Records State of New York* (*ERNY*) (Albany: J. B. Lyon Company, 1902), 3:1625.

not only to the Dort Church Order of 1619 but also to its sixteenth-century predecessors. The case raises questions about the validity, heritage, and Americanization or modernization of the Dort Church Order of 1619 and of its predecessors, in Dutch immigrant churches in New Netherland, the Middle Colonies, the US Eastern Seaboard, and the Midwest from the seventeenth to the twentieth centuries. The Synods of Emden (1571), Dordrecht (1574 and 1578), Middelburg (1581), and The Hague (1586) together constitute the legal precedents of the Dort Church Order of 1619.

This article seeks not only to clarify which church order was valid during these centuries but also to consider, as in the case with Freeman, whether a Dutch church order was applicable in new contexts. The article focuses on the general question of whether the Dort Church Order of 1619 was an "import article" and could be implemented in a new environment, a sort of "copy and paste" Reformed ecclesiology and church polity from the fatherland to overseas contexts. This includes an investigation of the legitimacy of this church order in the homeland in order to understand the background of its position in the church in the United States of America. Although the members of Dutch Reformed churches were British citizens after 1664, ecclesiastically, they still belonged to this church. From a public church in the Dutch colony, the Reformed church became an ethnic minority church under the supervision of the Classis of Amsterdam and the provincial synod of Holland, as far as church polity was concerned. That required finding a balance between Dutch heritage and Anglicization, later, Americanization.

The Freeman case

On behalf of their members, the joint consistory of the Dutch Reformed congregations of Breuckelen (Brooklyn), Vlakbosch or Midwout (Flatbush), Nieuw Amersfoort (Flatlands), and Nieuw Utrecht (New Utrecht) on Long Island requested the governor of New York and New Jersey, Edward Hyde (1661-1723)—Lord Cornbury—to approve the call of Freeman.

At that time, Freeman was on the payroll of the English government for a mission among the Mohawks, and he was pastor of the Schenectady Dutch Reformed congregation. Because Freeman was not appointed by the West Indies Company, they did not pay his salary. Therefore, the members of the congregation(s) on Long Island had to pay it. According to the church order, the consistory also needed the approval from the Classis of Amsterdam for calling a new minister.

(The classis is the Reformed "bishop."[3]) The classis is the board in a region composed of elders and ministers who are delegated by their consistories. Since 1636 this classis had been responsible for the overseas congregations. The fact that American congregations, although governed by this classis, had no representation at its meetings, did make a difference. The consistories of these congregations could not appoint a pastor or an elder to visit the meetings of the Classis of Amsterdam. So they did not have a voice in these meetings. It also explains why a British and Anglican governor played an important and confusing role in these Dutch Reformed congregations. He did not abide by the rule that a Dutch Reformed congregation in a British colony should be allowed to be governed by a Dutch ecclesiastical assembly.

The consistory of the Schenectady congregation did not want to give Freeman his certificate of discharge, a regular procedure according to the church order. It read the call of the consistories of Long Island and noticed that they did not want to pay enough salary to Freeman, that they did not pay the expenses incurred by Freeman's voyage to the German territories for his ordination by the Lingen Classis, and that Freeman had refused to obey and submit to the Classis of Amsterdam. The Schenectady consistory called Freeman again (with better terms!) because he had already preached his farewell sermon. It did agree that as soon as the consistories of Long Island would pay the same salary and offer the same terms, then it would grant Freeman a certificate of discharge. Freeman asked the consistories on Long Island to call him again, this time with improved terms. They declined his request and wrote the Classis of Amsterdam to send a new minister. Four months before the new minister, Vincentius Antonides (1670-1744), arrived, Freeman was married on Long Island. Antonides had been pastor in Burgum, the Netherlands, from 1693 to 1705.[4] Freeman's bride was not willing to join him in Schenectady; Freeman insisted that he had been legally called by the four congregations on Long Island. Therefore, when he received the call from the consistory of New Utrecht on 21 September 1705, he accepted it.

Later Lord Cornbury dropped his objections against Freeman. On December 26, 1705, he provided Freeman with a license stating that he was the pastor at Nieuw Utrecht, Vlackbosch, Breuckelen, and Boswijck.

---

3   C. (Leon) van den Broeke, *Een geschiedenis van de classis: Classicale typen tussen idee en werkelijkheid 1571-2004* (Kampen: Kok, 2005).

4   Russell Gasero, *Historical Directory of the Reformed Church in America 1628-2000* (Grand Rapids, MI: Eerdmans, 2001), 8.

This was only five days before Antonides, the new, legally appointed, pastor from the Classis of Amsterdam, reached New York City.[5] In this way, Cornbury tried to control the Dutch Reformed congregations in the British colony. In the end, only the consistory of New Utrecht called Freeman but without the permission of Classis Amsterdam. Also the greater consistory of these three congregations considered the ministry of Freeman unlawful, because he was called only by the consistory of New Utrecht and without the consent of Classis Amsterdam. Freeman preached twice on Sunday in New Utrecht and now and then in Boswijck (Bushwick), and he admonished the greater consistory to open the door for him.

On December 11, 1703, the greater consistory had requested the Classis of Amsterdam to call a new pastor. As soon as he reached the shore, on January 1, 1706, Antonides paid a visit to Cornbury. The governor, however, did not want to receive him. He believed there were already enough Dutch pastors. Antonides became the pastor of the other three congregations until 1744, the year he died. He was legally appointed by the classis. The greater consistory observed that the license provided by Cornbury to Freeman made him feel justified to take advantage of his power. Freeman organized elections for the offices of elder and deacon on his own. Although the consistory and congregants objected, Freeman ignored their protest. He was about to install the new elders and deacons, but Cornbury interfered and thwarted his initiative. Freeman feared that if he proceeded, he would lose the support of Cornbury.[6]

Antonides and the greater consistory had written an ecclesiastical protest against Freeman about what they regarded as an illegal election organized by Freeman. Their letter of February 15, 1706, included five objections from the perspective of Reformed church polity, with many references to the Dort Church Order of 1619 and its predecessors.[7] First, they held that Freeman was imposed upon

---

[5]   SLAC, *Historisch verhaal van saken voorgevallen in onse gemeente zedert den dood van D. Lupardus betreffende de beroepinge van een predikant* [Historical account of what occurred in our congregation, concerning the call of a Minister] (22 April 1706), 333. See also, *ERNY* 3:1607, and 1639-45.

[6]   SLAC, letter of Lord Cornbury to Bernardus Freeman (16 February 1706), 349; *ERNY* 3:1630.

[7]   SLAC, letter of the consistory of the joint congregations of Vlakbosch, Breukelen, and Nieuw Amersfoort to Freeman (15 February 1706), 345-48; *ERNY* 3:1625. The consistory of Vlakbosch had already written a letter of protest to him one day earlier; SLAC, letter of the consistory of Vlakbosch to Freeman (14 February 1706), 344; *ERNY* 3:1623.

the congregation, which, according to the Bible, is creating discord. Second, Freeman held elections for office bearers without the consent of the consistory, who considered his planned ordination of these newly elected elders and deacons illegal. A third objection was that such actions could result only in discord and disunity. The consistory asked Freeman if he intended to create a church within a church; this was illegal. Fourth, the consistory considered Freeman foolish if he thought that there was no consistory in place. They wrote that the elders and deacons were ordained for a period of two years. The church order, however, allowed that circumstances could change this term. Fifth, it offended the consistory that the governor's license made Freeman arrogant enough to ignore them and to use it to prove that he was the legal pastor on Long Island with the governor's approval. It was normal to have a kind of ecclesiastical license, extraordinary perhaps in this context, but understandable since the members and pastors of the Dutch Reformed Church were British subjects.

This sad story lasted for more than thirteen years, but it had a happy ending. In 1714, at a convention of delegates, the various congregations on Long Island agreed to set aside their differences on who was their legally appointed pastor; they accepted both Antonides and Freeman. Moreover, both ministers learned to work with each other in a dual ministry.

The validity of the Dort Church Order of 1619

The letters referenced show that the greater consistory applied not only the Dort Church Order of 1619 but also articles of its sixteenth-century predecessors, making clear that the American congregations sought to obey the Dort Church Order of 1619 *and* its predecessors. If the Dort order had been the most recent church order, it would have sufficed to use just that order, but the matter was more complicated than that. To learn more, we need to look at the Amsterdam Classis, as part of the Provincial Synod of Holland.

Officially, the States-General, the political assembly of all the provinces, never approved this Dort church order. In 1885, however, Frederik Lodewijk Rutgers (1836-1917), professor of church history and church polity at the Vrije Universiteit Amsterdam, deferred on this point to Gisbertius Voetius (1589-1676), who had been professor in Utrecht.[8] Voetius had concluded that the political authorities had

---

[8]   F. L. Rutgers, ed., *Gisberti Voetii Tractatus Selecti De Politica Ecclesiastica* pars 1, lib. 1, tract. 2, cap. 11, par. 4 (Amstelodami: J. H. Kruyt, 1885), 243.

indirectly approved this order. The churches maintained it *de facto*, while the political authorities did not prohibit it, even without political approval in some provinces. Also, the three Reformed confessions, the Three Forms of Unity—the Belgic Confession of 1561, the Heidelberg Catechism of 1563, and the Canons of Dort of 1619—were all approved by all the political authorities in the provinces. This implied, thought Rutgers, that they also approved the Reformed system of church polity which was assumed in these documents, despite lacking express political approbation.

In 1889 Rutgers stated that the decisions of the above-mentioned general synods could not be regarded separately; together, they made one corpus.[9] They did not develop one single church order but built upon the decisions of their predecessor(s). Therefore, Rutgers did not speak of one church order or of church orders (plural) but of the old church order in general.

Officially, the Particular Synod of Holland, to which the Classis of Amsterdam belonged, did not approve of the Dort Church Order of 1619, but there was no valid regional church order either. The provincial political authorities also did not expressly approve the Dort Church Order of 1619. In the end, they stopped imposing a political church order onto their provinces and decided in 1624 that the status quo in each classis could be continued. In practice, this meant using the Dort Church Order of 1619.[10] In 1626 this resulted in the decision of the Particular Synod of IJsselstein (South Holland) to stop the efforts of getting the approval of the provincial authorities and to obey the decisions included in the Dort Synod of 1618-19; this maintained the Dort Church Order of 1619. In short, the Classis of Amsterdam, in its responsibility for the overseas congregations, obeyed the Dort Church Order of 1619, and that implied that the earlier church orders were also in force as Rutgers asserted.

Seventeenth and eighteenth centuries

Even after 1664, both the Classis of Amsterdam and the American congregations followed the Dort Church Order of 1619 and its sixteenth-century predecessors. By the Articles of Capitulation and the Duke's Laws of 1665, affirmed later by the Charter of 1696, the

---

[9]   F. L. Rutgers, *De geldigheid van de oude Kerkenordening der Nederlandsche gereformeerde kerken. Met aantekeningen en aktenstukken* (Amsterdam: Ton Bolland, 1971; reprint Amsterdam: J. A. Wormser, 1890).

[10]   Art. 38 Acts of the South Holland Synod 's-Gravenhage, July 1624; ibid., 103.

British granted the Dutch Reformed population freedom of worship and religious toleration. The liberty of worship was, in the words of the Charter of the Reformed Protestant Dutch Church of New York in 1696, "according to the constitutions and direccons of the reformed Churches in Holland, approved and instituted by the nationall Synod of Dort."[11] It did not expressly name, but implied, the Dort Church Order of 1696. Later on, in the eighteenth century, during the road to and struggle for independence from Britain, the validity of the Dort Church Order of 1619 was questioned by the Dutch Reformed churches. This was related to the primary issue of ecclesiastical independence from the Netherlands.

The Plan of Union of 1771, a union convention hosted by the New York consistory, resolved "to adhere in all things, to the constitution of the Netherlands Reformed Church, as the same was established in the church orders of the Synod of Dordrecht . . . 1618 and 1619."[12] The history of Reformed Church polity from 1771 through 1792 is an expression of changing political and ecclesiastical contexts. From the 1740s on, the church suffered from divisions between the pro-Dutch party (Conferentie) and the pro-American party (Coetus). The issue centered on the education and ordination of ministers for the American congregations. The Conference wing wanted candidates for the ministry to be educated and ordained by the Classis Assembly of Amsterdam. The Coetus wing declared independence from this classis and committed itself to an American classis assembly within the Particular Synod of Holland. This situation remained unresolved until 1771 when John H. Livingston organized the Union convention.

The above-mentioned section of the 1771 Union Convention document mentions church orders (plural) of the Synod of Dordrecht instead of church order. This quotation made it clear what the union was about, bringing Coetus and Conferentie together in an independent church. In January 1772, the Classis Assembly of Amsterdam approved the Plan of Union. The Second Union Convention in June 1772 approved the long-sought-for rights of education and ordination and ruled that the church was allowed to organize itself into a general assembly and several particular assemblies. Due to the Revolutionary War (1775-83), the General Assembly was able to make a start on the implementation of the 1771 Plan of Union only in 1785. The General Synod of 1788 at

---

[11] http://www.upword.com/collegiate/charter.html (accessed 16 October 2015).
[12] Daniel J. Meeter, *Meeting Each Other: In Doctrine, Liturgy & Government* (Grand Rapids: Eerdmans, 1993); *ENRY* 6:4212.

New York, of what was now the Reformed Dutch Protestant Church, decided to translate into English the Articles of Church Government of the National Synod, held at Dordrecht, in 1618 and 1619:

> Which, being accompanied by such articles taken from the proceedings of this Rev. Body as have particular reference to the circumstances of the Church in this country, will exhibit the true nature and form of government of our Dutch churches in America.[13]

This shows the determination to continue adherence to the Dort Church Order of 1619, albeit in an English translation. In 1790 the committee reported that:

1. The distinct translation of the articles of Church Order of the Rev. Synod of Dordrecht . . . and of the Plan of Union adopted 1772 . . . be referred to a committee, who shall carefully compare the same with the original Dutch, and alter and amend all such English words and phrases as either are not pure or do not actually and appropriately express the true and literal meaning.
2. The same committee likewise prepare some observations upon the articles of Church Order, to be incorporated among them, in which the proper sense and meaning of them, if necessary, shall be briefly declared, or sufficient reasons be assigned why some articles are not inserted or cannot be carried out in our American churches.
3. If necessary . . . the same shall be issued in full or in part, and in what language, or whether both in Dutch and English, for the special benefit of our congregations.[14]

Some regulations were neither clear nor applicable in a new American context about 170 years later. The sources do not reveal which regulations were in question. A telling example, however, is the omission of the political authority ("magistrate") (part of the Dutch context) from the English-language version of the Dort Church Order of 1619. Due to the changed political context, the American Dutch Reformed church became independent from the mother church in the

---

[13]   *The Acts and Proceedings of the General Synod of the Reformed Protestant Dutch Church in North America, vol. 1: Embracing the Period from 1771 to 1812, Preceded by the Minutes of the Coetus (1738-1754), and the Proceedings of the Conferentie (1755-1767), and Followed by the Minutes of the Original Particular Synod (1794-1799)* (New York: 1859), 185.
[14]   Ibid., 210-11.

Netherlands. Therefore, the preface of the *Explanatory Articles of 1793* could state:

> Whatever relates to the immediate authority and interposition of the magistrates in the government of the Church, and which is introduced, more or less, into all the national establishments in Europe, is intirely [*sic*] omitted in the constitution now published.[15]

Apparently, the brethren did not consider this church order to be a petrifaction. At the special session of the general synod in 1791, a committee was appointed:

> To specify the subjects to be included in the Constitution of the Reformed Dutch churches of America, to be issued in accordance with the intentions of Synod, report, that after mature deliberation, it appears to them that such publication should be entirely restricted to what constitutes the Doctrine, Liturgy, and Government of said churches, that it may not only not form an unnecessarily large volume but also not perplex the English reader by the introduction of anything that does not essentially pertain to our ecclesiastical regulations.[16]

The constitution included not only government but also doctrine and liturgy. The report to the synod of 1791 also suggested that the Church Order and the Plan of Union be completely recast as a new church order adapted to North America. The synod wholly accepted the report of the committee. It requested the committee "to frame a draft of Church Government and Discipline, agreeably to the principles stated in the report." At the October meeting, half a year later, the committee submitted its draft, prepared by Livingston. The special session of the synod in 1792 charged another with the revision of the draft, article by article. Its report demonstrated a new, more conservative development. Although it would be accompanied by a number of "explanatory articles," the Dort Church Order of 1619 would be maintained:

> Not only was the translation of said articles *Syn. Nationis* completed, but in part, also, the draft of the explanatory articles; and *Deo volente*, they would be ready to be presented for approval at the next Synod in October.[17]

---

15   Meeter, *Meeting*, 50.
16   Ibid., 217-18.
17   Ibid., 14.

Finally, the draft of the Explanatory Articles was presented in October 1792 and adopted by the general synod, which requested that the constitution be published.[18]

Revisions were made in 1833, 1874, 1916, 1959, and 1968.[19] In 1868 the whole constitution was published in Dutch. This was a special request of the Classis of Holland, Michigan, that joined the denomination in 1850. It demonstrates not only the fact that not every immigrant knew English well but also the strong connection with the Dutch church. The current *Book of Church Order* (2015) does not contain the same chapters as the Dort Church Order of 1619:

Dort Church Order of 1619	Book of Church Order of 2015
1. The Offices	1. Government
2. The Assemblies	2. The Disciplinary and Judicial Procedures
3. The Doctrine, the Sacraments, and other Ceremonies	3. The Bylaws and Special Rules of Order
4. The Admonition and Discipline	4. Appendix: The Formularies

According to the minister of the Old First Reformed Church in Brooklyn, New York, Daniel Meeter:

> The Government is a far cry from the Rules of Dort, having gone through five major revisions and being now constantly, sometimes too hastily, revised. . . . The double purposes of preservation and change have continued to be at work, although during the last few decades, it would seem that change has had the upper hand.[20]

Meeter, however, is optimistic: "May the constitution help the Reformed church to answer the questions it faces now no less than it did two hundred years ago."[21] Allan J. Janssen agrees partially with Meeter that the *Book of Church Order* of the Reformed Church in America (RCA) is a large departure from Dort. In 1867 the Reformed Church in America became the new name of the Reformed Protestant Dutch Church. Indeed, the *Book of Church Order* of the RCA is not, as the Dort Church Order of 1619, organized around assemblies and offices. It does

---

[18]   *The Constitution of the Reformed Dutch Church in the United States of America* (New York: William Durell, 1793).
[19]   Meeter, *Meeting*, 150.
[20]   Ibid., 155.
[21]   Ibid., 191.

not have the connections to the political authorities who had authority in ecclesiastical affairs according to the Dort Church Order of 1619. It also does not include "customs and usages," and it faces constant revisions (nowadays the RCA has preaching elders and commissioned pastors).[22] By "customs and usages," Janssen meant the section of the Dort Church Order of 1619 which included directions on such matters as the celebration of the sacraments, the provision of what could be sung in public worship, visitation by elders and deacons, the nature of funeral sermons, provisions for days of fasting and prayer, and marriage.[23] On the other hand, Janssen pointed out that the government of the RCA does have classes and offices which remain fundamentally Dortian.

I only can relate a few examples of the differences between the 1619 Dort and the RCA Church Orders. First, due to much greater geographical distance in the United States, the classis assembly in the Reformed Church in America should convene at least annually, not every three or four months as in the Dort Church Order of 1619 (art. 4, Sessions of Classis, sec. 1).[24] Second, art. 6, Transaction of Business, sec. 4, is relatively new. Since 1994, persons other than office-bearers may serve on bodies responsible to the classis. Janssen clarifies: "It was maintained that gifts for the ministry are not limited to those ordained to office."[25] Third, associates in ministry (art. 6, Transaction of Business, sec. 5), became a new category in the church order that same year. They are "Christian educators who meet certain criteria established by the church and certified by the classis."[26] Although they are not officers and also not members of the classis, they are granted the right to speak and contribute to the ministry of the church. They are not, however, allowed to participate in decisions by their vote. Fourth, in 1979, the RCA made a judicial ruling to allow women to be ordained to the office of minister. In 1980 it added a "conscience clause" to the Book of Church Order (art. 5, Responsibilities of the Board of Elders, sec. 2h). It means that the consistory "shall not penalize nor permit to be penalized any member for conscientious objection to or support of the ordination of women to church offices."[27] At the same time, it meant: "nor shall it permit any member to obstruct by unconstitutional means the

---

[22] Email with Allan J. Janssen, 30 May 2016.
[23] Allan J. Janssen, *Constitutional Theology: Notes on the Book of Church Order of the Reformed Church in America* (Grand Rapids: Eerdmans, 2000), 12.
[24] Ibid., 114.
[25] Ibid., 120.
[26] Ibid., 120.
[27] Ibid., 86.

election, ordination, or installation of women to church offices" (art. 5, sec. 2h).[28] Last, the Dort Church Order of 1619 attributed the authority to examine candidates for the ministry to the particular synods. This power was shared with the classis (Explanatory Articles 47). The RCA Constitution of 1833 dropped this power, but a delegate from synod had to represent the synod at these examinations. In 1874 this rule was also dropped. It meant that the classis is the body that admits persons to the pulpit (art. 2, Responsibilities of the Classis, sec. 8).

Except for much greater geographical distances influencing the frequency of general synod meetings, most of the changes were responses to the modernization of the church rather than to the new American context. Similar changes have been enacted in the Reformed churches in the Netherlands.

The Seceders in the Midwest

The Dutch immigrants who moved to the Midwest after 1846 worked hard for a Dort foundation for their congregations. They had left the homeland where both the political and ecclesiastical contexts had changed considerably after 1619. Moreover, they had been persecuted by the authorities. In 1816 King Willem I had authorized a new church order for the Dutch Reformed Church in the new Kingdom of the Netherlands. Alongside a centralized state, the king created a national church with one church order with central authority. One of the results of the opposition to these changes was the Secession in 1834 from the state church. The Seceders longed for Dort and for a church following the Reformed confessions of the sixteenth and seventeenth centuries. They implemented the Dort Church Order of 1619. For two decades, however, the Seceders struggled with adopting this church order, a disagreement between adaptation and heritage. In 1854 the synod of the Seceder Churches decided not to revise the 1619 church order.[29] Some had wanted more flexibility, while others had wanted to implement it in its entirety, without any change.

An example of those wanting more flexibility was the group of H. P. Scholte (1805-1868), whose Utrecht Church Order of 1837 was not accepted. Apart from some minor changes, for example, clarity about

---

[28]   Ibid.

[29]   Art. 8. Handelingen Synode Zwolle 1854; *Handelingen en Verslagen van de Algemene Synoden van de Christelijk Afgescheidene Gereformeerde Kerk (1836-1869)* (Houten/ Utrecht, Den Hertog, 1984), 627; Van den Broeke, *Een geschiedenis*, 210-13.

who appointed the delegates to the particular synod, five new dogmatic articles, and eight other new articles were added to this church order. In 1841 the Seceder synod published the *Kerkelijke handboekje* which, just like its eighteenth-century predecessors, contained the synodical acts/ church orders of the five, sixteenth-century synods mentioned above.[30] The preface stated that the synod would retain the Dort Church Order of 1619 as the one and only rule of Reformed church polity.[31] At issue was not so much the validity of all the sixteenth- and seventeenth-century church orders as one corpus, as Rutgers had argued (see above), but rather, only the Dort Church Order of 1619. The predecessors of this church order were included only for reasons of clarification.

A. C. Van Raalte (1811-1876) initially favored Scholte's church order, but from 1838, the year of the schism in the Seceders' church in the Netherlands, he gradually began favoring the Dort Church Order of 1619 and opposed extensive revisions about such things as the position of lay preachers and the traditional garb of pastors. In 1846 Van Raalte left the Netherlands because of the oppression of the Seceders. He and the flock he led as their Moses longed for religious freedom in the United States. Crop failures in the Netherlands also created economic hardships at that time. After founding Holland Colony in 1847, Van Raalte continued to defend the Dort Church Order of 1619 against his opponents in their struggle over the church order. chcal church, the confederationon In its first meeting on April 23, 1848, the Classis of Holland, Michigan, decided that it was in complete harmony with the "Catechism, Formulas of Concord, Confession of Faith, Canons of Dort, and Church Order."[32] The minutes do not make clear which church order the classis had in mind. But because the brethren had decided to follow "our fathers" as they had expressed themselves in the *Kerkelijk handboekje*, this meant, as noted above, that they followed the Dort Church Order of 1619, in harmony with its predecessors.[33] Still, this was not clear to everyone.

---

[30] Synode der Afgescheiden Gereformeerde Gemeenten gehouden te Amsterdam Anno 1840; *Kerkelijk handboekje zijnde een kort uittreksel van de voornaamste acten der Nationale en Provintiale Synoden, betrekkelijk de zuiverheid der Leere, rust der Kerke, enz., alsmede de post-acta of nahandelingen van het Nationale Synode van Dordrecht, gehouden in de jaren 1618 en 1619: zeer dienstig en noodig voor predikanten en kerkenraden: met eene voorrede* (Amsterdam: N. Obbes, 1841).

[31] *Kerkelijk handboekje*, 3.

[32] Classis of Holland, Michigan, 23 April 1848; *Minutes 1848-1858* (Grand Rapids: Eerdmans, 1950), 22.

[33] Ibid., 46.

In 1851 Harm Krans, elder from Zeeland, Michigan, asked the Classis of Holland, Michigan, in reference to the term for elders, whether the Dort Church Order of 1619 had been adopted or not. The classis referred to the *Kerkelijk handboekje*, and stated "being convinced that we can prepare nothing better, clearer, or more useful, considers it proper to refrain from making new rules or ordinances. Hence all new resolutions on the subject are superfluous."[34]

The minutes of the classis of 30 April 1851 reveal that Krans was "informed that the Church Order also makes provision therefore stipulating that if the welfare of the church demands it, or if there are other circumstances making it imperative, an elder can retire, i.e., become inactive."[35] Indeed, according to art. 27 of the Dort Church Order of 1619 and to local ecclesiastical regulations, elders and deacons served for two or more years. Each year a proportional part of the consistory would retire. Congregations were free to decide to re-elect the same persons again, if circumstances were judged to be expedient for them to continue in the office.

Also, Gijsbert Haan, member of the church in Vriesland, Michigan, and, later, father of the Secession of 1857, which founded the Christian Reformed Church, discussed the position of the Dort Church Order of 1619 with the classis.[36] It was quite an issue. It reveals the struggle between adaptation and heritage. In Haan's case, he and his fellow seceders left the Reformed Protestant Dutch Church, because they wanted to stick to the confessional Dutch church of the sixteenth and seventeenth centuries.

Haan objected not only to the above-mentioned term of elders and deacons but also to the observance of festival days in relation to daily work or occupations.[37] This objection was discussed at length.[38] The minutes of 14 October 1851 point out:

> The rules of discipline have been adopted, namely, those which
> we find expressed in the Church Order of Dort, in connection
> with the earlier church orders of the Reformed Church and the
> expressed principles of the preface [in the *Kerkelijk handboekje of*

---

[34]   Ibid. (30 April 1851), 46.

[35]   Ibid.

[36]   Ibid. (14 October 1851), 58; Leon van den Broeke, *"Pope of the Classis"? The Leadership of Albertus C. Van Raalte in Dutch and American Classes* (Holland, MI: Van Raalte Press, 2011), 74-75, 95.

[37]   Classis of Holland, Michigan, 23 April 1848; *Classis of Holland* (1950), 21.

[38]   Ibid. (14 October 1851), 58-61.

1841]—adopted in such a manner that everyone was free to touch upon all points of dispute and that thus the adoption did not take place as a piece of make-believe but with the purpose of living according to it.[39]

Furthermore, it was considered:

That if individuals or churches are at fault, these, and not the entire government, ought to be subject to accusation, but that the government itself ought constantly to be held in the highest honor, without which the Reformed system of church government, yea any organization at all, is unthinkable.[40]

The classis had adopted the Dort Church Order of 1619. The minutes, however, show that in ecclesiastical practice not only this church order but in some cases also the Explanatory Articles of 1792 were followed.[41] These were written in America by the Reformed Protestant Dutch Church. As of 1850 the seceders were members of this denomination.

Van Raalte did not mention these articles in 1866 when he attended the meeting of the Seceders' Synod of Amsterdam. After twenty years, he had returned to his homeland for a visit. He explained to this synod the union of the Classis of Holland with the Reformed Protestant Dutch Church. He told this body that, with the exception of certain practices that sprang from the character of the country, this denomination was like the Dutch Reformed Church before 1816 in doctrine, discipline, and worship. He did not elaborate on these practices. He pointed out that it "recognizes the confessions of our Church [Seceders' church] as the expression of its faith and governs itself according to the Church Order of Dort."[42]

H. P. Scholte had a different opinion on church polity in general and on the Dort Church Order of 1619 specifically.[43] For this ecclesiological position alone, he had already run into trouble with the other fathers of the Secession. He did not seek the restoration of the Netherlands Reformed Church, but, both in the Netherlands and in Pella, Iowa, he argued for a church that was free, independent from

[39]   Ibid., 60.
[40]   Ibid., 61.
[41]   Van den Broeke, *"Pope,"* 56-57.
[42]   *Handelingen van de Synode der Christelijk Afgescheidene Gereformeerde Kerk in Nederland,* 1866 (Kampen: S. van Velzen jr., 1866), 955-57.
[43]   F. L. Bos, "Scholte, Hendrik Pieter," in *Biografisch Lexicon voor de Geschiedenis van het Nederlandse Protestantisme,* 2nd ed., D. Nauta (Kampen: Kok, 1983), 390-93.

the state, and congregational in its government. In the Netherlands, Scholte had been disciplined by the Synod of Amsterdam of 1840 for these views. This did not help to bring him back to the Presbyterian-synodical type of Reformed church government. In 1846 he emigrated with a group of followers to Iowa and founded Pella. He refused to seek the ecclesiastical affiliation with the Reformed Protestant Dutch Church and organized his own church along congregational lines with a consistory that was congregational and not Presbyterian-synodical in nature. Scholte was not the pastor; he was an elder alongside others and preached along with others. He became the economic and political leader of the larger community of Pella. Despite the congregational nature of this church and the democracy for its consistory, Scholte remained aristocratic and autocratic. In 1855 the consistory expelled him as a member of the church. The majority of the members sought affiliation with the Reformed Protestant Dutch Church. Scholte and his little flock had relied on one and only one rule for the affairs of the church: the Word of God—no law book and no church order.

Christian Reformed Church

In the minutes of the Classis of Holland, one can already see the preliminary elements for an upcoming secession (1857) from the Reformed Protestant Dutch Church. Again, the central issue for immigrants was how to deal with Americanization or modernization. There were two opinions within the Dutch Reformed communities in the Midwest: adherence to the church order and practices of the Seceders' church founded in 1834 in the Netherlands or adaptation to the new context with a broader mindset. Two years after the birth of the Classis of Holland, in 1850, its congregations joined the Reformed Protestant Dutch Church. Its opponents considered this union to be illegal from the standpoint of the church order.

There was, however, more going on: appointment of (lay) preachers, orthodoxy of the true church in the colony, singing of hymns rather than psalms, Freemasonry, neglect of catechetical preaching, and tensions between the local congregation and the denomination (classes and synods). Apart from Freemasonry, the other issues dated back to the Dutch situation. These issues were also encountered when the emigrants left the Netherlands for the United States. Then, it had less to do with Americanization and more to do with the tension between tradition and modernization. This tension led to the secessions of 1857 and 1881.

The True Dutch Reformed Church, later, the Christian Reformed Church (CRC), was formed. The schism reflected the theological division in the Seceders' church in the Netherlands. Bruins and Swierenga asserted in 1999 that RCA members in the Midwest were immigrants who sought to assimilate theologically, ecclesiastically, and culturally to the new context. The CRC members were colonists who remained focused on the Motherland for leadership and direction and who desired a little Holland, with old content in a new context.[44] That included the Dort Church Order of 1619, until today, although with revisions, especially in 1914, 1965, and 1978.[45] Just as the Reformed Churches in the Netherlands in 1905, so also the Christian Reformed Church in 1914 updated articles of the church order. One of the trends within the church in relationship to church order was the North American context: "Any comparative review of Christian Reformed Church government with its European antecedents demonstrates how clearly the church has become a part of its North American environment."[46] The current church order still reflects the Dort Church Order of 1619, in the (almost the same) number of articles, the division into the same four chapters, and in the fact that the content of these articles and chapters are substantially the same. Even this revised version

> is still a redaction and continuation of the original Church Order of Dort. The basic plan and church governmental principles . . . have been retained, and much of the material was dealt with in the original Church Order also, but the century-old document has been brought fully up-to-date as to organization, language, and content.[47]

Nonetheless, the CRC denomination regards church polity as living law: "Part of being wise about how to live together and function in healthy ways is being able to adjust to changes in the church and in our culture."[48] That is not only a juridical reality but also quite Reformed. The church order also refers to John Calvin, *Institutes*, IV.X.30:

---

[44] Robert P. Swierenga and Elton J. Bruins, *Family Quarrels in the Dutch Reformed Churches of the 19th Century* (Grand Rapids: Eerdmans, 1999), 103.

[45] *Church Order and Its Supplements* (Grand Rapids: Christian Reformed Church in North America, 2015).

[46] William P. Brink and Richard R. DeRidder, *Manual of Christian Reformed Church Government* (Grand Rapids: Board of Publications of the Christian Reformed Church, 1969), 4.

[47] Idzerd Van Dellen and Martin Monsma, eds., *The Revised Church Order Commentary: An Explanation of the Church Order of the Christian Reformed Church*, 3rd ed. (Grand Rapids: Zondervan, 1969), 20.

[48] *Church Order* (2015), 7.

As he has not delivered any express command, because things of this nature are not necessary to salvation, and, for the edification of the Church, should be accommodated to the varying circumstances of each age and nation, it will be proper, as the interest of the Church may require, to change and abrogate the old, as well as to introduce new forms. I confess, indeed, that we are not to innovate rashly or incessantly, or for trivial causes. Charity is the best judge of what tends to hurt or to edify: if we allow her to be guide, all things will be safe.[49]

There are many examples of revision in the church order of the Christian Reformed Church (CRC). Revisions usually just followed those of the Reformed Churches in the Netherlands; for example, the revisions of 1905 were adopted in 1914. Moreover, the authors of commentaries closely followed the Dutch Reformed experts in church polity like F. L. Rutgers, H. Bouwman (1863-1933), and Joh. Jansen (1873-1956).

Sometimes, however, the Christian Reformed Church made its own decisions. I will point out seven examples. First, only "male members who meet the Biblical requirements for office-bearers are eligible for office."[50] The addition of "male" was new in the revision of 1965, added expressly to exclude female congregants. Second, the revision of 1965 did not call committees of the classis "classical committees" anymore, but "interim committees," in order to distinguish them from "advisory committees" and "study committee."[51] Third, art. 24 clarified that the elders shall "engage in and promote the work of evangelism."[52] The previous version in art. 23 stated that the elders "exhort others in respect to the Christian Religion."[53] This article dates back to the political context of the Dutch Reformed Church in the seventeenth and eighteenth centuries, when it became the privileged church. In short, the meaning of art. 24 is that the church takes responsibility not only for church members but also has duties toward all.

Fourth, the 1914 revision stated that the classis shall convene "at least once in three months, unless great distances render this inadvisable."[54] The 1965 revision changed this into "at least every four

---

[49] http://www.reformed.org/master/index.html?mainframe=/books/institutes (accessed 11 November 2016).

[50] *Revised Church Order Commentary*, 26.

[51] Ibid., 56.

[52] *Manual of Christian Reformed Church Government*, 103.

[53] *Revised Church Order Commentary*, 107.

[54] Ibid., 180, 184, 379.

months, unless great distances render this impractical."[55] This must be understood against the background of the great distances in North America, as compared to the small scale and high population density of the Netherlands. Fifth, in the Netherlands, ministers never solemnize marriages because of the legal context. Only civil magistrates solemnize marriages. Afterward, the couple may go to a church where a minister will bless the marriage. This situation is different in North America; ministers are legally authorized to solemnize marriages. For this reason, the texts of the Dutch and American articles are different. Sixth, the Dort Church Order of 1619 stated that consistories are charged to make sure that there are good teachers. The 1914 revision in the church order of the Christian Reformed Church replaced "good teachers" with "Christian schools." Such schools were unknown in 1619. Seventh, a revision in 1914 stipulated that "funeral sermons and services shall not be introduced."[56] This article followed the 1905 version of the Reformed Churches in the Netherlands. This was changed by the CRC Synod of 1940 to "Funerals are not ecclesiastical, but family, affairs and should be conducted accordingly."[57] The meaning was the same, but it stated more clearly the Reformed vision of funeral law. Church funeral services could be conducted but within those limits. What is clear by now is that some revisions were made to update the text, to make it more clear and understandable and/or to Americanize it, for example, the great distances within a classis affecting the frequency of its meetings.

Both RCA and CRC denominations Americanized their church orders, the CRC more slowly than the RCA, present in North America for nearly four hundred years.

Concluding remarks

Although the history of (the acceptance of) the Dort Church Order of 1619 might be considered as rather complex, it became important, even without the express approval of the political authorities in the Dutch Republic. The Particular Synod of North Holland, including the Classis of Amsterdam, obeyed this church order. This classis was responsible for the overseas congregations. In the Americas, the Dort Church Order of 1619, including its predecessors, was also in force. That is clear from the case with pastor Freeman.

---

[55] *Manual of Christian Reformed Church Government*, 167.
[56] *Revised Church Order Commentary*, 270.
[57] Ibid., 270.

The Freeman case also teaches that simply referring to the church order is no guarantee that ecclesiastical problems would be solved. Moreover, it was a lesson in Reformed Church polity not only for Freeman but also for all the participants, including the English governor. The case also shows that such a church order, written for a specific country, could not simply be copied and pasted into another. The American congregations had to strike a balance between Dutch heritage and Americanization. The Coetus-Conferentie split, and the Explanatory Articles of 1792 are expressions of this tension between the Dutch and American-minded factions. Due to changing ecclesiastical and political contexts, the American congregations became independent from the Classis of Amsterdam in 1792, after which, more revisions were necessary. The Reformed Church in America became a more missional church. Nowadays, the *Book of Church Order* of 2015 is published not only in English but also in Korean, Spanish, and Mandarin, one demonstration of accommodation to changing contexts; translation alone, however, does not necessarily express accommodation to changing contexts if the content of church polity does not change.

This article could highlight only a few of the many changes in the church order of the RCA, but these examples represent many others. Of course, the church order changes, or in the words of Allan Janssen, "Church order is ecclesiology in action."[58] On its website, the RCA shows that it is fully aware of a constantly changing world: "We like to say we're 'Reformed and reforming according to the word of God.'[59] We embrace fresh ideas and hold on to what's best about our deep, rich past." Although the current Book of Church Order seems like a far cry from the Dort Church Order of 1619, the classes and offices are still fundamentally Dortian.

Obeying the Dort Church Order of 1619 is not a goal in itself. The aim of Reformed church polity is to serve the church so that it can fulfill its duties. Comparing church orders is not just checking whether the articles, composition, and contents are similar. Moreover, by highlighting some of the changes in Reformed church orders, the essence and the composition of the ecclesiological content are revealed. It is not just Dutch heritage, but it principally has to do with the foundations of Reformed or Calvinistic ecclesiology. Revisions of the church order need to fit within this framework. Revisions have to do

---

[58]   Janssen, *Constitutional*, 6.
[59]   http://about.rca.org/ (accessed 22 August 2016).

with the nature of the offices, the office of every believer, the (authority of) assemblies and their tasks and activities, and admonition and discipline. The church order of the CRC reflects the Dort Church Order of 1619, more so than the RCA, both in format and content. Between 1628 and 1792, however, the RCA applied this church order more closely for a long time, when it was legally part of the Dutch Reformed Church and even thereafter, with a different format and revisions. Moreover, when the congregations of the RCA in the Midwest were established, beginning in the first part of the nineteenth century, they, unlike the seventeenth century congregations, were not dependent on the Classis of Amsterdam. The political contexts also differed. The RCA congregations in the Midwest were founded more than half a century after the Revolutionary War. People experienced far more freedom of religion in the United States than in the Netherlands at that time. In the homeland, their experience was one of persecution and imprisonment. Across the ocean, they found a safe haven for their colonies and ecclesiastical Calvinistic heritage, which included the Dort Church Order of 1619 as a cultural import. This was especially the case in the CRC. It implemented the church polity developments in the Reformed Churches in the Netherlands and continued to obey the Dort Church Order of 1619.

Reformed ecclesiology, along with its accompanying church order, can function in North America but needs to adapt to changing contexts. It is not so much about preservation, as to what a specific context requires. If the Dutch political authorities would have allowed another synod after 1619, the Dort Church Order of 1619 would undoubtedly have been revised, just like the order itself was a revision of its sixteenth-century predecessors. Even when new contexts require accommodation, the (Dort) Church Order (of 1619) can be flexible, since it is an expression of Reformed church polity and ecclesiology. In the example of the Freeman case, a British governor wanted to control the number of Dutch pastors through licenses, despite the promised freedom of Dutch Reformed congregations. They were hindered by his politics of Anglicization, which caused division and discord. Such flexibility was also shown when the church order Americanized, for example, regarding the size of the classis in relationship to the frequency of its meetings. Such was also the case when, because of general modernization, the church order was revised, as in the Reformed Churches in the Netherlands. The above-mentioned examples, both in the RCA and CRC, also affirm this.

In juridical terms: *ius sequitur vitam* (law follows life), or theologically: *ecclesia reformata semper reformanda* (the Reformed church [is] always to be Reforming). That principle also applies to the (Dort) Church Order (of 1619). Reformed church polity, including the Dort Church Order of 1619, has moved between flexibility and fixed ideas.

Part Two

Dutch American Culture Moving West

CHAPTER 4

The Changing Map of the Dutch American Culture Region as Measured by the Spread of Dutch American Reformed Churches, 1664–1846

Henk Aay

A culture region changes through time and in space. An ethno-national minority culture abroad, situated in an open settlement zone, largely cut off from its homeland via continuing immigration, will expand geographically by natural increase. At first this spreading out will be more contiguous and in ethnic islands. In time the expansion will become more intermingled and highly scattered. Coincident with and related to geographic expansion are time-bound processes of exogenous and endogenous cultural change, such as intermarriage, assimilation, and adaptation. One possible endpoint of such processes might be described as a heritage culture: geographically, entirely mixed in with the majority culture and people of other ancestries and, in respect to cultural differences, largely assimilated, with a focus on ancestry and cultural memory and heritage, including heritage sites.[1]

In this article, I map the changing distribution of Dutch Reformed churches from the close of the New Netherland period in 1664 to the

[1] A useful textbook overview of geography and culture is found in Mona Domosh, Roderick P. Neumann, and Patricia L. Price, *Contemporary Human Geography: Culture, Globalization, Landscape* (New York: W. H. Freeman, 2015).

75

beginning of the new wave of Dutch immigration in 1847, noting in particular the leading edges and changing density of expansion, the further infilling of earlier settlement zones, and the gradual loss of geographic cultural cohesion through time. Assimilation and ethnic mixing ran concomitantly with these nearly two centuries of geographic expansion; all together, these wore away Dutch American cultural ways to eventually leave only cultural memory. The wave of new Dutch immigration brought an energetic, up-to-date, ethnic subculture into the Midwest and beyond and reintroduced it to selected places within the old Dutch American realm.

Dutch Reformed churches as centerpieces of Dutch American culture[2]

Where Dutch Reformed congregations from the seventeenth to the early nineteenth century were present in New York and New Jersey, they pointed to a more robust and complete Dutch and Dutch American culture.[3] With the disappearance of Dutch legal/political authority and institutions after the takeover by the English in 1664, the Dutch Reformed church, the only Dutch denomination in America, became the consolidating fulcrum for Dutch life and culture. As several scholars, especially Firth Haring Fabend, have shown, the Dutch Reformed Church was closely associated with the persistence of Dutchness from the seventeenth to the nineteenth century in America.[4] Through their preaching and education, Reformed clergy gave spiritual and moral, as well as Dutch, enculturation to their congregations and communities. This guidance was shaped, especially during the seventeenth and eighteenth centuries, not only by their customary mandatory university

---

[2]   By churches, I mean local congregations and preaching stations as recorded in Russell L. Gasero, *Historical Directory of the Reformed Church in America* (Grand Rapids, MI: Eerdmans, 2001).

[3]   Throughout this study, I will use the name Dutch Reformed Church to represent the various names given to it during the period from 1628 to 1846. These include the names Hervormde Kerk, the Dutch Church, the Low Dutch Reformed Church, and the Reformed Protestant Dutch Church. Today it is called the Reformed Church in America.

[4]   Firth Haring Fabend, "The Reformed Dutch Church and the Persistence of Dutchness in New York and New Jersey," in *Dutch New York: The Roots of Hudson Valley Culture*, ed. Roger Panetta (New York: Fordham University Press and Hudson River Museum, 2009), 137-58; Firth Haring Fabend, "The Synod of Dordt and the Persistence of Dutchness in Nineteenth-Century New York and New Jersey," *New York History* 77, no. 3 (July 1996): 273-300; David Steven Cohen, "How Dutch were the Dutch of New Netherland?" *New York History* 62 (1981): 43-60.

education in the Netherlands—training in Calvinist doctrine, pastoral care, and church polity—but also by their life and experiences in that country.[5]

After the British takeover of New Netherland in 1664, immigration from the Netherlands came to a near halt and remained negligible until the mid-nineteenth century when a second wave of Dutch immigration began, primarily into the American Midwest.[6] Dutch and Dutch American communities, however, continued to grow and expand into the seventeenth-, eighteenth-, and nineteenth-century American settlement frontiers in New Jersey and New York by natural increase and by the assimilation of local non-Dutch families (Batavianization) and several theologically like-minded immigrant groupings, such as the French Huguenots and German Palatines. Within and over against English colonial culture, the Dutch began to identify their cultural distinctiveness more self-consciously. Often, members of a Dutch Reformed congregation, regardless of their ethnicity, considered themselves as Dutch. Dutch Reformed churches were centerpieces in shaping and negotiating Dutch American culture for more than two hundred years.[7]

Dutch Reformed congregations could be organized only when there were enough families (some 30 or more) in a local area to support a church. And that could take several decades. Outside the cities of New York and Albany, churches were usually centered in clustered rural villages and towns and, as such, were part and parcel of a more

[5]   There were exceptions to this requirement. There were those who were exempted from having to follow an academic study in Reformed theology in the Netherlands. They were known as *Nederduytse clerici*, Dutch-speaking clergy. See Janny Venema, *Beverwijck, A Dutch Village on the American Frontier* (Albany, NY: State University of New York Press, 2003), 141.

[6]   Joyce Goodfriend, "The Social and Cultural Life of Dutch Settlers, 1664-1776," in *Four Centuries of Dutch-American Relations*, ed. Hans Krabbendam, Cornelis A. Van Minen, and Giles Scott-Smith (Albany NY: Suny Press, 2009), 121.

[7]   Firth Haring Fabend, "Being Dutch and Being the Reformed Dutch Church," in *Zion on the Hudson: Dutch New York and New Jersey in the Age of Revivals* (New Brunswick, NJ: Rutgers University Press, 2000), 8-19. Some broad-based, recent attention and interest in New Netherland and its legacy and contributions to the DNA of the United States pay scant attention to the role of the Dutch Reformed Church. A good example of this neglect is Russell Shorto's otherwise compelling book, *Island at the Center of the World* (New York: Random House, 2004). Other historians of New Netherland, for example, Jaap Jacobs and Janny Venema, take the place of the Dutch Reformed Church in New Netherland and its legacy quite seriously. Jaap Jacobs, *New Netherland. A Dutch Colony in Seventeenth-Century America* (Boston: Brill, 2005), 263-325. Venema, *Beverwijck*, 131-56.

diverse cultural life. Clearly without a congregation and a church building, many features of Dutch material culture and folkways were still present, but regular worship in the Dutch language and social activities organized by congregations brought the important cohesion of religion and gathered people together to interact, participate in, and reinforce Dutch American habits and institutions.[8] The Dutch Reformed Church could well be the only church in an area drawing people living from a five-to-eight-mile radius. Non-Dutch people were attracted to the locally dominant Dutch (Reformed) Church and/ or were drawn to qualities often associated with the Dutch: Fabend lists, among others, tolerance, charity, civic concord, literacy, and enlightened attitudes toward women.[9] They learned to understand and speak Dutch and adopt Dutch American mores and dispositions. In this way, such families and their descendants made Dutch American culture their own.

Collectively, the Dutch Reformed Church was also eager to preserve its Dutch language and heritage. Before the new wave of Dutch immigration beginning in 1847, it rejected a union with the German Reformed and the Scottish Presbyterians; after 1847, it rejected three more mergers: in 1892 with the German Reformed, and in 1930 and 1950 with the Presbyterians.[10] Moreover, it took more than twenty-five years of General Synod debate to finally decide in 1867 to drop the word "Dutch" from the name and officially become the Reformed Church in America (RCA).[11]

Mapping Dutch Reformed churches

If the seventeenth- to nineteenth-century Dutch Reformed churches were flagships of Dutch American culture, then mapping their spread will help to reveal the changing culture area of Dutch America. With several exceptions, not very much attention has been paid to mapping these Dutch Reformed churches and their attributes (members, baptisms, stewardship, etc.) in the United States (and a

[8]   Joyce Goodfriend provides a very useful summary of Dutch American culture in New York and New Jersey between the takeover by the English and American independence: Joyce Goodfriend, "The Social and Cultural Life of Dutch Settlers, 1664-1776," in *Four Centuries*, 120-31.
[9]   Fabend, *Zion on the Hudson*, 9.
[10] Herman Harmelink III, *Ecumenism and the Reformed Church* (Grand Rapids, MI: Eerdmans, 1968), in particular, 32-37; 38-52; 58-65; and 79-85.
[11] Gerald F. De Jong, "The Controversy over Dropping the Word Dutch from the Name of the Reformed Church," *Reformed Review* 34, no. 3 (Spring 1981): 158-70.

small number in Canada). Their international, national and regional distribution, their geographic growth and decline through time from the beginning to the present, and their (changing) locations in towns and cities would all be of interest. Exceptions include the *New Historical Atlas of Religion in America* (2001), as well as the work of cultural geographer Peter Wacker. The *Atlas* includes a section on Reformed denominations in the United States and maps national distributions of RCA churches by county for 1750, 1850, 1890, 1950, and 1990. [12] Wacker's work reconstructed the material landscape of, especially, New Jersey and mapped the locations of house types, barns, and churches of the several ancestral groupings that first settled the state, including the Dutch.[13]

In 1996 Don Luidens and Roger Nemeth, sociologists at Hope College in Holland, Michigan, received a Lilly grant to study congregational change in the Reformed Church in America during the previous one hundred and fifty years. As a foundation for this study, they compiled the *Reformed Church in America Denominational Membership Data, 1818-2000*, a database that recorded all the statistical information available for each congregation for every year from the denominational records.[14] Locational data included place, county, and state, but not the street address, of each church. Several students from Hope and Calvin Colleges extended the locational information back from 1818 to 1628 and forward from 2000 to 2015. The place information was converted into geographical coordinates. Using GIS software, RCA churches and their attributes could now be mapped for any year and geographic change through time in their locations and summary statistics documented.[15]

---

[12]   Edwin Scott Gaustad and Philip Barlow, *The New Historical Atlas of Religion in America* (Oxford: Oxford University Press, 2001).

[13]   Michael Siegel, Maxine N. Lurie, and Peter O. Wacker, *Mapping New Jersey: An Evolving Landscape* (New Brunswick, NJ: Rutgers University Press, 2009).

[14]   These records were taken from the Minutes of the General Synod of the Reformed Protestant Dutch Church (RPDC), later the Reformed Church in America (RCA), also known as the Orange Books; beginning in 1967, separate directories with this information were published as appendices to General Synod's annual minutes. *The Reformed Church in America Denominational Membership Data, 1818-2000* records eighty-nine different variables, including information about membership, baptism, education, and stewardship. It was employed to produce scholarly articles, different denominational studies, study materials for a conference about the RCA, and articles in the church press. The database is archived and may be accessed at the Association of Religion Data Archives (ARDA) at Penn State University. http://www.thearda.com/Archive/Files/Descriptions/RCAHIST.asp, last accessed 1/22/2016.

[15]   I am grateful to Hope College students Bekah Llorens and Nathan Longfield and Calvin student Matt Raybaud for adding geographic coordinates for each

This study examines only the changing distribution of RCA churches from the British takeover of New Netherland in 1664 to the new wave of Dutch immigration to the United States beginning in 1847.

The Dutch culture region at the close of Dutch sovereignty

While Dutch rule applied to the entire area claimed by the West India Company (WIC) in 1624 (approximately today's states of New York and New Jersey and parts of Connecticut and Delaware), the effective Dutch culture region constituted a very, very small area within New Netherland at the time of the takeover of the colony by England in 1664. [16] The only somewhat contiguous Dutch culture region was arrayed along today's Upper and Lower New York Bay, part of the estuary of the Hudson River, including the western tip of Long Island, the southern tip of Manhattan, Staten Island, and the North Jersey Shore. Twelve churches were founded in this core cultural area by 1670, most of them on Long Island, with only three churches elsewhere (1670 map).[17] And, unlike the later expansion of Dutch culture regions into New York and New Jersey, during English and then US rule which took the form of ethnic islands among English, Scots, Irish, and German communities, the culture area around the mouth of the Hudson River in 1670 was then a more contiguous Dutch region.

As in the Netherlands itself, however, Dutchness was complicated; many immigrants had come from the Netherlands, then called the United Provinces, to the colony; Dutchness was a layer of their identity, but they carried diverse ethnic origins and spoke a variety of languages and dialects. And this region of settlers emerged rather late in the short, forty-year history of New Netherland; in 1650, there were only two Dutch Reformed congregations, one on the southern tip of Manhattan and

---

congregation into the database and for extending the place information about congregations and their coordinates back to 1628 and forward to 2015. For this work they used Gasero, *Historical Directory of the Reformed Church in America*. Calvin College geography student Matt Raybaud produced maps from the expanded RCA database during the 2015 summer undergraduate research program, organized by the science division at Calvin College. He also helped produce the maps published in this study.

[16]   Even though the Dutch recaptured New Netherland in 1673 and held it for about a year, historians take 1664 as the year that the colony was taken over by the English.

[17]   Gerald Francis De Jong, "The Formative Years of the Dutch Reformed Church on Long Island," *The Journal of Long Island History*, part 1, no. 8 (Summer-Fall 1968):1-16; part 2, no. 9 (Winter-Spring 1969): 1-20.

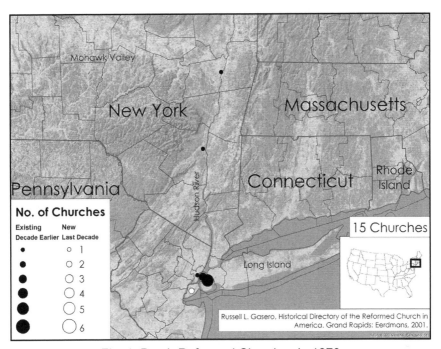

Fig. 1. Dutch Reformed Churches in 1670

one in Albany. Although the patroonships already planned to send over famers from the low counties and elsewhere, not many settlers arrived in the early years. But, as New Netherland later made the transition from a trading to a settlement colony, more immigrant families arrived to take up permanent residency as independent farmers and artisans.[18] Churches away from the cultural core surrounding Upper and Lower New York Bay, Albany, Kingston, and New Amstel (New Castle), were in 1670 distant Dutch enclaves situated along the Hudson and Delaware Rivers.

Cartographic schema for the expansion of the Dutch and Dutch American culture area during the English and Early American periods, 1664-1846

Figure 2 presents a generalized spatial model for the spread of Dutch Reformed churches and, by extension, the Dutch American culture region, from 1664 to 1846. Without further immigration,

[18] Jaap Jacobs, "Migration, Population, and Government in New Netherland," in *Four Centuries*, 85-96.

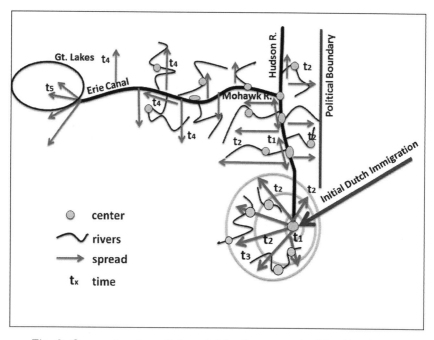

Fig. 2. Generalized spatial model for the spread of the Dutch and Dutch American culture region, 1664-1846

expansion was driven mainly by the rate of natural increase and the availability of suitable nearby farmland; assimilation of non-Dutch people into local Dutch settlements and their Dutch Reformed Churches was also at work. In effect, the large-scale geographic trading structure already realized in New Netherland was slowly and steadily occupied by Dutch settlement: the estuary region of the Hudson River as the base; the river itself, along with its tributaries, as the spine of the colony; and the Mohawk Valley, as a principal Indian trading artery reaching far inland. The Delaware and Connecticut Rivers, toward the borders of New Netherland, did not figure into this primary Dutch geographic colonial structure and, therefore, did not channel later settlement.

The advantages of this extensive network were especially apparent to the water-savvy Dutch: transportation (navigability), trade (especially furs), commerce, fishing, waterpower, and markets for agricultural goods; these benefits, of course, were just as relevant after the English takeover as before.[19] Subsequent Dutch population

---

[19]   Jaap Jacobs, "The Great North River of New Netherland": The Hudson River and Dutch Colonization," *Hudson River Valley Review* 30, no. 2 (Spring 2014): 2-15.

expansion proceeded from the toehold(s) of settlement achieved in New Netherland. The core area of the Hudson River estuary (described above) steadily expanded outward in a semicircle north, west, and south. Dutch settlers from Long Island, Staten Island, and Manhattan moved on to the mainland of Northern New Jersey and to what is today the southeastern funnel of New York State—the Bronx—and Westchester and Rockland Counties. From the original New Netherland settlement core, there was little room for expansion eastward; the Atlantic coast and English settlements were in the way, for example, on Long Island.

The spread was also up (and down) the Hudson River, first on and close to the river and later farther away from it, along its tributaries, such as the Wallkill and Rondout. The more open western frontier made settlement on that side of the river more extensive; eastward expansion from the Hudson River was more constrained, because of existing and encroaching English settlements up to and beyond the borders with Connecticut, Massachusetts, and New Hampshire. These borders were part of the Hartford treaty line of 1650, negotiated between England and the Netherlands.[20]

After the early forerunner of Schenectady, New York, already with a church in 1680, the Dutch American settlement frontier began also to turn westward in earnest along the Mohawk Valley, beginning in the 1730s, with German Palatines and, in time, spread farther west and to centers north and south of the river. Helped by the Erie Canal, central and, in turn, western New York, were the next frontiers at the turn of the nineteenth century; already here, whatever Dutch American culture still existed was geographically very scattered. Finally, beginning in the 1830s, and until the new wave of Dutch immigration commenced in 1847, the frontier of newly founded Dutch Reformed Churches moved to isolated locations in the future Midwest and during that expansion lost any areal cohesion. Therefore, one cannot speak of a Dutch American culture area anymore in central and western New York and in the Midwest before 1847, not as one could in the Hudson Valley and northern New Jersey.

The spatial model charts the outward expansion of the Dutch American culture area. But also at work, though not shown, are other, more internal, geographical processes. As population density increased from population growth, intensification of land use and urbanization,

---

[20]   Jaap Jacobs, "The Hartford Treaty: A European Perspective on a New World Conflict," *De Halve Maen* 68 (1995): 74-79.

earlier frontier zones saw a further thickening of churches; the Hudson Valley and Northern New Jersey are examples, as the detailed maps below will demonstrate. Alternatively, in the original core of Dutch settlement, the burgeoning and cosmopolitan New York City region, the Dutch population and its culture were quickly overwhelmed, first by British residents and then by the influx of many different European immigrant streams. Even though New York City could boast nineteen Dutch Reformed Churches in 1850, it had not been a Dutch city for 150 years. Dutch culture was Americanized far more quickly in such settings than elsewhere; here, Dutch Reformed Churches no longer indicated a more encompassing cultural presence.

To summarize: there were several geographic processes that changed the Dutch subculture: one is the gradual fading of a culture due to scattering, whether of individuals or communities; another is cultural intensification as a result of a growing population density of its members; yet another is the swamping of a subculture in large cities by a majority culture. But, overlaying these, several other general processes contributed to the decline and extinguishing of Dutch American culture, regardless of geographical circumstances. Without the influx of new immigrants from the Netherlands into existing and new Dutch communities during this period, there was no reinforcement and updating of Dutch material and nonmaterial culture. At the same time, and inevitably, Anglicization and, later, Americanization, everywhere, slowly and persistently, gathered momentum and impact as macro-cultural influences. As with other ethnic groupings, Dutch Americans, generations later, became unhyphenated Americans. For the descendants of the seventeenth-century Dutch settlers, even in the most persisting culture areas, by the middle of the nineteenth century, Dutchness had become no more than a nostalgic cultural memory. With the exception of certain Dutch-derived ecclesiological practices and Reformed confessions, Dutchness was no longer operative: "By the time of the Civil War, Dutchness in the Hudson Valley had become for many only a quaint memory."[21] Even so, that, to a greater or lesser degree, Dutchness remained a working cultural system for two hundred years and through from eight to ten generations is quite remarkable; the Dutch Reformed Church played a pivotal role in this preservation.

---

[21] Fabend, "The Reformed Dutch Church and the Persistence of Dutchness," 155.

The maps: Dutch and Dutch American culture on the move[22]

The maps depict the locations of Dutch Reformed churches under three circumstances at the beginning of each decade: churches present a decade earlier, churches organized during the last decade, and churches discontinued during the last decade. For example, the 1780 map of Dutch Reformed churches (below) shows the locations of all the churches present before 1771, the locations of churches organized between 1771 and 1780, and the locations of churches that closed their doors between 1771 and 1780. The maps have as background the physical geography (landforms, elevation, and water features) and the present-day boundaries of states and counties. The text accompanying the maps describe the geographical patterns of the newly organized as well as the shuttered churches.[23]

1680 map

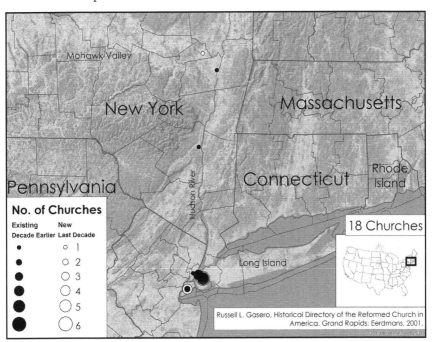

Fig. 3. Dutch Reformed Churches in 1680

[22] Historian Gerald F. De Jong contributed much to our understanding of the growth of the Dutch presence and of the Dutch Reformed Church in early America. Gerald F. De Jong, *The Dutch in America, 1609-1974* (Boston: G. K. Hall, 1975), 48-66; Gerald F. De Jong, *The Dutch Reformed Church in the American Colonies* (Grand Rapids: Eerdmans, 1978), 28-45; 83-105.

[23] Churches outside the United States are not included.

By 1680, just into the English period, the primary Dutch culture region at the mouth of the Hudson was strengthened further by additional churches on Staten Island and western Long Island. And among the most isolated Dutch communities away from this base, the future of the influential turn to the west along the path of the Mohawk Valley and its tributaries, had already been signaled with the establishment of a congregation at Schenectady, twenty years after the founding of a Dutch farming settlement there. The Mohawk valley had been one important source region for the fur trade with the Native Americans in New Netherland.

1690 map

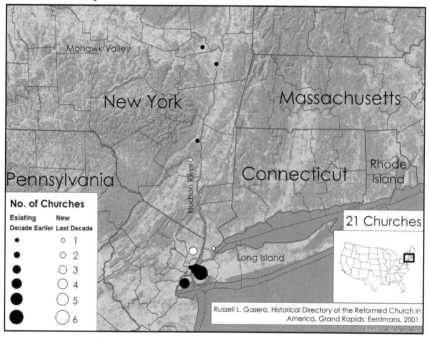

Fig. 4. Dutch Reformed Churches in 1690

All in all, church development during the 1680s further expanded and consolidated the core Dutch culture area. In a relocation process that lasted many decades, Dutch families were moving from Western Long Island and Staten Island to available land in northern New Jersey, first along the coast, where they drained wetlands with dikes to harvest salt hay.[24] Like the Huguenots, early Dutch settlers there also founded

---

[24]   Stephen Marshall, "The Meadowlands before the Commission: Three Centuries of Human Use and Alteration of the Newark and Hackensack Meadows," *Urban*

a church in Hackensack, New Jersey. At the original nucleus, New York City saw its Dutch Reformed churches increase from two to three.

The map of 1690 records the founding of churches by French Calvinist Huguenots during the previous decade: in New Rochelle and New Paltz in New York and Hackensack in New Jersey; only New Paltz, New York, however, was outside the core Dutch area. Persecuted by Catholic authorities in France, they were part of a worldwide diaspora that earlier already had led to their emigration from France to New Amsterdam and Brooklyn in New Netherland. As with other persecuted religious groups that had emigrated from Europe and bought and were granted land by the authorities, the Huguenots at first created their own separate settlements. With the exception of New Rochelle, these Huguenot communities in time intermarried with the Dutch population and adopted the prevailing Dutch language and culture.

The 1680s also witnessed the first closing of a Dutch Reformed church. After the English takeover, the frontier village of New Amstel, Delaware, founded in 1651, by Peter Stuyvesant, on the site of the former Fort Casimir, no longer had the necessary population to support a church.

1700 map

During the 1690s, the expansion of Dutch settlements out from the original core of Manhattan, Western Long Island, and Staten Island continued unabated. Churches were founded north of Manhattan in the Bronx on the Harlem River; in Tarrytown, in Westchester County, New York; and in Tappan in Rockland County, New York. To the west and southwest, five new churches were started in northeastern New Jersey: Belleville and Passaic both on the Passaic River; Homdel and Marlboro, next to each other along the Jersey Shore; and Somerville in the Raritan Valley of central New Jersey. One congregation dropped out: the French Reformed Huguenot Church merged with the Dutch Reformed Church in Hackensack, New Jersey. Away from this Dutch cultural core, no additional churches were established farther up the Hudson Valley.

It is not at all surprising that for more than forty years after the English conquest of New Netherland, the growth of the Dutch culture area, as measured by the founding of Dutch Reformed churches, was centered on the lands surrounding the estuary of the Hudson River.

Habitats 2 (December, 2004). http://www.urbanhabitats.org/v02n01/3centuries_full.html#cite83.

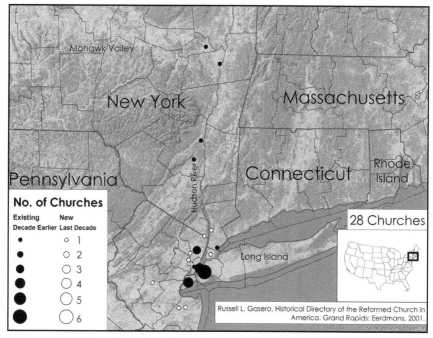

No. of Churches

Existing   New
Decade Earlier Last Decade

● ○ 1
● ○ 2
● ○ 3
● ○ 4
● ○ 5
● ○ 6

28 Churches

Long Island

Russell L. Gasero, Historical Directory of the Reformed Church in
America. Grand Rapids: Eerdmans, 2001.

Fig. 5. Dutch Reformed Churches in 1700

This was where the vast majority of the Dutch originally settled in
New Netherland, and, as their communities grew, they would seek out
suitable nearby sites to stay connected. No longer in command of trade
or defense, there were fewer opportunities for the Dutch to settle in
more peripheral locations.

1710 map

By 1710 the pattern of geographical expansion of Dutch culture
had transitioned to two fronts: the by now well-established extension
and infilling around the original New Netherland nucleus and now, for
the first time, new, although isolated, settlements and their churches
in the Hudson Valley itself. These include Saugerties, on the west side,
north of Kingston, originally a settlement of Palatine immigrants from
Germany, as well as Schaghticoke, on the Hoosic River, a tributary of
the Hudson. This was the first Dutch Reformed church to be organized
north of Albany.

Like the Huguenots, the Palatine Germans were persecuted
Protestants, many of Reformed conviction. With permission of the
British Crown, they settled in its colonies, including New York. The

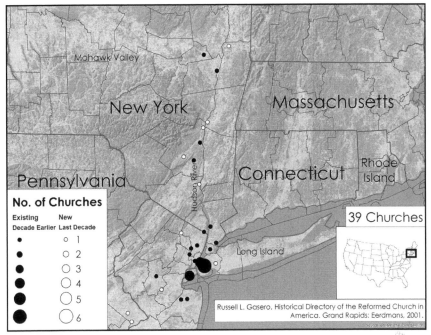

Fig. 6. Dutch Reformed Churches in 1710

Dutch Reformed Church organized congregations in the Palatine settlements there and sent Dutch pastors to serve their churches. In time, many adopted Dutch ways.

The continuing spreading out and infilling out from the settlement core also continued: east to Jamaica, Long Island, New York; west and southwest to Oakland and Franklin Park, New Jersey; and reaching as far southwest as North and South Hampton (Churchville) and Neshaminy, just over the New Jersey line in the extreme southeastern corner of Pennsylvania. The Neshaminy congregation would not make it into the next decade.

1720 map

From 1711 to 1720, a string of Dutch Reformed churches was organized along the east side tributaries of the Hudson (from south to north): Montrose, Fishkill along Fishkill Creek, and Claverack and Kinderhook along Kinderhook Creek. And there was more budding off and infill in northern New Jersey: Fairfield (along the Passaic River) and Readington and New Brunswick on the Raritan River. At the historic nucleus, the small churches on Staten Island contracted by two due to a merger.

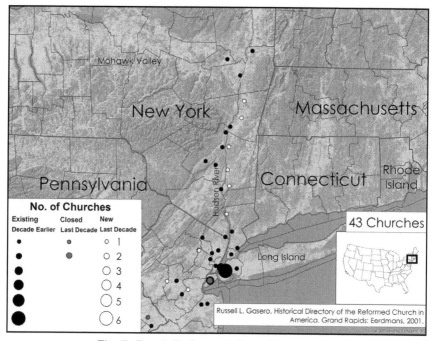

Fig. 7. Dutch Reformed Churches in 1720

1730 map

The most striking development during the 1720s was the opening of another front of church founding, this time along the Mohawk Valley, with the organization of churches west of Schenectady. The settlers were not Dutch but, again, German Palatines, who now resettled on land of their own from work camp Palatine settlements, such as Germantown and Livingston on the Hudson River. There they had moved closer to Dutch Hudson Valley culture. Along the Mohawk River, the Palatines organized a number of Dutch Reformed congregations: two in Schoharie, New York, along Schoharie Creek, a tributary of the Mohawk; another in Palatine Bridge, New York, right on the north side of the Mohawk River; two more congregations in German Flats, New York, farther west along the south side of the Mohawk; and one in Herkimer, New York, on the other side of the river from German Flats. Land grants to such groups were often ahead of the principal pioneer zones. This was clearly not an extension of the Dutch culture area *pur sang*, yet as German Calvinists and Lutherans, they had become familiar with the Dutch Reformed Church. In time these German Reformed congregations were also served by Dutch pastors and

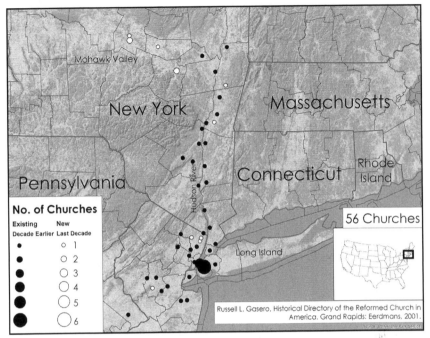

Fig. 8. Dutch Reformed Churches in 1730

absorbed Dutch Reformed theology, church polity, and some Dutch ways. As Dutch settlers later also moved into the Mohawk Valley, there was more interaction between them and the German Palatines.

The other geographical patterns of church founding during this period are by now more familiar. New Jersey saw more infill and budding off of settlements in Northern New Jersey: Schraalenburgh, Dumont, and Ridgewood, in the northeast corner, and Belle Mead (Harlingen) in the center. And, more infill along the Hudson, again, along the east bank: Germantown and Livingston, New York (both Palatine settlements), and Nassau, New York (formerly part of the patroonship of Rensselaarwijck).

1740 map

The westward spread of churches along the Mohawk River largely came to a halt during the 1730s, with the exception of the organization of a church in Middleburgh, New York, just south of Schoharie. In the Hudson Valley, the founding of churches switched to the west side, with some farther out from the river: West Coxsackie and Catskill (both fronting the Hudson); Stoneridge on Roundout Creek, a tributary of the

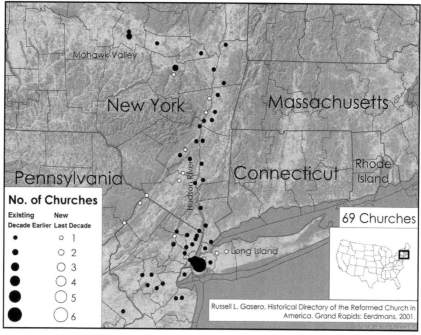

Fig. 9. Dutch Reformed Churches in 1740

Hudson; and Wallkill and Montgomery, both along the Wallkill River. On another western frontier, Dutch settlers organized Dutch Reformed Churches along the Delaware River in Pennsylvania, New Jersey, and New York: Bushkill in Pennsylvania, Montague in New Jersey, and Port Jervis in New York. And in the southwest corner of Pennsylvania, far beyond the developing Dutch culture region, a short-lived mission station was founded in Smithfield. Meanwhile, the expansion and infill from the central Dutch core continued with Elmhurst, Manhasset, and Brookville on Long Island, New York (the last two into the English zone), and Pompton Plains, New Jersey, to the west.

1750 map

Only five churches were organized during the 1740s. Napanoch and Pine Plains, New York, as well as Lebanon, New Jersey, were all on the outer perimeter of the Dutch culture zone: the first two, east and west of the Hudson, respectively, and the third, in western New Jersey. West Nyack, New York, added to the historic cultural core. In the Mohawk Valley, Schenectady already added a second congregation.

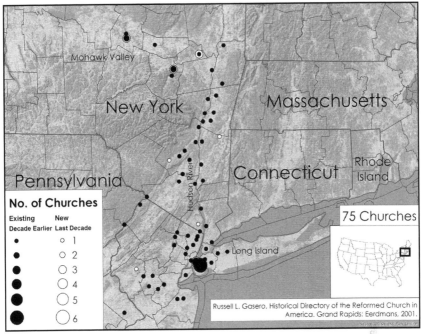

Fig. 10. Dutch Reformed Churches in 1750

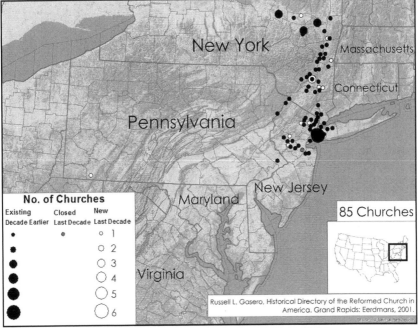

Fig. 11. Dutch Reformed Churches in 1760

1760 map

The decade of the 1750s again saw little church organization west of Albany, with the exception of a new congregation at Fonda, New York, on the north bank of the Mohawk River, west of Schenectady. The distribution of churches in the Hudson corridor continued to thicken with a second church in New Paltz and four new congregations on the east side of the river: from north to south, Schodack, West Copake, Wappinger Falls, and Hopewell Junction. Around the historic core of Manhattan, Long Island, and New Jersey, four additional churches were organized in northern New Jersey: Patterson, Montville, Bedminster, and Neshanic. New York City itself went from three to four Dutch Reformed churches.

1770 map

During the 1760s, the center of church organization again shifted to the periphery, particularly to the Mohawk Valley. Seventy years after Dutch settlers from Albany founded Schuylerville, a Dutch Reformed Church was organized in the village, the most northerly church

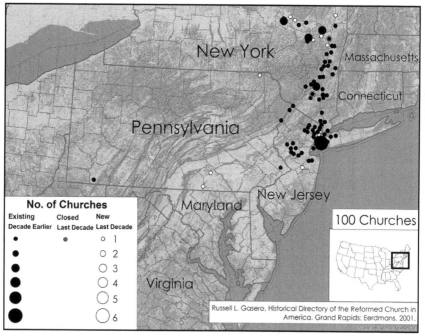

Fig. 12. Dutch Reformed Churches in 1770

along the Hudson. Churches established in the Mohawk corridor were Guilderland Center, south of Schenectady, and West Berne, east of Schoharie, and St. Johnsville, on the Mohawk River, both settled by German Palatines, as was Manheim, also right on the Mohawk River, east of German Flats. While it witnessed the organization of an increasing number of Dutch Reformed congregations, the Mohawk corridor as a whole, unlike the Hudson, did not become known for a more distinctive and dominant Dutch American culture in the post-Revolutionary War period. The earlier German Palatine populations, while influenced by Dutch ways, had a different cultural background. The frontier zones in upstate New York in the post-Revolutionary War period, until the early part of the nineteenth century, were far more culturally diverse than the Hudson Valley and Northern New Jersey had been earlier. Migrants especially from New England, but also from New Jersey, Pennsylvania, and Maryland, flooded into the area.[25]

The very peripheral new locations of churches in Pennsylvania, were quite short lived (until the turn of the century), because they lacked a sufficiently large core of Dutch or German Calvinists and were very remote: Conewago, Hanover, and Susquehanna. Along the Hudson corridor, there was modest growth: a second church in Albany, as well as in Wallkill, and a new congregation in Selkirk, south of Albany. At the historic center, churches were organized in Millstone and Ridgefield, New Jersey (on the Hackensack River), and in Red Hook Landing in Brooklyn and Spring Valley, New York. The French Calvinist church in New Rochelle, New York, closed.

1780 map[26]

The upheavals and divisions during the Revolutionary War resulted in the founding of fewer churches. New churches were organized not in the frontier zones but in already established areas, largely in New York State, such as Waterford and Lansingburgh, at the confluence of the Hudson and Mohawk Rivers; Hillsdale, close to the Massachusetts line; and Spring Valley, in Rockland County, part of the core Dutch area.

---

[25] James W. Darlington, "Peopling the Post-Revolutionary New York Frontier," *New York History* 74, no. 4 (October 1993): 341-81.

[26] From 1780 on, there were an increasingly large number of churches organized every decade, too many to name and situate in the discussion of each map. I will hereafter describe the geographical expansion in more regional terms.

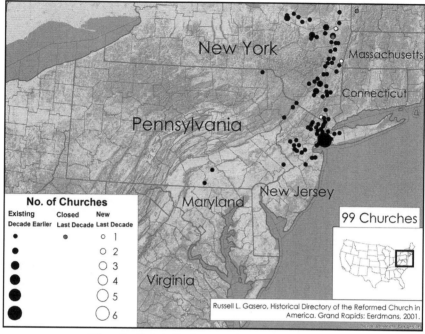

Fig. 13. Dutch Reformed Churches in 1780

1790 map

Church founding recovered during the 1780s with some seven churches in the Upper Hudson and Lower Mohawk Valleys in and around Albany and Schenectady. Further expansion occurred in northern New Jersey, part of the historic Dutch nucleus. An outlier congregation was organized in Hardy, Virginia; by the following decade, as had others on the periphery, it too had left the Dutch Reformed fold and became Presbyterian.

1800 map

As the settlement frontier during the 1790s moved into central and western New York, including the Finger Lakes Region, Dutch (and German) American settlers also relocated into this new border zone and organized a number of widely scattered congregations that, in a very loose form, pushed the Dutch American culture zone westward from the Mohawk Valley. But the most explosive consolidation of the Dutch American culture area during this decade, as in the previous decade, took place east of this new frontier; some eighteen more congregations

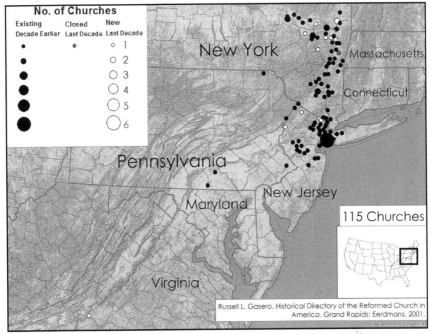

Fig. 14. Dutch Reformed Churches in 1790

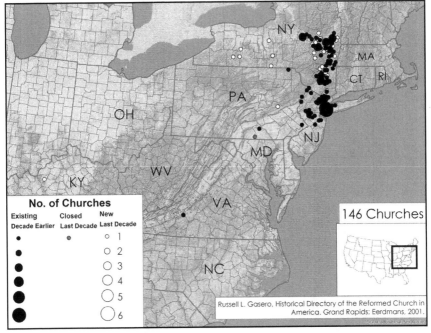

Fig. 15. Dutch Reformed Churches in 1800

were organized in the Upper Hudson and lower Mohawk valleys, many farther out from the axis of the corridor. By contrast, things were very quiet in the historic core area of southeastern New York and northern New Jersey. Two outliers, Hardy, Virginia, and Conewago, Pennsylvania, became Presbyterian congregations.

1810 map

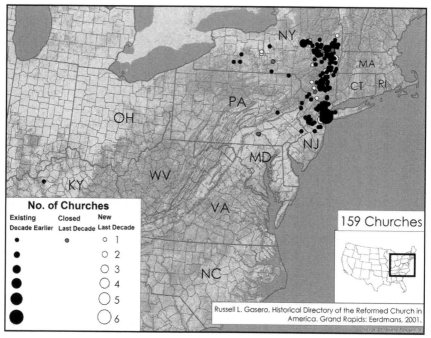

Fig. 16. Dutch Reformed Churches in 1810

The dynamic nature of the distribution of Dutch Reformed Churches during the first decade of the nineteenth century is shown on the map in several ways. For one, more individual places gained additional churches: New York City went from four to six; and other places, such as Staten Island, Saugerties, and Nassau, New York, now had two. Several more churches were organized in the Finger Lakes region, continuing the spread of Dutch American heritage into central New York. There was moderate growth (some nine congregations) throughout the Hudson and Mohawk corridors, particularly farther west in the Hudson Valley.

This map and others following also identify a growing number of churches that had left the denomination, such as the congregation in Knowlton, New Jersey, that joined the Presbyterian Church. Dropouts pose a methodological complication when the local presence of only a Dutch Reformed Church is used to identify Dutch American culture. Even if a congregation leaves the denomination due to secession, merger, joining another denomination, or disbandment, the local presence of Dutch American culture still continues in some fashion, although it may be argued that, without a local Dutch Reformed Church, a centerpiece of the culture goes missing. Nevertheless, leaving these dropouts out on subsequent maps does eliminate some of the geography of Dutch American culture.

1820 map

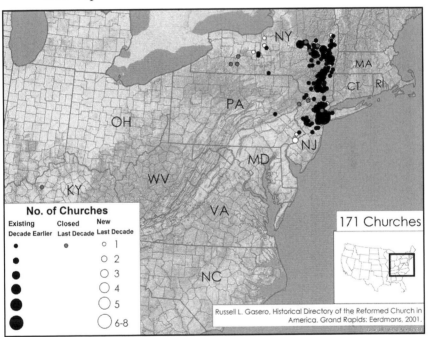

Fig. 17. Dutch Reformed Churches in 1820

The years from 1811 to 1820 brought moderate growth of some twenty-five new churches throughout the entire established Dutch American culture area. On the periphery, three congregations emerged across the border with New Jersey in extreme southeastern Pennsylvania, two of them in Philadelphia. Three more churches arose on the New York settlement frontier, several more in the Finger Lakes region.

1830 map

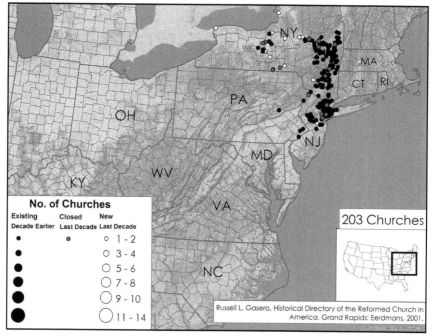

Fig. 18. Dutch Reformed Churches in 1830

During the 1820s, the growth of churches in the historic core was quite vigorous, especially in the large cities, with New York City going from eight to thirteen and Brooklyn from six to eight congregations. Elsewhere, the Mohawk Valley saw a further thickening of churches (nine); central New York, now a more mature settlement zone, added six churches; and, for the first time, the Dutch Reformed Church had a presence in the pioneer settlement region of western New York. Two churches were founded along the Lake Ontario coast: Henderson and Six Mile Creek (Olcott), New York, both relatively short lived. The 1830 map also locates a number of congregations that seceded from the denomination beginning in 1822 over, among other matters, theological differences and slaveholding; they formed the True Dutch Reformed Church. [27] Even though these churches were no longer part of the denomination, they very much remained part of the Dutch American heritage.

[27]   Harmelink, *Ecumenism and the Reformed Church*, 29-30.

1840 map

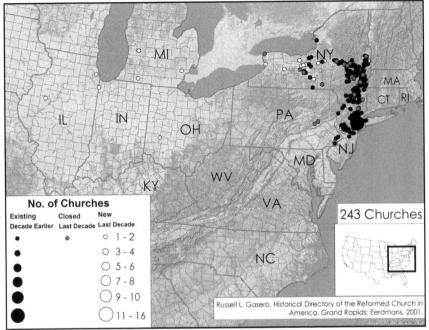

Fig. 19. Dutch Reformed Churches in 1840

The states of Ohio, Indiana, and Illinois and the territory of Michigan were established and opened for settlement during the 1810s and 1820s. During the 1830s, a number of disparate population centers in this emerging western region had Dutch American population thresholds considered large enough to attempt organizing Dutch Reformed Churches: three in Michigan (Centerville, Grand Rapids, and Redford) and three in Illinois (Brunswick, Cicero, and Fairview). Redford and Brunswick already dropped out during the following decade.[28] The rest of the churches founded during this decade were located in the earlier settlement zone of western New York; elsewhere, there was little church formation except for multiple churches in the same place, for example: Brooklyn, from eight to twelve; the Bronx, from one to two; and New York City, from thirteen to sixteen. The number of church dropouts/closings (fourteen), resulting from mergers, secession, and unviability remained high, a trend started in the preceding decade. Again, these losses do not necessarily reflect a local decline in Dutch American culture.

---

[28] Gerald F. De Jong, *Non-Immigrant Reformed Churches in the Middle West before the Civil War* (Chicago: Particular Synod of Chicago, 1978), 5-22.

1846 map

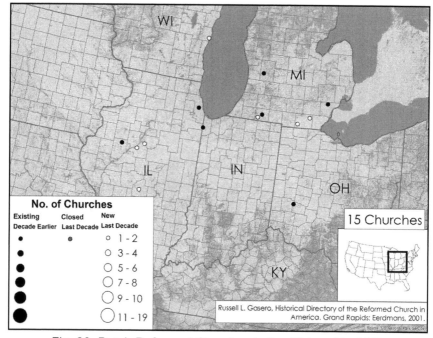

Fig. 20. Dutch Reformed Churches in the Midwest in 1846

This map is included to show the distribution of new churches organized in the Midwest between 1841 and 1846, just before the new wave of Dutch immigrants began to arrive in this area in 1847. Before that influx began, eight additional "old Dutch" nonimmigrant churches were founded in rural areas: four in southern lower Michigan and two each in Illinois and Wisconsin.[29] Three of these (Caledonia and Sun Prairie, Wisconsin, and Allegan, Michigan) had already closed their doors the same decade and several others (Vanderveer, Illinois, and Medina, Michigan) in the decade following. Still others (South Macon and Constantine, Michigan, and Pekin, Illinois) made it into the early twentieth century and then closed. The high failure rate of these "old Dutch" churches in the Midwest undoubtedly had to do with the small number of charter members who had been part of a Dutch Reformed Church farther east and the difficulty these churches experienced attracting new members in areas where this denomination was quite unknown. Unlike in the East, the word "Dutch" in "Reformed

[29]   Ibid.

Protestant Dutch Church," would have kept many from considering joining such a congregation; many would have expected it to be an ethnic, Dutch language church.

During this decade, Dutch immigrants and Dutch American migrants were moving into the same settlement zone: immigrants, into more compact Dutch-only areas, and migrants, more scattered and intermingled. The migrants were near the end of their cultural journey as Dutch Americans. The immigrants gave a brand new Dutch cultural impulse to the Dutch Reformed Church, mainly in the Midwest. And, like the Dutch immigrants of the seventeenth century before them, the new immigrants, albeit under different conditions, were embarking upon similar and related processes of geographic consolidation and dispersion and cultural separation and assimilation. In this developing culture region, Dutch Reformed churches would again become centerpieces of a new American Dutchness.[30] In the areas of Reformed theology and church life, it did not take long for differences between "Old" and "New" Dutch to take institutional form. The establishment in 1857 in the Midwest of the True Dutch Reformed Church (later the Christian Reformed Church) cemented some of those differences.

Conclusions

The physical geography of New Netherland was the basis of its commercial and settlement geography: the estuary, main trunk, and tributaries (especially the Mohawk) of the Hudson River. The geographic expansion of the Dutch and Dutch American culture region after the British takeover in 1664 and American Independence in 1776 followed this geographic arrangement. In broad chronological outline, the pioneer Dutch settlement zones shifted from lands around the Hudson River estuary to lands along the Hudson River and, later, along its tributaries. Then the new settlement zones shifted to lands along the Mohawk River and later along its tributaries. Later still it spread to widely scattered locations in central and then western New York State and, finally, to even more dispersed locations in what would become America's Midwest. In time further infill and consolidation occurred in these settlement zones.

Although the organization of Dutch Reformed Churches lagged behind the initial settlement, the years and location of their founding

---

30   James D. Bratt, *Dutch Calvinism in Modern America. A History of a Conservative Subculture* (Grand Rapids, MI: Eerdmans, 1984).

can be used to reconstruct the settlement history and geography of the changing Dutch American culture area. Moreover, the presence of Dutch Reformed churches betrayed a more full-fledged Dutch American culture. And for nearly two hundred years, they served as guardians and perpetuators of that changing culture. In the long run, however, for those who were and who became Dutch American during the seventeenth and eighteenth centuries, Dutchness was no match for Americanization, except for those features that were part of America itself, such as individual freedom, tolerance, free trade, and equality. At different rates, depending on location, and accelerating throughout the nineteenth century, Dutchness for these Americans slowly changed from cultural ways to cultural memory and legacy.

CHAPTER 5

Helping Hands: Old Dutch Aid Young Dutch

Robert P. Swierenga

The "Old Dutch" who settled New Netherland in the seventeenth century were distant cousins of the "Young Dutch" who emigrated in the mid-nineteenth century to the American Midwest.[1] Both shared a Netherlandic cultural heritage and Dutch Reformed theological confessions, but being separated for two centuries by an ocean led to profound differences in language, culture, and religious practices. Simply stated, the Old Dutch had become Americanized to the point of being Dutch only by heritage and faded memory. Most of them had long lost their mother tongue and were changed by the colonial wars, the American Revolution, and religious revivals, specifically the First and Second Great Awakenings.

[1] Jacob Van Hinte coined the phrases Old Dutch and Young Dutch to differentiate the seventeenth-century Dutch in New Netherland/New York from the nineteenth-century Dutch immigrants in the Midwest. The terms mark the two-hundred-year chronological gap between the cousins and are not meant to be pejorative or ageist. Jacob Van Hinte, *Netherlanders in America: A Study of Emigration and Settlement in the Nineteenth and Twentieth Centuries in the United States of America*, in Dutch, 2 vols. (Groningen: Noordhoff, 1928), gen. ed. Robert P. Swierenga, chief trans. Adriaan de Wit (Grand Rapids: Baker Book House, 1985).

The Young Dutch, for their part, had experienced a religious upheaval of their own, the Secession of 1834, when pietistic, orthodox members of the national Dutch Reformed Church withdrew and formed the Christian Seceded Church. The dissenters suffered a short but intense time of religious persecution by governmental and religious authorities and experienced social ostracism, economic boycotts, and occupational blacklisting. Beginning in 1846, the seceders, led by their pastors, began immigrating to the United States for religious freedom and economic opportunities.

The Old Dutch readily offered well-meant advice and considerable financial assistance to the Young Dutch, but they expected a quid pro quo—help in planting Dutch Reformed churches on the western frontier on the backs of the immigrant settlers, in order to further the home mission program of the Reformed Protestant Dutch Church (RPDC). The Young Dutch, for their part, begged for money constantly and soon tired the Old Dutch by asking for more "snowflakes." The relationship proved to be ambivalent, as one might expect of distant cousins long separated by geography and culture.

The New Yorkers were chagrined by the carping of the pietistic immigrants about a perceived heterodoxy, especially a dalliance with Freemasonry and the revivalist beliefs and practices of the Second Great Awakening.[2] Upwardly mobile, Old Dutch Reformed businessmen and professionals joined Masonic Lodges, the quintessential American civic institution, which their Calvinist cousins in England, Scotland, and the Low Countries condemned as un-Christian, oath-bound societies that substituted humanism for Christianity.

The Dutch in the East also sang "man-made" hymns rather than "God-given" Psalms, and worse, some hymns expressed Arminian theology. Preachers neglected to base sermons regularly on the fifty-two Lord's Days of the Heidelberg Catechism. Elders were negligent in faithfully visiting the families in their districts, and they failed to discipline members who committed public sins. Worse, the Old Dutch had little empathy for the discrimination and even persecution the Seceders suffered at the hands of the Dutch government and church leaders. In short, the Knickerbockers were too American in theology and practice and had lost much of their "Reformedness." Proof was the move in 1867 to drop the word "Dutch" from the name of their

[2]   Firth Haring Fabend, *Zion on the Hudson: Dutch New York and New Jersey in the Age of Revivals* (New Brunswick, NJ: Rutgers University Press, 2000).

denomination, the Reformed Protestant Dutch Church, in favor of the de-ethnicized Reformed Church in America (RCA).[3]

Another flash point was the decision in the 1870s of the Young Dutch in Holland, Michigan, to establish their own seminary, Western Theological Seminary, to prepare Dutch-speaking pastors for the immigrant churches. The Old Dutch saw this expression of ethnic chauvinism as a threat to the denomination's New Brunswick Seminary in New Jersey. The narrowness of the newcomers, in short, was at odds with the genial cosmopolitanism of the Old Dutch.

Help in migrating

Money and advice from the Old Dutch proved invaluable in the emigration. Already before embarking, the Reverends Albertus C. Van Raalte and Anthony Brummelkamp wrote a lengthy letter to the Old Dutch in New York to introduce their movement and ask for help. Their appeal, which they published in pamphlet form, explained the reasons for the Secession of 1834, described the sufferings of the faithful, and noted the harsh economic and social conditions in Holland. "Our hearts' desire and prayer to God is, that in one of those uninhabited regions in America there may be a spot where our people . . . may find their temporal conditions secured . . . [and] we would desire that they, settling in the same villages and neighborhoods, may enjoy the privilege of seeing their little ones educated in Christian schools."[4] One can sense the emotional heartstrings that this letter plucked among Old Dutch parishioners.

After the *Southerner* docked in New York harbor on November 17, 1846, Van Raalte was warmly welcomed in the Dutch tongue by Rev. Thomas De Witt of the city's Collegiate Reformed Church and Rev. Isaac Wyckoff of the Second Reformed Church in Albany. De Witt had visited the Netherlands only a few months earlier and learned of the coming flood of Hollanders. De Witt and Wyckoff formed Dutch

---

[3]   Fabend, *Zion*, 225-28, argues that the denomination's founding document, the Constitution of 1793, deleted key parts of the authoritative Synod of Dort (1618-19), and its preface copied the First Amendment's disestablishment clause by allowing for freedom of conscience on the part of every individual. These changes evidenced "a new American stage" in the Reformed Dutch Church, which was further enhanced by the Second Great Awakening.

[4]   "Appeal to the Believers in the United States of North America" (May 1846), cited in Henry S. Lucas, *Netherlanders in America: Dutch Immigration to the United States and Canada, 1789-1950* (Ann Arbor: University of Michigan Press, 1955; reprinted, Grand Rapids: Eerdmans, 1989), 61.

Rev. Thomas De Witt,
Collegiate Reformed Church,
New York City
(*Joint Archives of Holland*)

emigrant aid societies in New York City and Albany, respectively, to assist the newcomers. De Witt gave Van Raalte directions to Wisconsin by way of Albany, Buffalo, and the Great Lakes. With this help, Van Raalte was able to negotiate cheap travel inland.[5]

The party left New York by steamboat for Albany, where Wyckoff gave Van Raalte his complete attention. Wyckoff even offered to send three men to select a prime location in the Great Lakes states and purchase land for the Hollanders. Van Raalte politely refused; he would scout out the land himself. But the enthusiastic welcome by the Old Dutch was confirmation that God approved of his decision to emigrate.

Van Raalte labored under serious handicaps. He could speak only broken English and knew little about American geography and topography; yet he had to act quickly to choose a location, or his followers would scatter. To make an informed decision, he had to learn about flora and fauna, soil quality, transportation routes, methods of buying land at state and federal land offices (which presupposed a knowledge of the rectangular land survey system), and prospects for

[5]   This and the following paragraphs follow Van Raalte's two lengthy letters to Anthony Brummelkamp in Arnhem of his first month in America, written on 27 Nov. 1846, while aboard the *Great Western* in Buffalo, and on 16 Dec. 1846, after arriving in Detroit. The letters were published in Amsterdam as *Stemmen uit Noord-Amerika* (1847). John Dahm translated this important document, which Herbert J. Brinks and Zwanet Janssens published under its English title, *Voices from North America* (Calvin College: Heritage Hall Publications, 1993).

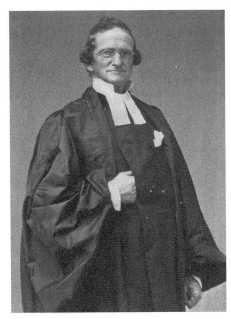

Rev. Isaac N. Wyckoff, Second
Albany Reformed Church
(*Joint Archives of Holland*)

economic growth in various regions. Clearly, he had to rely on new friends he could trust.

It was natural for Van Raalte to turn to "the faithful believers in these parts," that is, the Old Dutch, who shared the same basic confessions—the Belgic Confession (1561), the Heidelberg Catechism (1563), and the Canons of Dort (1618-19). A common heritage of faith and blood was a stronger bond than one of blood alone.

Wyckoff gave Van Raalte letters of introduction to a Presbyterian minister near Buffalo, who in turn wrote letters of recommendation to Presbyterian and Congregational clerics in Detroit, Chicago, and elsewhere. The Reformed Protestant Dutch Church worked closely with these denominations in home mission projects in the West, since they shared common doctrines. Van Raalte felt most comfortable with these Calvinist denominations, although in western Michigan, he also relied on Methodist and Baptist ministers and lay leaders.

In Detroit Van Raalte came to trust a prominent attorney, Theodore Romeyn, whose father and brother were Dutch Reformed ministers in New York. Romeyn's brother had written to alert him to Van Raalte's coming. Romeyn and his Michigan friends jumped into action to snare for Michigan this vanguard of a huge stream of stout settlers. The relationship was mutually beneficial. Van Raalte told his

Detroit attorney Theodore Romeyn (*courtesy of the Burton Historical Collection, Detroit Public Library*)

brother-in-law that Romeyn "opens the way for me to the highest and most respected officials in the state."[6]

The pledge of help by Romeyn and his friends, fellow Calvinists all, disposed Van Raalte to choose West Michigan. They were "God-fearing, upright gentlemen," he wrote his wife.[7] "Pray fervently and earnestly," Van Raalte wrote Brummelkamp, "for the Lord's leading in this matter. . . . A great deal depends on our choice." The Lord answered his prayer before this letter reached the Netherlands. He never got farther than Kalamazoo—the first stop on his western trip.[8]

Romeyn sent him to Rev. Ova Hoyt, pastor of First Presbyterian Church in Kalamazoo, a man who shared a "cordial interest in the Holland immigration." Hoyt introduced Van Raalte to Judge John Kellogg of Allegan, a large land investor in northern Allegan County, who happened to be in town. Kellogg took Van Raalte to the Old Wing Indian Mission on the Black River, which drained into Lake Michigan at Black Lake (later Lake Macatawa). They arrived on Old Year's Night of 1846.

[6]   Van Raalte to Brummelkamp, 30 Jan. 1847, in A. Brummelkamp, ed., *Holland in Amerika, of de Hollandsche Kolonisatie in den Staat Michigan* (1847), trans. Henry ten Hoor and Nella Kennedy, typescript, p. 4, Joint Archives of Holland.

[7]   Albert Hyma, *Albertus C. Van Raalte and His Dutch Settlements in the United States* (Grand Rapids: Eerdmans, 1947), 94-95.

[8]   Brinks and Janssens, *Voices from North America*, 20-22, 29 (quote), 33-34; Hyma, *Van Raalte*, 70.

Rev. Ova Hoyt of First Presbyterian
Church, Kalamazoo
(*Joint Archives of Holland*)

Besides showing Van Raalte the region, Kellogg introduced him to Rev. William Ferry of First Presbyterian Church in Grand Haven, the county seat, and to Henry Pennoyer, the county treasurer and a member of Ferry's congregation. Kellogg also took Van Raalte to Rev. Andrew Taylor of the First Reformed Church in Grand Rapids, where elder George Young surprisingly spoke fluent Dutch. Young convinced Van Raalte that the Black Lake watershed was superior to any place in Wisconsin or Iowa. That Young and Romeyn shared the dominie's Dutch Reformed faith made them persuasive salesmen. The rest is history.

Within three weeks, Van Raalte was back in Detroit, accompanied by his new friends, Taylor, Kellogg, and Hoyt, who traveled the considerable distance across the state to endorse the dominie's decision for Black Lake. Here they again met with Romeyn, his pastor George Duffield at First Presbyterian Church, and others to clinch the decision. Romeyn sent a detailed report of Van Raalte's decision to Wyckoff in Albany and requested him to direct new arrivals to Michigan where helpful committees awaited. These rapid-fire developments of January 1847 convinced Van Raalte and the Young Dutch that the Old Dutch were on their side. Indeed, many immigrants in letters to the Netherlands praised Old Dutch families they met en route westward for lodgings, temporary employment, and food.

When the immigrants built their colony, George Harrington, a New York Yankee already living in the area, taught them how to wield

Judge John Kellogg
of Allegan
(*Joint Archives of Holland*)

axes to fell trees and clear the land, to build brush fences and log cabins, and to drive ox teams. Harrington's wife, Margaret Van Alstyne, was of Old Dutch ancestry.[9] She was a rare find. But there were hundreds of Old Dutch in southern Michigan along the immigrant route. Two RPDC churches were located west of Toledo at Ridgeway and Medina with 140 and 70 members, respectively, and three were south of Kalamazoo, at Centerville, Constantine, and Mottville, with 460 souls.[10]

In the summer of 1847, when Van Raalte and his business partner, Henry D. Post, one of the first Americans in Holland, erected the first sawmill, known as the Colony Mill, De Witt's Collegiate Church collected $600 for the millworks. The mill provided the colony with lumber for building homes and barns.[11] When farmers suffered a complete crop failure in 1858 due to drought, Van Raalte sent a request to the Board of Domestic Missions for relief funds "to prevent many in the Holland Colony from starving."[12]

[9]   Gerrit Van Schelven, "Chronicles of the Dutch Settlers: George Harrington," *Allegan Gazette*, 12 Dec. 1914; Eugene Fairbanks, "Obituary of George S. Harrington Jr.," *Holland City News*, 12 May 1921.

[10] *Acts and Proceedings of the General Synod of the Reformed Protestant Dutch Church*, June 1850: 66 (table).

[11] *Grand Rapids Eagle*, 2 Feb. 1849; Peter T. Moerdyke, "Pioneer Industries," P. T. Moerdyke Papers, box 4, Holland Museum (HHTC).

[12] *Christian Intelligencer*, 9 Sept. 1858.

Samuel B. Schieffelin
(*Joint Archives of Holland*)

Buying land

Once Van Raalte chose the Black Lake watershed for his colony, he quickly acquired several thousand acres of land, before Americans could preempt him and drive up the price. Henry Pennoyer, Ottawa County treasurer and a leading member of First Presbyterian Church in Grand Haven, helped him buy some 3,800 acres of delinquent tax titles for pennies on the dollar at the Ottawa County courthouse. Wyckoff served as a middleman to enable Van Raalte to buy from eastern investors three large tracts in and around Holland, all with low down payments and six-year mortgages. Time is money and credit was hard to come by on the frontier. One key 261-acre tract lay at the mouth of Black Lake, owned by Nathan Silsbee of Salem, Massachusetts. The other two mortgagees were members of De Witt's Collegiate Church, James Suydam and Samuel Schieffelin, the latter a wholesale drug distributor. When Van Raalte was later pressed to repay the $5,000 debt, the two men bailed him out by extending the terms. The dominie was still making periodic mortgage payments to these long-suffering friends on his deathbed in 1876.[13] Suydam and Schieffelin gave generously to Reformed Church causes.[14]

---

[13]   Louis G. Vander Velde, "Glimpses of the Early Dutch Settlements in Michigan," *Michigan Historical Collections, University of Michigan* 1 (Nov. 1947): 1.

[14]   Robert P. Swierenga, "Albertus C. Van Raalte as a Businessman," 291, 305-6, in *A Goodly Heritage: Essays in Honor of Reverend Dr. Elton J. Bruins*, ed. Jacob E. Nyenhuis

With crucial help from the Old Dutch and the Presbyterian layman Pennoyer, Van Raalte, with a relatively small purse, gained a treasure in real estate that increased in value at his death to $200,000 ($6 million in today's dollars).[15] He had become a rich man indeed! But his land investments were highly leveraged in the early years, and the strain showed at times, including when he suffered a business bankruptcy in 1849.[16]

Union of 1850

The "payoff" for Wyckoff and the Old Dutch was the decision in 1850 of Van Raalte and his ministerial colleagues, Cornelius Vander Meulen, Seine Bolks, Martin Ypma, and Hendrik Kleyn, to merge the seven congregations of the Dutch-speaking and independent Classis Holland with the RPDC. (Two congregations, Drenthe and Grand Rapids, had no regular minister.) Wyckoff had come to the colony in June 1849 to personally lobby for the merger. Within a year, the deed was done. That the process was rushed seems clear in retrospect, at least from the settlers' side.

What motivated the two parties? For Van Raalte and the immigrant churches, the union was dictated by the desire for ecclesiastical unity with brothers and sisters who shared the same theological confessions. The church in the East, for its part, wanted to plant congregations on the frontier, exactly where the immigrants were settling. They also wanted to bring fresh blood to struggling RPDC congregations founded by Old Dutch settlers in the Great Lakes states. In 1850 the English-speaking Classes of Michigan counted six churches with 805 souls and the Classis of Illinois five churches with 956 souls. The Dutch-speaking Classis of Holland with a thousand souls boosted the Midwestern wing of the denomination by one-third.[17]

Equally important, in Van Raalte's words to the Board of Domestic Missions, was the "heartfelt gratitude" the Young Dutch felt

(Grand Rapids: Eerdmans, 2007); Receipt, William Schermerhorn for Peter Schermerhorn from A. C. Van Raalte, per George Young, and P. Schermerhorn to H. D. Post, 2 Oct. 1848, HHTC; Mortgage Assignment, Courtland Palmer to James Suydam and Samuel B. Schieffelin, New York, 10 Mar. 1857, Van Raalte Collection, Archives Calvin College.

[15] The US Consumer Price Index (1913-2010) has risen by a factor of 20, so it is conservatively estimated that the US dollar inflation rate since the 1850-70 era is a factor of 30.

[16] Swierenga, "Van Raalte as a Businessman," 300-307.

[17] *Acts and Proceedings*, June 1850: 67 (table).

for the "fraternal fellowship" extended "in the painful condition of our alienage, who, as we sat at your docks, intermingles[d?] with thousands of immigrants, were not ashamed of us, but afforded us refreshment and relief for our souls." The advantages of union were obvious for the "needy and stressed" newcomers: linkage with an American denomination with experience, leadership, and affluence, in exchange for money and advice.[18]

After the Civil War, in 1869, when Van Raalte founded the Amelia Colony in Virginia, his old friend, Schieffelin, again was involved. Schieffelin owned a large tract of land in Amelia and offered it much below the going price of $50 per acre. Eighty people from Michigan comprised the first Amelia group. After only four months, Van Raalte's wife, Christina, in poor health, insisted that the couple return to Holland with their children and grandchildren. The Virginia colony failed within a decade, severely damaging the dominie's purse and prestige.[19]

Pillar Church

In 1854 Van Raalte's congregation decided to build a large frame church in the heart of the village, on Ninth Street and College Avenue, kitty corner from the later Hope College campus. The original log church was unsuitable and very overcrowded. The new church to seat fifteen hundred cost $5,000: $2,000 for the exterior and $3,000 for the interior. Four carpenters in the congregation did the construction, using trees from the wood lot of another member. They raised enough money for the building but could not finish the pews and six huge pillars, which were very labor intensive. In the extremity, Van Raalte appealed to the Collegiate Church for a $1,000 loan. The church, the wealthiest in the denomination, overwhelmed the colonists by *donating* the money. This allowed the congregation to begin worship in the sanctuary a year early, in 1856. The pillars were finished over the next eighteen months.[20]

---

[18]   William O. Van Eyck, *The Union of 1850: A Collection of Papers by the Late Wm. O. Van Eyck, Esq., on the Union of the Classis of Holland with the Reformed Church in America, in June 1850* (Grand Rapids: Eerdmans, 1950), 3 (quote); Adrian Van Koevering, *Legends of the Dutch: The Story of a Mass Movement of Nineteenth Century Pilgrims* (Zeeland, MI: Zeeland Record, 1960), 506-20 (quote 514), contains all the official documents.

[19]   Janet Sjaarda Sheeres, *The Not-So-Promised Land: The Dutch in Amelia County, Virginia, 1868-1880* (Grand Rapids: Eerdmans, 2013).

[20]   Swierenga, *Holland, Michigan: From Dutch Colony to Dynamic City*, 3 vols. (Grand Rapids: Eerdmans, 2014), 1:200.

1870 engraving of Pillar Church (*Joint Archives of Holland*)

Christian schools

Van Raalte led his followers to America for religious freedom, including the right to establish Christian schools. The first priority was preparatory schools to train preachers, teachers, and missionaries of Reformed persuasion. Faculty could be found only among the Old Dutch since Van Raalte was the sole university graduate in the colony, and he had his hands full with his church and running the colony. In 1851 General Synod's Committee on Education sent Walter Taylor to staff Holland's Pioneer School for "higher education," which offered a classical education heavy on Latin and Greek language and literature. In 1853 General Synod transferred the care of the institution to the Board of Education, which obligated the denomination to support it.

When ill health forced Taylor to resign from Holland Academy in 1854, the synodical education committee sent replacements, notably John Van Vleck, who after five years, was succeeded by Rev. Dr. Philip Phelps Jr. General Synod paid the salaries of these teachers, since students paid little or no tuition.

Meanwhile, in 1853 Van Raalte carried a letter from Classis Holland to the Particular Synod at Albany stating that Christian elementary schools were necessary because the public schools were a "mixed multitude" that fostered a "colorless Protestantism" and opened the way for Catholicism. Holland had a public school, as did most of the outlying villages at Zeeland, Drenthe, Vriesland, and Overisel.

Walter Taylor, first principal of
Pioneer School and its successor,
Holland Academy
(*Joint Archives of Holland*)

John Van Vleck, second
principal of Holland Academy
(*Joint Archives of Holland*)

Dr. Philip Phelps Jr., first
president of Hope College
(*Joint Archives of Holland*)

Schieffelin made it his life quest to fund Christian parochial schools in immigrant churches by establishing a $7,000 trust fund. The General Synod sanctioned his project in 1854, provided the churches made support for the schools "voluntary," not mandatory. The Reformed Protestant Dutch Church was committed to public education, but Christian elementary schools were tolerated among the immigrants, given their Old World convictions. The immigrant churches readily tapped the "free money" and founded parochial schools, beginning with Kalamazoo, followed by Grand Rapids, Holland, Grand Haven, Muskegon, and Pella.[21]

The Seceder immigrants were finally realizing their dream of educating their young children in the Reformed faith. This nascent Christian day school movement, however, fizzled out. The parochial school at Van Raalte's First Reformed Church, for example, ran for only six years, from 1857 to 1862. Much to Van Raalte's keen disappointment, the congregation would not sustain it, since the public school stood across the street and was staffed by a Christian woman of New England stock, Elvira Langdon, a native of Vermont. Van Raalte had hired a recent immigrant, twenty-year-old Hendrika Van Zwalewenburg, augmented the next year by Cornelia Falconer of New Jersey Old Dutch stock to teach in English.[22]

Holland Academy, meanwhile, had severe money problems. With Synod's endorsement, Van Raalte made three financial missions to Reformed churches in the East (1856, 1857, 1859) to tap benefactors—Schieffelin, Suydam, Abraham Van Nest, Myndert Van Schaick, and William Mandeville, among others. Many spurned his appeals, but some responded generously. Van Raalte recorded the successes meticulously in his "Traveling and Begging Guide."[23]

---

[21] Elton J. Bruins, "The Educational Endeavors of the Reformed Dutch Church, 1628-1866," *Reformed Review* 59 (Winter 2005/2006): 179-82; Dennis Voskuil, "When East Meets West: Theological Education and the Unity of the Reformed Church in America," in *Tools for Understanding: Essays in Honor of Donald J. Bruggink*, ed. James Hart Brumm (Grand Rapids: Eerdmans, 2008); Dennis Voskuil, "The Vexed Question: Hope College and Theological Education in the West," in *A Goodly Heritage: Essays in Honor of the Reverend Dr. Elton J. Bruins*, ed. Jacob E. Nyenhuis (Grand Rapids: Eerdmans, 2007); Harro W. Van Brummelen, *Telling the Next Generation: Educational Development in the North American Calvinist Christian Schools* (Lanham: University Press of America, 1986), 55; *Classis Holland Minutes, 1848-1858* (Grand Rapids: Eerdmans, 1950), 11 Apr. 1855:174-75, 176 (quote); 17 Dec. 1856: 232 (quote); Swierenga, "For God and Country: Michigan's Dutch Reformed Christian Schools," *Michigan History Magazine* 100, no. 6 (Nov./Dec., 2016): 28-32.

[22] Swierenga, *Holland, Michigan*, 1:372, 531-38.

[23] Elton J. Bruins and Karen G. Schakel, *Envisioning Hope College: Letters Written by Albertus C. Van Raalte to Philip Phelps Jr., 1857-1875* (Grand Rapids: Eerdmans, 2011), 3n.

Van Vleck Hall, 1915 (*Joint Archives of Holland*)

Before going east in June 1856 to attend General Synod in Ithaca, New York, and engage in fundraising in New York and New Jersey churches, Van Raalte put his fellow parishioners to the test. He gave a challenge gift of $500 and demanded that they match it within twelve days, or he would accept an urgent call from the Pella congregation. The threat had the desired effect; $2,500 in pledges came in, and Van Raalte declined the call to Pella.

The positive response to the local and eastern campaigns gave Van Raalte the confidence to lay the cornerstone of the academy building on May 13, 1857. By 1858 he had raised $6,000 (of the needed $7,000) for the four-story brick structure. Construction was already underway before all the money was in hand. Van Vleck, who had "mothered" the project from start to finish, donated the final $1,000 to complete the building, even though his salary was in arrears.[24]

In 1859 Schieffelin made a $1,000 challenge gift for the Holland Academy, and Van Raalte went east a third time as a "begging" man—

[24] Wynand Wichers, *A Century of Hope, 1866-1966* (Grand Rapids: Eerdmans, 1968), 42-44, 49; Classis Holland Minutes, 112; Van Vleck to Mr. and Mrs. Abner Hasbrouck, 22 July 1858, printed in *Holland Sentinel*, 29 Mar. 1979; Consistory minutes, First Reformed Church, 6 Mar. 1857, transl. by William Buursma; Van Vleck Hall Fundraising Brochure, Hope College Advancement 1980. Van Raalte had had previous dealings with the merchant Suydam and druggist Schieffelin. In 1853 they rescued him from personal bankruptcy and purchased a land mortgage from him that he could not repay. See Swierenga, "Van Raalte as a Businessman," 291, 305-6.

W. Charles Scott, president
of Hope College, 1878-93
(*Joint Archives of Holland*)

his words—to raise matching gifts. Van Raalte prepared the churches by publishing a letter in the *Christian Intelligencer* setting forth the needs of the academy for a second teacher, more land, and lab equipment, costing $3,000, all to further the mission of providing leaders for immigrant churches and schools. Eleven students had already enrolled at Rutgers College and New Brunswick Seminary and "many more in the Academy have the ministry in view," Van Raalte reported happily.[25]

His demeanor changed, however, when on December 1, 1859, the *Intelligencer* published an article, titled "The Holland Academy," penned by "W.," likely W. Charles Scott, a New Brunswick Seminary junior classmate of Philip Phelps Jr., who ironically in 1878 succeeded Phelps as president of Hope College, which had been founded in 1866. Scott charged that the colonists were milking the eastern churches and not carrying enough of the load themselves.[26] It was the same complaint heard by immigrant churches in Canada in the 1950s from Christian Reformed leaders in the United States. Van Raalte, in an invited response, noted that the academy was the "property" of General Synod, established to train up "an evangelizing ministry for the West." Moreover, the principal eastern donors "knew perfectly well what they were doing and why they were doing it."

In the early 1860s, Phelps appealed to these same wealthy easterners for funds to allow the academy to become the denomination's

<hr />

[25]   Bruins and Schakel, *Envisioning Hope College*, 23 (quote), 345 (quote).

[26]   *Christian Intelligencer*, 10 Nov. 1859; Bruins and Schakel, *Envisioning Hope College*, 345-69, includes all the relevant documents.

Rev. Albertus C. Van Raalte (*r*) and son-in-law Pieter
Oggel (*Joint Archives of Holland*)

"Western College." General Synod in 1865 declared the "new college"
to be of "paramount importance" and recommended an endowment
of $85,000. Hope College began with a $30,000 endowment, the
minimum amount required to charter a Michigan college, and the
denomination continued to pay most of the professors' salaries for
decades. The endowment reached $50,000 in 1870, with $18,000—more
than one-third—coming from immigrant churches in the West, thanks
to a canvas by Professor Pieter Oggel, Van Raalte's son-in-law, in the
year before his death in 1870. The Young Dutch showed the "wise men
from the East" that they could carry their share of the load. In 1873
the endowment target was raised to $100,000, with 50 percent to come
from western congregations. The target proved unrealistic and was not
reached. Whenever income fell short of operating costs, the college
tapped the endowment to balance the books. The college was $10,000
in debt in 1873, with another $3,000 due for professors' salaries and
$600 due President Phelps in a matter of weeks. From 1867 to 1879,
Hope College received an average of $4,000 per year from the RCA's

Hope Haven University letterhead (*Joint Archives of Holland*)

Board of Education. Altogether, since 1851, the board had appropriated more than $67,000 to the Pioneer School and its successors, Holland Academy and Hope College.[27]

Hope Haven University

President Phelps conceived of a cockamamie plan to support a "scientific school" by planting a peach orchard as a cash crop. General Synod bought a tract of land on the west edge of the city, but it proved to be too small for the purpose. So in 1867 Synod purchased from Jacob Van Putten 830 acres of woodlands between Point Superior and Indian Point (later known as Waukazoo Woods) along the northern shore of Black Lake. The council (as Hope's board of trustees was then known) invested $5,000 of its endowment as a down payment on the $9,400 purchase. The faculty, except for Phelps, saw Hope Haven Farm as a pipe dream. Council president Van Raalte backed Phelps; the farm would "be a noble basis for the security and growth" of the college; it was an investment for the future.[28]

In 1869 Van Raalte went east to raise $5,000 to replenish the endowment, and after two months of discouragement, James Suydam again came through. Van Raalte then successfully pressed him for another $5,000 to develop the orchard. In gratitude, Van Raalte had the farm named after Suydam, who might not have appreciated the gesture. Eastern businessmen questioned the financial acumen of a

---

[27] *Acts and Proceedings*, 1864: 47, 87-89, 91; 1865: 66 (quote); 1868: 379, 416-17, 470; 1870: 109; 1873: 733; 1879: 332.

[28] Ibid., 1870: 108-9; Robert P. Swierenga, *Park Township Centennial History, Ottawa County, Michigan: Holland's Water Playground* (Holland: Van Raalte Press, 2015), 13.

Waukazoo Inn (*Joint Archives of Holland*)

council of clerics. Hope College was a "hopeless case," many thought, and the western seminary was a needless duplication of New Brunswick Seminary. In 1878 William H. Moore, Phelps' friend and Union College classmate, donated $4,000 to improve the farm, but it continued to be a financial drain. Clerics and professors could not run a farm. In 1901 Hope College sold the farm at a good price of $25,000 to John C. Everett of Chicago, who had the deep pockets to develop Waukazoo Inn at Indian Point, which became one of the largest resorts in west Michigan, a rival of Ottawa Beach and Macatawa Park.[29]

The Reformed Church in the East continued to spread its largess to western schools via its board of education. Hope College in the 1880s and 1890s received $2,400 a year for operating costs. North Western Classical Academy, founded in 1882 in Orange City, Iowa, enjoyed the same amount and an endowment of $20,000. Pleasant Prairie Academy, founded in 1894 in German Valley, Iowa, for Ost-Frisian Reformed churches in northcentral Iowa, received a $1,000 annual subsidy and an equal amount from Classis of Pleasant Prairie congregations. Wisconsin Memorial Academy, founded in 1901 in Cedar Grove, also received $1,000 a year from the board and more from churches of Classis Wisconsin. The academies were feeder schools to Hope College. Northwestern evolved into a junior college in 1928 and a senior college in 1959, when the academy closed. Wisconsin Memorial Academy

[29]   Wichers, *Century of Hope*, 87 (quote).

closed in 1937. Pleasant Valley continued as a German Reformed high school until it closed in 1958.[30]

Holland Harbor

Van Raalte chose the Black Lake watershed because of its potential harbor, but it took twenty years of effort to dredge the mouth and build breakwaters and a channel. Only when the US Army Corps of Engineers took over harbor maintenance after the Civil War could the settlers step down.

In the first decade, the colonists learned by trial and error that lake storms would destroy any pier, and breakwaters had to be constructed of the largest granite boulders and shaped into an arrowhead to lessen siltation at the entrance. Tree trunks and shovels would not do the job; it required heavy equipment, notably steam dredges. Van Raalte turned first to the state and federal governments for funds, but his appeals fell on deaf ears because of small government convictions by Democratic presidents Franklin Pierce and James Buchanan. The Dutch could not even get $10,000 for a lighthouse. A team of US Topographical Engineers surveyed the harbor in 1849 and recommend a new channel, but the estimated cost of $106,000 (multimillions in today's dollars) was preposterous for the poor settlers.

In 1858 the Holland Harbor Board under Van Raalte decided not to wait for government funds and to do the job themselves. They issued $20,000 in harbor bonds underwritten by a township tax levy in Holland, Zeeland, and Fillmore Townships.

Selling harbor bonds meant going east, where the money was. In the summer of 1858, the harbor board sent John Roost (Jan Roest), "a wholehearted Republican," to sell bonds in Old Dutch congregations. Only with "indefatigable perseverance" and the backing of De Witt and Wyckoff was Roost able to peddle $5,000 worth of bonds. Church members had already been tapped out by Van Raalte to complete Pillar Church and Van Vleck Hall. And Roost lacked a salesman's natural bent and fluency in English. He wrote Van Raalte: "I find it verry [sic] hard to sell bonds. I have not sold any in New York or Brooklyn, notwithstanding I tried verry [sic] hard." Roost, homesick for his wife and children, was losing interest. "If there is a person of ambition, he might have mine place, and I shall be glad to go home and leave the hard work of begging

---

[30]   *Acts and Proceedings*, 1882: 116; 1985: 93; 1897: 943-45; 1937: 93; Gerald De Jong, *From Strength to Strength: A History of Northwestern, 1882-1982* (Grand Rapids: Eerdmans, 1982).

for somebody else." Later that year, Van Raalte himself went east to take over the sale of the harbor bonds. He was a master at fundraising and understood the importance of laying out a vision. Van Raalte sold the remaining $15,000.[31]

The Civil War hindered the project, but a year after the war, Holland had a serviceable harbor. Congress had appropriated $55,000 for Holland harbor and US Army Engineers were tasked in 1867 to maintain all Great Lakes harbors.[32]

Holland Fire of 1871

During the night of April 8-9, 1871, Holland was destroyed by a forest fire that farmers southwest of town had set to clear stubble from their fields. Holland was one of many Great Lakes cities that burned down that week, including Chicago the same day. The "fire monster" fanned by unexpectedly strong winds swept in and burned every building on the heavily populated west side of town and the entire downtown area. Three quarters of the homes were destroyed (only the east side was spared), leaving three hundred families (1,300 souls) homeless and destitute. Seventy-five stores and shops in the business district were lost, all three hotels, five of seven church edifices, and thirteen of fifteen factories. Total damages came to $900,000 ($20 million in today's dollars), and only one-fifth was covered by insurance, mainly businesses. The devout Dutch declined fire insurance, both because of the cost and the belief that it showed a lack of trust in Divine Providence.[33] The fire wiped out the labors of the first twenty-five years, which pioneers had accomplished with great scrimping and saving.

Dutch Americans responded to Holland's plight, especially the Old Dutch in the East, who took pity. President Phelps, a native of Albany, went east on an aid campaign. Up and down the Hudson Valley and in New Jersey, the churches responded to his message, with collections that swelled to an astounding $40,000, all reported in the weekly *Christian Intelligencer*.[34] Van Raalte went to western Illinois and

---

[31] Van Raalte to Samuel B. Schieffelin, New York City, 8 July 1858; Van Raalte to Samuel Pruyn, New York City, 8 July 1858; Van Raalte to John Roost, 15 July 1858; Roost to Van Raalte, 11 Sept. 1858; Roost (Albany, NY) to Van Raalte, 11 July 1859, all in HHTC; Van Raalte to Philip Phelps Jr., 19 Nov. 1859, in Bruins and Schakel, *Envisioning Hope College*, 28-29; *Grand Rapids Daily Eagle*, 6 Sept, 4, 12 Oct. 1858; *De Hollander*, 19 Nov. 1859.

[32] Swierenga, *Holland, Michigan*, 1:697-98.

[33] According to the National Consumer Price Index, 1913-2014, the inflation factor is 22.

[34] Van Raalte to Phelps, 25 Oct. 1871, in Bruins and Schakel, *Envisioning Hope College*, 272-73.

Pella and raised several thousand dollars. Grand Rapids and Grand Haven churches also contributed generously. The state of Michigan provided $70,000 in construction materials to rebuild. Within eighteen months, the city was reborn, but it took many years for tree saplings to provide any shade.[35]

Van Raalte raised tens of thousands of dollars in the East for colonial lands, Holland harbor, Pillar Church, Holland Academy and Hope College, and various business ventures. Holland Colony would have survived and prospered without this help from the Old Dutch, but it would have been a more difficult slog. The assistance at critical times saved the newcomers who were in tight spots, but the lasting effects were slight. With or without General Synod, the Young Dutch would have planted churches across the western frontier, since few colonies could thrive without a church at the center. All the parochial day schools were short lived. On the other hand, the Reformed colleges and Western Theological Seminary absolutely needed RCA financial assistance in the early years. But even with that, only Hope, Northwestern, and Central (a Baptist college that was incorporated into the RCA in 1916) survived the Great Depression.

Long-term implications

In the long run, the Old Dutch Reformed churches needed the Young Dutch more than the other way around. The founding of a large number of new Dutch congregations across the western frontier made a profound difference in the future of that denomination. Indeed, without the "no" votes of the immigrant classes, the RCA would have merged with the German Reformed Church in 1893 or the Presbyterian Church in the twentieth century, which General Synod put to a vote twice—in 1950 (United Presbyterian Church) and in 1969 (Presbyterian Church United States, formerly Southern Presbyterian Church).[36]

If the RCA had merged with the Presbyterians, it would then have lost its historic Dutch confessions and heritage, just as the German Reformed Church, after a merger with the Evangelical and Reformed Church, became subsumed under the banner of the United Church of Christ. Ambivalent or not, the Old and Young Dutch cousins helped one another preserve a sense of Dutchness, and together they furthered the Kingdom of God in America.

---

[35] Swierenga, *Holland, Michigan*, 3:128-35.

[36] Herman Harmelink III, *Ecumenism and the Reformed Church* (Grand Rapids: Eerdmans, 1968), 52, 94; *Acts and Proceedings*, 1949: 165-69; 1950: 148-51; 1968: 273-97; 1969: 105.

Are the terms "Old Dutch" and "Young Dutch" still meaningful?

Old Dutch and *Young Dutch* are still meaningful today in the sense that the Eastern wing of the RCA reflects its American heritage and the Western wing its immigrant ancestry. The passage of time is of the essence. Old Dutch churches stretch back over 350 years, while Young Dutch churches go back 170 years at most. According to a 1976 RCA membership survey, the Particular Synod of New Jersey reported 26 percent Dutch or Part Dutch, Albany 24 percent, and New York only 12 percent. By contrast, the Particular Synods of Michigan reported 78 percent Dutch or Part Dutch, Chicago 69 percent, and West (from Iowa west) 58 percent. The Dutch ethnicity of the Eastern RCA was less than half that of the Western RCA, and the ratio would have been even lower if not for nineteenth-century Dutch Reformed immigrants who stayed in the East and joined RCA congregations.[37] Clearly, the Old Dutch are largely assimilated, but ethnicity continues to be an enduring legacy of the Young Dutch.

---

[37] Donald Luidens, "Portrait of a Denomination [RCA]," *Church Herald* 35 (1978): 4-5.

CHAPTER 6

El Dorado in the United States: Dutchmen, Dutch Americans, and the Quest for Gold in Indian Country, 1609–1880

Pieter Hovens

Throughout the history of humankind, the pursuit of material wealth was a force that energized governmental, commercial, and private endeavors to explore, colonize, and exploit foreign lands and peoples. From 1609 to 1890, the quest for gold captured the imagination of a number of Dutchmen and Dutch Americans, drawing them to different regions of North America. They searched for and dug the precious ore in New Netherland, the Upper Midwest, and in various parts of the Far West. Here they encountered Native tribes, the aboriginal inhabitants of the New World. Dutchmen and Dutch Americans played a variety of roles in the historic search for gold in North America on the various mining frontiers. They came from the ranks not only of low-skilled urban and rural classes but also of professionals, such as civil servants, military men, lawyers, and scientists, some of whom also became publicists, both promoters and critics of the rush to "El Dorado."[1] The exploits of some of them, the relations between prospectors and Indians, and their views on Indian policy are explored here for the first time, based on archival

---

[1] Europeans believed that somewhere in the New World there was a place of immense wealth known as El Dorado.

documents, historic newspapers, and published accounts from the United States and the Netherlands.[2]

In 1492 Christopher Columbus sailed westward across the Atlantic and arrived in a New World, at least for Europeans. It was not long before Spanish reports reached Europe about the native peoples of these lands, their possession of hoards of precious metals, and Indian chiefs decked out in gold jewelry. This caused Spanish adventurers to leave their ordinary lives behind to pursue their luck on the other side of the Atlantic. When Spain conquered the Indian civilizations of Mexico and Peru and brought back fortunes in gold and silver to their mother country, the rivalry with other European maritime powers keen on capturing that wealth intensified.[3]

Early European voyages to the Americas were driven by geopolitical and economic considerations. The expectation of the discovery of precious metals, notably gold, was more often than not a force also operative in such endeavors. The French and British were disappointed when they did not find gold in their North American colonies. The New World across the Atlantic was also soon equated with golden treasure in the Netherlands. Dutch allegorical portrayals of America in the fifteenth century soon showed Indians dredging for gold and central figures decked out in gold and jewels. In various contemporary literary texts of a philosophical and historical nature, the New World was also identified as a land of gold, a country reigned by El Dorado, the Gilded Man. Depending on the point of view of the artist or author, the gold land was either regarded as an unspoiled Garden of Eden or a morally corrupt environment, where real gold as well as golden opportunity could cause the fall of man from God's grace.[4]

New Netherland, 1609-1664

The Dutch colony of New Netherland on the Hudson and Delaware Rivers (1609-64) was never a major destination for gold seekers. Throughout its short history, however, a number of reports about the presence of the precious metal in New Netherland surfaced and fired the imagination of those who heard about them. When Henry Hudson was exploring the river in 1609 that would eventually bear his name, his shipmate Robert Juet wrote in his journal on July 17 that

---

[2]   A more extensive publication is planned for the near future.

[3]   Charles R. Boxer, *The Dutch Seaborne Empire* (New York: Knopf, 1965).

[4]   Benjamin Schmidt, *Innocence Abroad: The Dutch Imagination and the New World, 1570-1670* (Cambridge: Cambridge University Press, 2001), 129, 135-37, 244-45, 261-65.

Indians told them about the presence of gold, silver, and copper mines farther north. The *Halve Maen*'s crew was continually on the lookout for precious ores but found nothing of significance.[5] In 1624 the directors of the West India Company adopted pre-emptive provisional regulations for colonists, stating that any precious minerals belonged to the company and that the finder of gold and other ores would be rewarded with 10 percent of the net value of what was mined for six years.[6] A more liberal approach was adopted in 1638. The various reports about the discovery of gold in New Netherland proved to be disappointments. Most scientific analyses of specimens from the Delaware and Raritan Rivers, the Kittatinny Mountains, and elsewhere proved negative. What was hoped to be gold turned out to be pyrite, "fools gold." In a few instances the gold content was too low for mining to be profitable.[7]

An interesting episode took place in 1645 when director Willem Kieft visited the patroonship (estate) of Rensselaerwijck and Fort Orange for a meeting with the Mohawks. The patroonship's *schout* (sheriff), Adriaen van der Donck, had enlisted the services of headman Agheroense, who was fluent in several Iroquois languages as well as in Mahican. The Dutchmen witnessed the chief painting his face before the official meeting began. They were struck by the bright yellow color of the paint and immediately thought it might contain gold. Could this be El Dorado, the Gilded Man from the Gold Country? They purchased the face paint from Agheroense and obtained additional yellow mud from its source in the Catskill Mountains. This specimen, however, was lost in a shipwreck, and later chemical analysis proved negative.[8]

Although the precious metal was present in New Netherland, it was buried deep under layers of rock not eroded by water, thus explaining the absence of placer gold in riverbeds. Furs yielded by far the highest profits of any commodity obtained from New Netherland, and the beaver has therefore been referred to as the four-legged gold mine of the Dutch.[9]

---

[5] Robert Juet, *Henry Hudson's Reize onder Nederlandsche Vlag naar Noza Zembla, Amerika en Terug* (The Hague: Martinus Nijhoff, 1921), 28.

[6] A. J. F. van Laer, ed., *Documents Relating to New Netherland, 1624-1626* (San Marino, CA: Henry E. Huntington Library, 1924), Document A, articles 10 and 11.

[7] Herbert C. Kraft, *The Dutch, the Indians, and the Quest for Copper* (South Orange, NJ: Seton Hall University Museum, 1996), 37-39, passim.

[8] Adriaen van der Donck, *A Description of New Netherlands* (Syracuse, NY: Syracuse University Press, 1968), 35-36.

[9] E.g., Reed Sparling and Ted Spiegel, *Hudson Valley Voyage: Through the Seasons, through the Years* (Fishkill, NY: Involvement Media, 2007), 17.

The Upper Midwest and the Dakotas, 1840-77

In the 1840s, many Dutch emigrated and settled in Michigan, Wisconsin, Iowa, and Minnesota, but they were seldom aroused by reports of gold finds in their states. Usually the discoveries proved to be small and unprofitable. In 1874 illegal prospectors discovered gold in the Black Hills of South Dakota, officially Indian territory. Lt. Col. George Armstrong Custer confirmed the discovery, and soon thousands of fortune seekers hurried to the region.[10] But the Dutch immigrant newspapers such as *De Volksvriend* from Orange City, Iowa, and even some national newspapers in the Netherlands (*De Tijd* and *Algemeen Handelsblad*) informed their readers of the danger of armed resistance by the Sioux and Cheyennes against the invasion of their lands. Any sign or act of opposition of the native tribes against white encroachment onto their land and interest in gold was termed *verraderlijk* (treacherous) in *De Volksvriend*.[11] Eventually the Indians defeated Custer and his army at the Battle of the Big Horn in 1876. The Black Hills Gold Rush (1874-77) was short lived and had little impact on the Dutch and Dutch American farmers who had settled in the Great Lakes and Midwestern states.[12] By that time the emigrants had begun to take root in American soil and society, although they maintained a distinct Dutch identity.

The California Gold Rush

In early 1848, gold was discovered at Sutter's mill on the American River in northern California's Sacramento Valley. When President Polk publicly confirmed to Congress the genuine nature of the find in December 1848, the unprecedented California Gold Rush was on. Fortune seekers dashed to the gold fields in droves, crossing the plains and western deserts en masse or arriving by ship after crossing Central America overland or by rounding Cape Horn. They were a brand of men that had little consideration for either the natural environment or the Indians and their rights to the land they had occupied for thousands of years.

The Dutch mass media were quick to pick up the news. National and provincial newspapers reported about every new discovery and the high quality of the ore; the fastest and safest ways to reach the gold fields; the skyrocketing price of tents, tools, clothing, and food;

[10]   Watson Parker, *Gold in the Black Hills* (Lincoln: University of Nebraska Press, 1966).
[11]   Cf., Black Hills article in: *De Volksvriend*, 20 August 1874.
[12]   John D. McDermott, ed., *Gold Rush: The Black Hills Story* (Pierre: South Dakota State Historical Society Press, 2004).

working conditions and health hazards; the need to employ Indians for the heavy physical labor, and so on. Several papers also noted that the rising demand for food and goods was an economic opportunity for the Dutch and that entrepreneurs in Rotterdam and Amsterdam were already cashing in on the profitable trade. From 1850 to 1855, about ninety Dutch ships had anchored at San Francisco.[13] Cornelius Vanderbilt (1794-1877), American businessman of Dutch ancestry, made his fortune partially in this way.[14]

Several guides to the California gold fields were published in Dutch.[15] In early 1849, the Dutch who had settled in Pella, Iowa, witnessed a steady and increasing stream of gold seekers trekking through their own town and area en route to California. Many Dutch settlers in Pella profited from this mass migration which continued for several years, selling meat, produce, and trade goods at elevated prices to the passing travelers. Only a few Dutchmen from the Upper Midwest joined the "forty-niners" to California, even from Pella.[16] They had found their place of refuge. More people went to California directly from the Netherlands, although in comparison to other nations, their number was small. Also a small number of Dutch Americans whose earlier generations had settled in the northeastern United States joined the trek. Many ran out of money or became ill. The luckiest returned home to their families, penniless, but alive, but some died in the gold fields of various afflictions associated with life and work in harsh and unsanitary conditions.[17]

Walter Van Dyke: prospector and publisher in Northwestern California, 1849-63

Among the Easterners flocking to California in 1849 was Walter Van Dyke, a descendant of a Dutch American family from

[13] Jacob Van Hinte, *Netherlanders in America: A Study of Emigration and Settlement in the 19th and 20th Centuries in the United States of America* (Grand Rapids, MI: Baker Book House, 1985), 630.

[14] C. Carl Pegels, *Prominent Dutch American Entrepreneurs: Their Contribution to American Society, Culture, and Economy* (Charlotte, NC, Information Age Publishing, 2011), part 3.

[15] N. N., *Gids naar California* (Amsterdam: Van Heteren, 1849). C. L. Plasberg, *Californië* (Arnhem: Stenfert Kroese, 1849).

[16] Henry S. Lucas, *Netherlanders in America: Dutch Immigration to the United States and Canada, 1789-1950* (Ann Arbor: University of Michigan Press, 1955), 696. Brian W. Beltman, "The California Gold Rush and a Few Dutch Argonauts from Pella," *Origins* 18, no. 2 (2010): 29-35. Jan Nollen, *De Afscheiding: een Gedenkschrift.* (Orange City, IA: De Volksvriend Printing House, 1898), 53-54.

[17] Lucas, *Netherlanders in America*, 193-94, 390-91. Van Hinte, *Netherlanders in America*, 274-75, 629-32, 1071.

New Netherland that was still being extended by new kinsmen from the Netherlands in the early nineteenth century. Van Dyke was born on October 3, 1823, in Tyre, Seneca County, New York. He attended Earlville School and Clinton Liberal Institute and obtained a law degree in Cleveland in 1848.[18] He recalled that the country was "electrified" by the accounts of the discovery of gold in California. A number of friends and acquaintances decided to try their luck out West and persuaded him to come along. In May 1849, they left Cleveland by boat, and in Chicago, they outfitted for the overland trek. On August 31, they spent a night with friendly Sioux and Cheyenne Indians on the Platte River near Fort Laramie. They traversed the Sierra Nevada during a severe snow storm. Crossing Paiute territory was daunting since these Indians had a reputation of being hostile to white trespassers. They reached Las Vegas without being troubled, although most of their stock had perished. In February 1850, they reached the colonized and fertile country again.[19]

After unsuccessfully prospecting on the American River near Sutter's Fort, Van Dyke sailed north to the Klamath River on the bark *Tarquin*. A trading post had just been opened, and the small white settlement on Humboldt Bay began primarily as a supply center for the gold mining camps on the Klamath, Trinity, and Salmon Rivers. The towns and ports of Eureka, Union (Arcata), and Trinidad had just been established. At the mouth of the Klamath River, the *Tarquin* struck rocks and went down immediately. Local Indians and some white pioneers rushed to the scene and rescued the crew and passengers. In the black sands of the Klamath River estuary, Van Dyke found gold, and with several associates formed the Gold Bluff Company and began to exploit the sands. When the yield proved disappointing, Van Dyke sold his interest in the venture in 1851 and settled in Trinidad to practice law.[20]

The Indians living on the coast and the Lower Klamath River had been warning the prospectors and settlers against the hostile Indians on the Upper Klamath and Trinity Rivers. Van Dyke sagely remarked:

> Not much attention was paid to those warnings, however, they being looked upon as a sort of ruse, to ingratiate the Indians

[18]   James Miller Guinn, *Historical and Biographical Record of Los Angeles and Vicinity* (Chicago: Chapman, 1901), 628-29.

[19]   Walter Van Dyke, "Overland to Los Angeles, by the Salt Lake Route in 1849," *Annual Publication of the Historical Society of Southern California* 3, no. 2 (1894): 76-83.

[20]   Walter Van Dyke, "Early Days in Klamath," *Overland Monthly and Out West Magazine* 17, no. 104 (191), 174-81. Guinn, *Historical and Biographical*, 628.

with the newcomers at the expense of their enemies—a device not limited to savages by any means. For this reason, the whites had been less cautious than prudence would dictate under the circumstances.[21]

During the summer of 1851, the Indians of the interior attacked a small mining camp and killed several prospectors. The white settlers in the region soon organized retaliatory raids, during which, they killed all of the Indians they encountered and destroyed their villages, irrespective of whether they were involved in the attack.

The federal government dispatched Indian agent Colonel Redick McKee to the area. In early October 1851, he gathered all the Klamath and Hoopa Indians at Durkee's Ferry at the junction of the Trinity and Klamath Rivers. The treaty negotiated was signed on October 6, and Van Dyke was an official witness, signing the official document. The treaty stipulated peace between Indians and whites; the conciliation of future interethnic conflicts by American authorities in an unbiased manner; the cession of all tribal lands to the federal government in exchange for a reservation forever guaranteed as inalienable Indian property; the relocation of all tribal members to the reservation within three years; the provision by the federal government of education and instruction in farming; and compensation payment to the Indians for two years, including five hundred pairs of Mackinaw blankets, five hundred pairs of pants, five hundred white cotton shirts, five hundred red flannel shirts, five hundred cotton dresses, three thousand yards of calico and sewing materials, butcher knives, garden hoes, axes, and iron kettles.

It took until 1853 before a fort was established on Humboldt Bay to protect the miners and settlers from hostile Indians in northwestern California. Van Dyke procured the land for the government, but he regarded the coastal location for keeping the Indians of the interior in check as ill-advised and was proven right by continual inland interethnic troubles.[22]

Van Dyke established and edited several regional newspapers in the early 1850s and editorialized on Indian-white relations.[23] As a concerned citizen, he frequently wrote to state authorities to voice the concerns of settlers and miners. Newspaper reports and several

[21]   Van Dyke, "Early Days," 178.
[22]   Ibid., 178-80.
[23]   W. W. Elliott, "History of Humboldt County Newspaper Enterprises," *History of Humboldt County, California* (San Francisco: Wallace W. Elliott & Co., 1881), 215-18.

letters have survived and document Van Dyke's involvement in Indian affairs. The earliest letter dates from March 10, 1852, and is addressed to Governor John Bigler. In it Van Dyke recounts the many incidences of murder among the Indians and whites, and urgently requests the establishment of an army garrison at the junction of the Klamath and Trinity Rivers and in Scott Valley. A similar letter was sent to General Hitchcock of the Department of the Pacific, and Van Dyke requested a speedy reply.[24]

During the course of 1852, the army undertook some action, and Brigadier General George Wright of the Department of the Pacific informed Walter Van Dyke of measures taken. Colonel Lippitt had been put in charge of Humboldt County and the wider region, with ten companies of infantry and one artillery company at his disposal. Three hundred Indians were rounded up and taken to Forth Klamath, awaiting their transportation to a reservation.[25] The removal, however, of a small number of Indians did little to alleviate the situation. Some escaped from Fort Klamath and returned to their homeland. White vigilante groups raided Indian villages and captured Indian women and children to be sold into slavery. Indians retaliated, and the cycle of violence intensified during the course of the 1850s.

California governor John P. Downey called for the organization of defensive companies consisting of local volunteers, and Van Dyke became engaged in that endeavor in Humboldt County. On November 26, 1861, he wrote to the governor that Indian troubles in his region were worse than ever. He pointed out that, through dealings with unscrupulous traders, stealing from isolated ranches, and attacks on lone travelers, the natives had obtained a substantial number of firearms with which they had become increasingly adept. This emboldened them to attack small groups of settlers or travelers and defend themselves, whereas they formerly fled if they feared punishment or reprisal. Van Dyke stressed that the Indian threat could be overcome only by disarming the natives and removing them to a reservation where they could do no more harm. He suggested that the local voluntary defense companies should be replaced by regular army troops to control and defeat what he called the "savages." Two companies would be needed: one stationed on the Mad River and its tributary, Redwood Creek, and the other on Van Dusen's Fork of the Eel River. They would be able

---

[24]   Letters Received by the Office of Indian Affairs, 1824-1881, National Archives, Washington (1958), 866-75.
[25]   Ibid. (12 June 1862), 1134.

to defeat the Indians during a winter campaign and, by spring, clear the region of aboriginal inhabitants. They could be resettled on a reservation under supervision by a capable and honest Indian agent, and peace could be assured if sufficient assistance was provided to the natives to become self-sufficient again. Colonel Whipple had told Van Dyke in confidence that he was willing to act as special agent to secure the rounding up and removal of the Indians, and Van Dyke wholly endorsed his appointment.[26]

Downey's successor, Leland Stanford, issued an order on June 19, 1862, to issue thirty rifles and additional required equipment to Walter Van Dyke to supply the volunteer company for the maintenance of law and order in Humboldt County, notably to control Indian depredations.[27]

On November 25, 1862, Van Dyke reported back to the governor. It was not good news. He related that the Indians from the Humboldt region had become so audacious that they had caused white settlers in outlying and isolated settlements to flee their ranches and seek refuge in the towns. Some had even left northwest California altogether to find more peaceful surroundings. The Indians had killed the beef and dairy herds of the settlers for food. The balance of power was shifting fast to the advantage of the native inhabitants, while the white population suffered economically and became increasingly vulnerable. The Indians had acquired so many firearms and so much ammunition that they did not fear the settlers. They were aware of the fear their raids instilled in the whites and used their newly gained power to keep the pressure on the newcomers, gaining back lost ground. They had even given up their traditional means of subsistence such as hunting, fishing, and gathering, and instead lived on the spoils of their raids. They seemed to have lost all fear of whites as shown by their disregard for human life and indiscriminate murdering of settlers. That this behavior might have been revenge and retaliation against the white frontiersmen who had invaded and taken their land seemingly did not occur to Van Dyke or many of his contemporaries on the northwestern frontier in California.

The Dutchman characterized the current situation as a crisis, the outcome of which would be either the departure of the white settlers from the region, thus leaving this part of the state in Indian hands, or

---

[26] Van Dyke to Governor Downey, 26 Nov. 1861; in: Military Department, Adjutant General, Indian War Papers: F3753:597; California State Archives, Sacramento.

[27] Governor Stanford to Executive Department, 19 June 1862 (California State Archives, n.r. F3753:614).

the forced removal of the natives to an area where they were under the control of authorities and not in the way of settlement. In Van Dyke's opinion, no part of the state had suffered so severely and for so long from Indian depredations. This situation required swift and effective action by the government. Van Dyke notes that it was the federal government that had induced the settlers to go west, provided them with cheap land, and now bore the responsibility to aid them in their hour of need. Experience had shown that it was impossible for both races to live together or even adjacent to each other. The option of a reservation in their ancestral lands was unacceptable. In Van Dyke's view, northeastern California was fit for white settlement only; the Indian problem would be solved once and for all by their complete removal from the region. A discussion among the members of the volunteer militia had resulted in that unanimous recommendation. Moreover, the authorities needed to restrict movement of the Indians when placed on reservations to prevent their absconding and returning to their homeland or roaming the countryside as a nuisance for settlers. The experience with deporting Indians to the Klamath Reservation had thus been unsuccessful. Van Dyke and the settlers abhorred the lack of results of this policy and the waste of government resources. They clamored for a permanent solution, possibly resettlement of the Indians on a reservation in southern California or in Oregon or Washington Territory. George Hanson, California superintendent of Indian affairs, however, had made it clear that he was not authorized to deport Indians out of state and could make arrangements for reservations for tribes only in the regions in which they lived originally. Van Dyke closed his letter by expressing the hope that he had demonstrated the urgency of a change of policy by the state of California and of a solution to the Indian problem once and for all.[28]

On January 7, 1863, Governor Leland spoke to the Senate and Legislative Assembly and addressed Indian hostilities and the untimely and ineffective response by the army. He was quite frank and spoke about the "miserable management of Indian affairs," asking for support in demanding from the authorities in Washington, DC, effective action with regard to the protection of the citizens of their state and the reparation of damages and losses incurred by settlers as the result of Indian raids.[29] Van Dyke moved to Southern California that year where

---

[28] Van Dyke to Governor Stanford, 25 Nov. 1862; in: Military Department, Adjutant General, Indian War Papers: F3753:623; California State Archives, Sacramento.

[29] Weekly *Humboldt Times*, 24 January 1863.

he practiced law, served in the State Assembly and Senate, and sat on the Supreme Court. He died on Christmas Day 1905 and was buried at Mountain View Cemetery in Oakland.[30]

Henry DeGroot: mining reports from the American West, 1855-65

Henry DeGroot was a member of an American family from New York with firm roots in the Netherlands. Although his father had died young, Henry was able to pursue academic studies and obtain a law degree at Union College in nearby Schenectady. In New York City, he joined the *Tribune* as a junior writer. When reports about the discovery of gold in the Sierra Madre of California reached the eastern seaboard, Horace Greeley sent DeGroot westward to cover the news.[31]

On February 28, 1849, DeGroot arrived in California and soon thereafter interviewed John A. Sutter and several other prospectors who had made the promising finds. His factual articles based on these interviews and his own experience in the field found a receptive audience back home. The Dutchman characterized the new arrivals as "an excited, eager, and rushing crowd, going for everything within reach," that "ended the old civilization."[32]

In 1850 DeGroot brought his family out west and settled in San Francisco. He embarked on a dual career, prospecting for precious metals while simultaneously establishing local newspapers and writing articles on mining for his own local and large urban newspapers. Often he was among the first in the field when new discoveries of gold and other precious metals became known. He was said to have visited every mining district in California and Nevada. Eventually he lost much money in unprofitable investments. He lived mostly on the income from writing for newspapers and publishing pamphlets and books on mining.[33]

In 1860 DeGroot was exploring the Washoe River district in western Nevada for precious minerals. Back in San Francisco, he published the first of several editions of *Sketches of the Washoe River Silver Mines*, as well as a

---

30   Oscar T. Shuck, *History of the Bench and Bar of California* (Los Angeles: Commercial Printing House, 1901), 495-99. D. K. Trask, "In Memoriam: Walter Van Dyke," *Minutes of the Superior Court of Los Angeles County* (1916), 779-81.

31   F. E. Birge, "Henry DeGroot," *Overland Monthly* 11 (1893): 261-63. J. F. Pinkham, J. F. and W. P. Harrington, "Doctor Henry DeGroot," *Obituary Records of the Society of California Pioneers* 3 (1893), 13, 15.

32   Henry DeGroot, *Recollections of California Mining Life* (San Francisco: Dewey & Co., 1884), 15.

33   Pinkham and Harrington, "Doctor Henry DeGroot," passim.

map of the mining district, of which an edition in French also appeared.[34] He had learned cartography for additional skill as a mining journalist and continually studied the technical aspects and innovations to better inform his readership. In his little book about Nevada and Utah mining, he mentions only casually the presence of Mono Indians in the Mono Lake region and Paiutes on the Walker River.

DeGroot spent at least some time with the Monos, as he collected a vocabulary of the Washoe tribal language. He told how the Monos collected insects that had gathered in huge quantities on the surface of the lake saturated with minerals but otherwise devoid of aquatic life. The Indians collected the fly-like creatures along the lake's shores with wicker scoops in such quantities that it was their staple food in the otherwise barren environment. DeGroot characterizes the Monos as "a quiet, feeble, and inoffensive people" who remained extremely poor and simple in their habits and customs because of the starkness of their natural environment. Besides the lake's insects, they subsisted on roots and berries and hunted hares with bows and arrows. They dressed themselves in animal skins, usually obtained from hares but occasionally from deer. The Monos usually kept their distance from white travelers and settlers.

The Paiutes on the Walker River were of larger stature and stronger build. They lived in dome-shaped huts constructed from willow and sage. DeGroot found them honest and peaceful, always with a friendly disposition toward white newcomers, who in turn learned to appreciate the industriousness, honesty, and sobriety of the Paiutes. Some were engaged in wage labor for white settlers. Throughout his treatise, DeGroot mentions the presence of the aboriginal population that had settled this region long before the Euro Americans arrived. He clearly is in favor of settling Indian land claims before white settlement was to take place and advocates "good treatment and a just policy. The policy of the federal government of creating reservations and assigning the different tribes to them seems to have had his support.[35]

In 1862 DeGroot investigated reports about the discovery of gold in the La Paz area on the Arizona side of the Colorado River north of Fort Yuma and sent his reports to the *San Francisco Bulletin*. He and his party traveled along an Indian trail that ran from Agua Caliente (Palm Springs) to the Pima villages in south central Arizona. En route they encountered

---

[34]   Henry DeGroot, *Sketches of the Washoe River Silver Mines* (San Francisco: Hutchings and Rosenfield, 1860). Henry DeGroot, *California: Description Physique de l'Utah Occidental et Dernieres Decouvertes Metallurgiques dans cet Etat* (Geneva: Impremerie J. G. Fick, 1860).

[35]   DeGroot, *Sketches*, 6-9, 11, 16, 18.

only a few Cahuilla Indians; the others had fled in the wake of the murder by Omos, an Agua Caliente Indian, of San Bernardino County deputy sheriff Rush Dickey. Cahuilla chief Juan Antonio had promised to bring the culprit in, since they were intent on maintaining friendly relations with the white newcomers. The heat was stifling, and drinking water was hard to come by. En route they traded with the Indians they encountered for feed for their horses and mules and for food for the rapidly exhausting men. At La Paz, DeGroot took notice of the scattered and limited finds of gold. Although the miners were predominantly Mexican, they also included Indians: Yaquis from Sonora and Yumas, Mohaves, and Paiutes from the Colorado River Valley. Especially the Yaquis seemed physically adjusted to a similar natural environment farther south that enabled them to earn a good income. Back in San Francisco, DeGroot published a booklet about the Colorado River mines in which he tried to convince his readers that this find did not warrant a gold rush.[36]

For many years DeGroot wrote for daily news media and the *Mining and Scientific Press*, for which he also occasionally acted as editor. He also began writing more technical and scientific reports for agencies, including the California State Mining Bureau and the US Geological Survey.[37] DeGroot's serious research, practical experience, and factual reporting resulted in widespread recognition by the public, as well as by businessmen and mining professionals, of the quality of his work and a distinguished career. Later in life he tried his hand at poetry, and one long poem, the *Colloquy of the Old Timers*, survives. It records the conversation of two aging prospectors about the good old days when life was full of promise and excitement. They discuss encounters with Indians, including a shootout with Apaches and a violent encounter with a Brulé Sioux.[38] At the age of seventy-three, DeGroot died on March 28, 1893, in Alameda, when he was hit by a train he had not heard coming from behind. The Society of California Pioneers arranged for his funeral, honoring the man and his work.[39]

From 1848 the various California gold rushes resulted in a massive influx of fortune seekers from other parts of North America, Europe, and

---

[36] Henry DeGroot, *Guide to the Colorado Mine* (San Francisco: H. H. Bancroft, 1863); Gerald Thompson, "Henry deGroot and the Colorado River Gold Rush, 1862," *Journal of Arizona History* 37, no. 2 (1996): 131-48.

[37] Mining Bureau Records, Receipt Books, 1889-1903 (California State Archives, Sacramento).

[38] The poem was published in the *Golden City* newspaper (El Dorado County, CA) but has survived only as a typewritten copy in the archives of the California State Library (STX q811D3).

[39] Pinkham and Harrington, "Doctor Henry De Groot," passim.

even Asia. In their obsession to become rich quickly, these men destroyed every obstacle in their path: mountains, forests, and rivers, as well as the aboriginal occupants of the land. The latter, in the best of cases, were forcibly removed onto small reservations (called *rancherias*); they were chased from their lands to become impoverished rural folk, and in quite a few cases, they were physically exterminated. Hubert Howe Bancroft, who authored the main study of the history of the state in seven stout volumes in the 1880s, concluded, "The California valley cannot grace her annals with a single Indian war bordering on respectability. It can boast, however, a hundred or two of as brutal butchering on the part of our honest miners and brave pioneers. . . . The poor natives of California had neither the strength nor the intelligence to unite in any formidable numbers; hence, when now and then one of them plucked up courage to defend his wife and little ones or to retaliate on one of the many outrages that were constantly being perpetrated upon them by whites, sufficient excuse was offered for the miners and settlers to band and shoot down any Indians they met, old or young, innocent or guilty, friendly or hostile, until their appetite for blood was appeased."[40] After analyzing the documentary evidence, several ethnohistorians concluded that this era of Indian-white relations in California approached genocide, not in massive campaigns, but in numerous local episodes, as part of the popular mass enterprise of conquest and exploitation of natural resources.[41] In the end, the number of Dutch rushing to California after the discovery of gold in 1848 was limited. The 1850 census lists 63 settlers as of Dutch descent, while 439 were registered in 1860, and for the next ten years, this number remained stable

John J. Van Bokkelen and Stephen Van Buren Boyce: gold, Indians, and law enforcement in the Pacific Northwest, 1845-75

The Van Bokkelen family had its origins in the United States around 1800 when a Dutch mariner by the name of Hogerwaard Van Bokkelen, a captain on intercontinental sailing ships, settled in New York. His son, J. J. (Jacobus Jan/John J.), was born on October 24, 1816, in Brooklyn, New York. After his formal schooling, John worked as a

---

[40] Jack. D. Forbes, *Native Americans of California and Nevada* (Healdsburg, CA: Naturegraph, 1968), 52-53.

[41] Albert L. Hurtado, *Indian Survival on the California Frontier* (New Haven, MS: Yale University Press, 1988); Kimberly Johnston-Dodds, *Bearing Archival Witness to Euro American Violence Against California Indians, 1847-1866* (Sacramento: California State University, MA thesis, 2009).

clerk for different companies in his native city, as well as in Alabama and North Carolina, but his health was poor. The family physician suggested that the climate in California would be beneficial. On his arrival there, the news about the discovery of gold prompted him to go prospecting in the Pilot Hill and Big Bar districts. He failed to find the precious metal and returned to San Francisco where he received an appointment as customs inspector.[42]

Gold fever, however, had J. J. Van Bokkelen in its grasp, and in 1851, he did some prospecting on the Queen Charlotte Islands, home of the Haida Indians. Here he was equally unsuccessful, but he tried his luck again in 1852 in California. In 1853 he accompanied Captain Thomas Coupe on the *Success* to Whidbey Island. At Penn Cove they established the town of Coupeville on Saratoga Passage, near three (Lower) Skagit villages and a native burial ground.[43] In 1853 Van Bokkelen prospected for coal on Vancouver Island and at the nascent settlement of Whatcom on Bellingham Bay.[44]

Wishing to open up the country for white settlers and contain the Indians on small reservations, the federal government, represented by Governor Isaac Ingalls Stevens, entered into treaty negations with the tribes of western Washington. A series of treaties were signed in 1854-55. On January 22, 1855, near Everett, the Treaty of Point Elliott was concluded. This included the Skagit, the Snoqualmie, and other Lutshootseed Indians who were destined to be settled on the small Tulalip (Snohomish), Lummi, and Swinomish Indian Reservations.[45] From 1855 to 1862, Indian affairs in the Puget Sound region were overseen by Robert Fay from the Penn Cove Special Indian Agency on Whidbey Island.

In the winter of 1855-56, war broke out between the hard-pressed Indians and the growing number of white settlers in the Puget Sound area. The latter congregated for safety in blockhouses. Van Bokkelen enlisted under the command of Captain Isaac N. Ebey, became captain, and was promoted to major of the Northern Battalion. Van Bokkelen was at Whatcom to organize and execute the construction of a stockade on Peabody Hill to protect white settlers from Indian attacks. On one occasion, the major led the whole battalion on a foray

42   Noel V. Bourasaw, "J. J. Van Bokkelen: Washington Territory Pioneer," *Skagit River Journal of History and Folklore* 2004 (www.skagitriverjournal.com; accessed 5 Dec. 2015).

43   Douglas Deur, *Ebey's Landing National Historical Reserve: An Ethnohistory of Traditionally Associated Contemporary Populations* (Seattle, WA: National Park Service, 2009), 80-84.

44   David B. Richardson, *Pig War Islands* (Orcas, WA: Orcas Publishing Company, 1971), 44. Bourasaw, "J. J. Van Bokkelen."

45   Deur, *Ebey's Landing*, 103-7, 230-35.

up the Snoqualmie River, but no confrontations with hostile Indians occurred. This expedition was backed by the federal government and represented by territorial governor Isaac Ingalls Stevens, since Snoqualmie Pass was a major communication venue between the Indian tribes of the interior and the coast and needed to be checked. Van Bokkelen was ordered to identify favorable locations to build forts to prevent the interior Indians from attacking settlers on Puget Sound. The major accomplished his commission, aided by Chief Pat Kanim of the Snoqualmie tribe who was disposed to be friendly toward the white newcomers. Three small strongholds were constructed, and the larger Fort Tilton accommodated two hundred soldiers. The Indian coalition eventually faltered, but in the turmoil, Colonel Ebey was captured by northern Indians and decapitated.[46]

Van Bokkelen settled in nascent Port Townsend in 1857. Several hundred Clallam and Chemakum Indians remained in the area, stalling their removal to the Skokomish Reservation. Frequently Van Bokkelen had to deal with unscrupulous whiskey traders illegally supplying the region's natives. With some associates, he took another chance on striking it rich in 1858 when Indians took his party inland in their canoes on the Skagit River, portaging strenuously past the log jams into unknown territory. The Upper Skagit Indians they met were friendly, but the yield in gold was disappointing, and J. J. Van Bokkelen abandoned treasure hunting for the rest of his life.[47]

Port Townsend, Kitsap County, was a community of about three hundred inhabitants. Van Bokkelen again worked as customs inspector, a position also referred to as port master.[48] In March 1859, he made the acquaintance of newly arrived entrepreneur James Swan, who had developed an interest in the native tribes of the Pacific Northwest. For a while Swan was the Dutchman's guest, and they became friends. Their personalities must have been compatible, and their interest in Indians was mutual. While Van Bokkelen had become involved in Indians affairs through his explorations for gold and his work as a customs inspector,

---

[46] Edmund T. Coleman, "Puget Sound and the Northern Pacific Railroad," *Washington Historical Quarterly* 23, no. 4 (1932), 245-47. Lelah Jackson Edson, *The Fourth Corner: Highlights from the Early Northwest* (Bellingham, WA: Cox Brothers, 1951), 55-57. Deur, *Ebey's Landing*, 10-114, 119; Yvonne Prater, *Snoqualmie Pass: From Indian Trail to Interstate* (Seattle, WA: Mountaineers Press, 1981), 25-27.

[47] N. N., *An Illustrated History of Skagit and Snohomish Counties* (Chicago: Interstate Publishing Company, 1906), 100. Margaret Willis, ed., *Chechacos All: The Pioneering of Skagit* (Mount Vernon, WA: Skagit County Historical Society, 1973), 22-23; Bourasaw, "J. J. Van Bokkelen."

[48] Edson, *The Fourth Corner*, 86.

Swan had been assisting Governor Stevens with his treaty negotiations with the tribes of Washington Territory in the mid-1850s. On a visit to the capital, Swan was enlisted to collect Indian artifacts from the Northwest Pacific tribes by the Smithsonian Institute's director, Spencer F. Baird, and secretary, Joseph Henry. In 1860 Van Bokkelen became city clerk and then city auditor of Port Townsend. Subsequently, he served as Jefferson County sheriff for eight years and represented the people of his county for two terms in the territorial legislature.[49]

Stephen V. (Van Buren) Boyce (Buijs-Buys-Boyce) was also of Dutch origin, a descendant of the seventeenth-century New Netherland immigrant Aert (Adriaen) Pieterse Buys from the town of Beest in the province of Gelderland. Stephen Boyce was born on January 28, in either 1825 or 1829, in Greene County, New York. He ran away from home when he was twelve, stayed with an uncle, and travelled westward, working and learning a variety of trades. In 1851 in San Francisco, gold fever caught him, and he prospected near Placerville and Georgetown. In 1858 Boyce heard about the gold rush on the Fraser River and took his family north to Victoria on Vancouver Island. He journeyed inland and worked the Cariboo gold fields for two years. Subsequently the family moved to San Juan Island to open a post to trade with the Coast Salish Indians. Because the British authorities refused him a license, he took up farming near False Bay. Intermittently between 1860 and 1874, he served as justice of the peace and sheriff. Among white settlers, as well as Indians, he gained respect for his evenhanded and just dealings. The Indians called him Hyas Tyee, meaning Great Man.[50]

In 1872 settler William Fuller was found murdered on his property, and in March 1873, farmer Harry Dwyer and his wife suffered the same fate. Sheriff Boyce investigated both cases, and four Indians were arrested. Joe Nuanna, aka Kanaka Joe, a seventeen-year-old, half Indian (because of a Stikine Tlingit mother from Alaska), half Hawaiian (Kanaka) had no alibi, and some of the personal belongings of one victim were found in his possession. He was taken to Port Townsend for trial and convicted to death. On the night before his execution, Nuanna admitted the Dwyer killings and the Fuller murder. The trial and the confession, however, are still a matter of some controversy. Sheriffs Boyce and Van Bokkelen accompanied him to the gallows on San Juan

---

49 James P. Swan, *Almost Out of the World: Scenes from Washington Territory* (Tacoma: Washington State Historical Society, 1971), xix, 11-15.

50 Harvey K. Hines, *An Illustrated History of the State of Washington* (Chicago: Lewis Publishing Company, 1894), 524-25. Clayton Francis Boyce, *Four Generations: A Family History* (at: www.michaelboyce.com; accessed 1 Dec. 2015).

Island on March 6, 1874. Before the noose was placed around his neck and the verdict executed, he turned to the crowd that had gathered and declared "I am very sorry for what I have done. All hands, goodbye."[51]

Epilogue

In addition to the protagonists of our story, there were other Dutchmen and Dutch Americans who searched for El Dorado in the American West and who were at one time or another confronted with the native inhabitants, directly or indirectly, such as stockman Nelson Van Tassel (1821-1904) from New York State, banker James De Fremery (1826-1899) from Holland,[52] Dutch American civil servant William Vandever (1817-1893),[53] and journalist John J. VandeMoer (1849-1926) from Amsterdam. A review of the involvement of Dutchmen and Dutch Americans in the various gold rushes in North America, however, demonstrates that the glint of metal in the rocks was generally not the thing that caught their attention and mobilized them in droves to leave their homes for possible distant fortunes. Rather, their El Dorado consisted of cheap land for farming and an environment as free as possible from government interference with their way of life and religious beliefs. Between 1820 and 1920, this more mundane El Dorado attracted almost three hundred and forty thousand emigrants from the Netherlands who settled in the Great Lakes region and the Upper Midwest and in ethnic enclaves across the Plains and the Pacific Northwest. Today many of their communities prosper and have retained a measure of Dutch identity and heritage, proof that they have found their own El Dorado in the American West.[54]

---

[51] E.g., *Seattle Weekly Intelligencer*, 24 May, 14 June, 13 Dec. 1873, and 7 March 1874; *Victoria Daily Standard*, 6 Nov. and 12 Dec. 1873; Richardson, *Pig War Islands*, 159-75.

[52] Pieter Hovens, "Collectors, Collections, and Museums: Native North Americana in the Netherlands," in *North American Indian Art: Masterpieces and Museum Collections in the Netherlands*, ed. Pieter Hovens and Bruce Bernstein (Leiden and Altenstadt; National Museum of Ethnology and ZKF Publishers, 2015), 25-26.

[53] Douglas F. Anderson, "More Conscience than Force: US Indian Inspector William Vandever, Grant's Peace Policy, and Protestant Whiteness," *Journal of the Gilded Age and Progressive Era* 9 (2010), 167-96.

[54] The author wishes to acknowledge the assistance of the staff from the California State University Library in Chico; the California State Library and California State Archives in Sacramento; the Society of California Pioneers in San Francisco; the Washington State Library in Olympia; the Hayden Library of Arizona State University in Tucson; the Charles C. Myers Library of the University of Dubuque in Dubuque, Iowa; the Western History Collections at the Denver Public Library; the Iowa State Historical Society in Des Moines; and the Hamaker Library of Northwestern College in Orange City, Iowa.

Part Three

The Dutch and Indians under
English Colonial Rule

CHAPTER 7

Prisoners and Profiteers: Commerce and Imperial Loyalty on the Albany Frontier, 1689–1713

Erin Kramer

Cadwallader Colden, a leading eighteenth-century New York politician, did not hide his disdain for the commercial and political elite of Albany, New York. At the beginning of the second part of his *History of the Five Indian Nations, Depending on the Province of New-York*, he plainly states of Albany's Dutch inhabitants:

> It is true, that the Plantations were first settled by the meanest People of every Nation, and such as had the least Sense of any Honour. The *Dutch* first Settlers, many of them I may say, had none of the Virtues of their Countrymen, except their Industry in getting Money, and they sacrificed every Thing, other People think honourable or most sacred, to their Gain.[1]

His assessment sets up the major themes of the narratives that follow his introduction: the values of honor and virtue and the

---

[1] Cadwallader Colden, *A History of the Five Indian Nations, Depending on the Province of New-York in America and are the Barrier between the English and the French in that Part of the World*, 3rd ed. (1755), 1:100-101.

149

detrimental allure of easy money. Throughout his *History*, he juxtaposes those who possessed "honour" with those who sought personal gain: the French Canadian governor, Louis de Baude de Frontenac—virtuous—; Peter Schuyler, the mayor of Albany—a profiteer. Colden finds strong leadership in the Mohawks and among the other Iroquois (or Haudenosaunee) nations, but he repeatedly notes the failures of New York's colonial officials. By his account, a good leader is one who is disinterested and puts his financial interests aside for the benefit of those he rules. Colden's is a classic eighteenth-century Enlightenment morality tale in a New World setting, in which the ethnically Dutch merchants and politicians become corrupt and their town—Albany—is saved only by the virtue and good sense of those nearby, namely, the Iroquois.[2]

Historians have revisited the history of Albany's fur traders and point to Colden's political partisanship in assessing (and generally dismissing) his claims.[3] Their revisions have dispensed with the anti-Dutch ethnic prejudice and political maneuvering of Albany's critics. Colden used the language of his time to criticize his political enemies; he articulated an important and common eighteenth-century fear that the merchant class was suspect because it prioritized financial gains of buying and selling over loyalties to people and place.[4] Colden's partisan criticisms were not based in reality, but even historians sympathetic to Dutch merchants have rearticulated the eighteenth-century belief that commercial and landed interests were necessarily at odds with

[2]   A recent biography of Colden examines his intellectual life as both an Enlightenment thinker and genteel, elitist politician. See John M. Dixon, *The Enlightenment of Cadwallader Colden: Empire, Science, and Intellectual Culture in British New York* (Ithaca, NY: Cornell University Press, 2016).

[3]   Thomas Elliot Norton, *The Fur Trade in Colonial New York* (Madison: University of Wisconsin Press, 1974), 7-8 and 63-64, and David A. Armour, *The Merchants of Albany, New York, 1686-1760* (New York: Garland Publishing, 1986), vii-viii. For New York's partisan politics in the eighteenth century, see Patricia Bonomi, *A Factious People: Politics and Society in Colonial New York* (New York: Columbia University Press, 1971).

[4]   In her biography of four generations of Livingstons, Cynthia Kierner argues that patronage and personal interest were the dominant and accepted forces in New York politics in the middle decades of the seventeenth century but that such self-interested politicking had gone out of style by the opening decades of the eighteenth century. Her timeline of New York political discourse would indicate that Colden used the lens of his era to judge the political behavior of Albany's leaders in the past, leaders who acted in ways consistent with the standards of their time. See Cynthia A. Kierner, *Traders and Gentlefolk: The Livingstons of New York, 1675-1790* (Ithaca, NY: Cornell University Press, 1992).

each other.[5] Looking at the city of Albany during the early period of Anglo-French warfare—from the start of King William's War (1689-97) through the end of Queen Anne's War (1702-13)—allows us to reevaluate the claim that commerce and settlement worked at cross-purposes on the North American frontier.

The latter decades of the seventeenth century and much of the eighteenth century saw almost unceasing hostility between the French and English, and European conflicts spilled over into the North American colonies. In the colonial theatre of war, native peoples became embroiled in imperial contests, and colonists found themselves in the middle of intertribal struggles. Prolonged war brought physical, political, and economic uncertainty and instability to the region; all of which are conditions supposedly antithetical to commerce. For those interested in territorial gain, these hardships were worth the promise of the spoils of war, but for traders, war was little more than an economic disruption.[6] Nonetheless, Albany's leading merchants and traders enthusiastically participated in England's wars against New France. Near the start of King William's War, Robert Livingston, an Albany trader deeply involved in Iroquois diplomacy and New York politics, wrote "wee must turn our tradeing into warring and instead of loading our Canoes with goods for Canida for Beaver as formerly wee must load ye Canoes with provisions and ammunityon to be revenged of our cruel and perfidious Enemies."[7]

This paper will highlight Albany's response to the threat of war as a way of re-examining the contention that landed and commercial interests stood in opposition to one another. Exploring how one Dutch commercial town loaded its trading vessels with ammunition and participated in England's imperial contests during the period from 1689 to 1713 complicates our understanding of the relationship between settler and commercial imperialism.

Situated 150 miles inland, at the edge of first the Dutch and then the English settlements, bordered by the Iroquois and the French, Albany was a space unparalleled in Anglo America. The town's singular

---

[5]   See especially Donna Merwick, *Possessing Albany, 1630-1710: The Dutch and English Experiences* (New York: Cambridge University Press, 1990) and *The Shame and the Sorrow: Dutch-Amerindian Encounters in New Netherland* (Philadelphia: University of Pennsylvania Press, 2006).

[6]   One example of this argument is in Merwick, *Possessing Albany*, 263.

[7]   E. B. O'Callaghan et al., eds., *Documents Relative to the Colonial History of the State of New-York, procured in Holland, England, and France* (Albany: Weed, Parsons, and Co., 1853-87), 3:706.

history, distinct geography, and diplomatic centrality provided the context for the actions of its leadership during the age of imperial wars. Initially a fur trade and military outpost, and then established as a *bijeenwoninge* (settlement) called Beverwijck in 1652, the village quickly became home to several hundred families. Beverwijck (named Albany after the English took over in 1664) was a significant city with its own artisans, tradesmen, and infrastructure, but the calendar of the fur trade produced the rhythms of its daily life.[8] In late seventeenth-century and early eighteenth-century Albany, political, diplomatic, and economic leadership were confined to a few families (most of whose fortunes originated in the fur trade) that had consolidated their power over just a few decades. Many of the town's elite had humble beginnings either as servants of the nearby Rensselaerswijck patroonship or from their middling Dutch family origins. Through strategic marriages and a pattern of economic diversification which invested profits from trade into landed estates and other resources such as timber and wheat, the first and second generations of Albany's top merchants were able to rapidly expand their wealth and influence. The new elite also served as the town's officials and magistrates and were responsible for diplomacy with native peoples, particularly the Iroquois.[9] After colonial rule was transferred to the English, Albany's leading merchants were able to negotiate the codifying of a powerful monopoly over the fur trade into the city's 1686 charter. Only a tiny handful of relative newcomers, such as Robert Livingston, managed to join the ranks of the elite once the monopoly was in place; for the most part, a few Dutch trading families dominated the city's politics throughout much of the seventeenth and eighteenth centuries.

Certainly, the Albany traders looked out for their own personal financial interests. More often than not, however, the commercial life of Albany's ethnically Dutch leadership fell in line with England's

---

[8]   The definitive account of Beverwijck's culture and development during the Dutch period is Janny Venema, *Beverwijck: A Dutch Village on the American Frontier, 1652-1664* (Hilversum, the Netherlands: Uitgeverij Verloren; Albany, NY: State University of New York Press, 2003). See also Merwick, *Possessing Albany.*

[9]   The Schuylers are one example of an Albany family that rose to prominence from middling origins. Philip Pietersz Schuyler, the son of a baker, emigrated to New Netherland to serve the Rensselaerswijck patroonship as a gunstock maker but also dabbled successfully in trade. In addition to his relative skill in the fur trade, he benefitted from marrying up and reinvesting in land. The Schuylers quickly became one of the wealthiest families in Beverwijck, and successive generations of Schuylers would dominate Albany's political, economic, and diplomatic life. See Venema, *Beverwijck,* 254-63.

overall imperial goals and frontier strategy of protecting their borders, strengthening ties with the Iroquois, and diverting the Great Lakes fur trade away from the French.[10] In the years after English conquest, the city's economy expanded to become the center of the Anglo American fur trade and the heart of frontier diplomacy.[11] The policies of Albany's elite leadership ultimately ensured the success of England's imperial goals in the region, albeit at times through complex, roundabout ways not entirely of their own design.

The long-term strategic goals of England's expansion in the New World could be at odds with short-term imperial policy, and interethnic economic transactions and partnerships did not often follow the rules of mercantilism.[12] Moreover, poor and middling Albanians had always participated in a small-scale exchange economy that ran parallel to the large-scale economics of the fur trade.[13] At times, this small-scale economic activity was legal, and, at others, it was prohibited. Between the Albany merchants who were known to skirt the bounds of mercantilism and the smaller-scale transactions of less wealthy individuals, smuggling was persistent, if not common. Even though the two sides—on the one hand, Albany's elite merchants, and on the other, middling newcomers and small-scale traders—often cried foul of one another; they formed an interdependent system of trade and diplomacy that accounted for Albany's successes. This paper focuses on the interests and decisions of Albany's elite leadership, but the poor and middling individuals who made up the bulk of the population also contributed to economic prosperity and regional stability. Macro trends of geopolitical strategy and long-term economics do not fully encompass Albany's participation in the Anglo-French wars of the late seventeenth and early eighteenth centuries either. Dutch Albanians participated in expeditions against

[10] See especially Armour, *Merchants of Albany*; and Norton, *Fur Trade in Colonial New York*.

[11] Holly Rine has explored the foundations of Albany's diplomatic centrality in great detail. See Holly Rine, "Intercultural Contact and the Creation of Albany's New Diplomatic Landscape, 1647-1680," PhD diss. (University of New Hampshire, 2004).

[12] Eugene Richard Henry Tesdahl, "The Price of Empire: Smuggling Between New York and New France, 1700-1754," PhD diss. (University of Colorado, 2012), 58-59.

[13] For an analysis of small-scale, daily transactions between settlers and Indians during the Dutch period, see Susanah Shaw Romney, *New Netherland Connections: Intimate Networks and Atlantic Ties in Seventeenth-Century America* (Chapel Hill: University of North Carolina Press, 2014), 145-72. For the tensions between small-scale or middling merchants and the growing Albany monopoly, see Cathy Matson, *Merchants and Empire: Trading in Colonial New York* (Baltimore, MD: Johns Hopkins University Press, 1998), 93-96.

Canada, outfitted soldiers and provisioned them, were taken prisoner, and used their financial networks to negotiate for prisoner releases.

The starkest example of the theater of war coming to the Albany region was the attack on nearby Schenectady. On the night of 8 February 1690, French soldiers and a group of Indian allies killed sixty of the town's inhabitants and took twenty-seven hostages before burning the village.[14] Albanians blamed the French success on New York's political instability because the attack took place in the context of an internal political uprising known as Leisler's Rebellion. In the wake of England's Glorious Revolution of 1689, Jacob Leisler, a New York merchant, seized power over the colony's government supposedly in the name of the crown of William and Mary. His administration ultimately divided the leadership of Albany and Schenectady into Leislerian and anti-Leislerian factions which harbored deep resentment toward each other on the eve of the French attack. After the Schenectady massacre, each political faction placed blame on the other as to who was responsible for the town failing to keep an adequate watch.[15] Schenectady was the upper Hudson River region's version of the destruction that northern New England towns had also met during much of the late seventeenth and early eighteenth centuries. Although they had never faced a large-scale attack by the French and their allies, Albanians lived with the memory of Schenectady during the age of imperial wars and constantly expected another devastating French raid.

In the days following the attack on Schenectady, the Albany leadership sprang into action, shaken by the threats to their physical security that came at a moment of great political uncertainty. They decided to set aside factional politics and focus on raising a force capable of a Canadian expedition by sending emissaries to New England and New York in hopes of obtaining military assistance and provisions. In their instructions to Reynier Barents, tasked with appealing to Leisler's government, the council urged him to "beseech them [in New York] to

---

[14] For details of the Schenectady attack in the context of that town's early history, see Thomas E. Burke Jr., *Mohawk Frontier: The Dutch Community of Schenectady, New York, 1661-1710* (Ithaca, NY: Cornell University Press, 1991), 102-7.

[15] E. B. O'Callaghan, ed., *The Documentary History of the State of New-York* (Albany: Weed, Parsons, and Co., 1850-51), 1:188-95. For more on Leisler's Rebellion, see William Voorhees, "'In behalf of the true Protestants religion': The Glorious Revolution in New York" (PhD diss., New York University, 1988); Bonomi, *A Factious People*, 75-81; and Alan Tully, *Forming American Politics: Ideals, Interests, and Institutions in Colonial New York and Pennsylvania* (Baltimore, MD: Johns Hopkins University Press, 1994), 15-25.

lay aside all animosities and divisions and that every one exert his power to crush the Common Enemy."[16]

Throughout February and March of 1690, the Albany council set to the task of provisioning the soldiers that would doubtless soon arrive from neighboring colonies. They gathered supplies and raised funds for necessities, often from their own pockets.[17] The leadership had little hope of recouping such costs, as Robert Livingston learned when he had to take his accounts all the way to the board of trade in London for restitution, eventually granted to him in 1695.[18] Albany's leading citizens scrambled to cobble together a group of soldiers with enough provisions to launch a land attack, while petitioning other colonies to arrange a naval assault on Quebec. Any military action against New France would require assistance from outside the city, which is why Albany's leadership also sent for their closest Iroquois neighbors, the Mohawks, to ask for military aid in the immediate aftermath of the Schenectady massacre.

In the late seventeenth century, the Iroquois proved fearsome— and crucial—allies to the English, representing what historian Jon Parmenter has called a "revolutionary change in Iroquoian approaches to warfare."[19] Formerly, the Iroquois fought mourning wars of their own that did not involve their Dutch and English trading partners, and the Iroquois-English alliance did not entail a military partnership until the Iroquois agreed to assist in King Philip's War (1675-76), a brief but devastating conflict between Narragansetts and New England settlers.

Thereafter, the Iroquois and the English depended on one another for military aid. Swapping out a trade partnership for a military alliance ultimately proved uncomfortable for both sides; each had its own limitations and interests which prevented an unequivocal partnership.[20]

---

[16] O'Callaghan, *Documentary History of New-York*, 2:97.

[17] Ibid., 108-12.

[18] O'Callaghan, *Documents Relative to New-York*, 4:127-41.

[19] Jon Parmenter, "After the Mourning Wars: The Iroquois as Allies in Colonial North American Campaigns, 1676-1760," *William and Mary Quarterly*, Third Series 64, no. 1 (January 2007): 39. The seventeenth-century Iroquois mourning wars have been traditionally called the Beaver Wars, which name implies that such conflicts were fought primarily for economic purposes. Historians of the Iroquois have questioned the economic motivations of seventeenth-century intertribal warfare. See especially José António Brandão, *"Your fyre shall burn no more": Iroquois Policy Toward New France and its Native Allies to 1701* (Lincoln: University of Nebraska Press, 1997).

[20] Parmenter, "After the Mourning Wars": 39-40. The Iroquois-English alliance(s), which also drew in relationships among neighboring peoples, is commonly referred to as the Covenant Chain. Daniel Richter and James Merrell succinctly describe the

In the early days after the attack on Schenectady, the allies needled each other about how best to proceed and who was responsible for avenging the deaths of sixty Dutch settlers. The Mohawks were incensed that Albanian townspeople seemed to be abandoning the area for the safety of New York City. They admonished the Albany leadership to "pray take good heart Doe not Pack and goe away if ye Enemy should hear yt it would much Encourage them."[21] The English reminded the Mohawks of their January visit to Albany when they had requested lead and powder and promised to send a party of scouts into the area around Schenectady. Had those scouts kept vigilant watch, the French would not have made it past Mohawk surveillance, Albany's leaders argued.[22] With mutual suspicions clouding negotiations, promises of military action often fell short.

Similar disparities characterized the Anglo-Iroquois military alliance throughout King William's War. The Iroquois had never received the full cooperation or assistance from their allies at Albany which they believed they had been promised. Albany's leadership, for its part, struggled to effectively raise the men, money, and provisions needed to launch a full-scale land campaign against the French and consistently failed to offer speedy assistance to its allies.

Historians disagree about the extent to which the disappointing military alliance with the English during King William's War was disastrous for the Iroquois. Daniel Richter maintains that "the [Iroquois] Five Nations stumbled from defeat to defeat" as a consequence of colonial political ambivalence and inconsistency.[23] Indeed, the English left the Iroquois to fight the French on their own for an additional four years after the Treaty of Rijswijk in 1697 ended the European

Covenant Chain as "a complex set of alliances among Indians and English in which Iroquois and New Yorkers played dominant but seldom dictatorial roles." See introduction to Daniel K. Richter and James H. Merrell, eds., *Beyond the Covenant Chain: The Iroquois and their Neighbors in Indian North America, 1600-1800* (Syracuse, NY: Syracuse University Press, 1987), 5. In the same volume, Richard Haan disputes the notion of a single Covenant Chain alliance and instead describes Anglo-Iroquois relations as "fluid" throughout the late seventeenth and early eighteenth centuries. The factional nature of the Iroquois Confederacy that the English scarcely understood, he argues, prevented the Iroquois from pursuing a single, unified diplomatic policy toward the English. See Richard L. Haan, "Covenant and Consensus: Iroquois and English, 1676-1760," in *Beyond the Covenant Chain*, ed. Richter and Merrell, 41-57.

[21]   O'Callaghan, *Documentary History of New-York*, 2:92.

[22]   Ibid.

[23]   Daniel Richter, *The Ordeal of the Longhouse: The Peoples of the Iroquois League in the Era of European Colonization* (Chapel Hill: University of North Carolina Press, 1992), 163.

conflict, which supports Richter's view that the English proved fickle allies for the Iroquois in King William's War. Jon Parmenter, on the other hand, insists that the Iroquois policy of neutrality, which took root in the Grand Settlement of 1701 (the negotiated peace among the Iroquois, French, and English, which lasted until the start of the Seven Years' War in 1754), emerged from Iroquois successes rather than defeats. During the years of neutrality, the Iroquois did not become embroiled in European and colonial conflicts; instead they were able to thrive in settlements between the two warring colonial powers. Parmenter sees neutrality as a final assertion of Iroquois autonomy over their own territory and mobility. Not subject to the whims of peripheral colonial neighbors, the Grand Settlement was, in his view, an indigenous beginning, rather than a colonial end.[24] Whether inspired by the disappointments of new military alliances or shaped by Iroquois interests, the policy of neutrality initiated with the Grand Settlement of 1701 placed the Iroquois in a position of unique power between the French and English empires. The Iroquois were strengthened by their aims of peace at the beginning of the eighteenth century, rather than weakened by their losses in seventeenth-century warfare.

One feature of Iroquois neutrality that would have a profound effect on Albany's role in future wars with New France was the cessation of hostilities between the Laurentian Iroquois living near French settlements (such as in the village of Kahnawake, just south of Montreal) and the League Iroquois who lived to the north and west of Albany along the Mohawk River. These two groups—united by kinship and ethnicity but separated by religion and political alliance—shared intelligence and usually declined to engage each other in battle, with some exceptions during King William's War. Starting after 1701, however, the League and Laurentian Iroquois succeeded in maintaining their alliances with colonial powers while avoiding any conflict with one another.[25] When European war once again spilled over into the North American colonies at the start of Queen Anne's War in 1702, the

---

[24] Jon Parmenter, *The Edge of the Woods: Iroquoia, 1534-1701* (East Lansing: Michigan State University Press, 2010), 271.

[25] Parmenter, "After the Mourning Wars": 47-51. The Laurentian Iroquois, who were predominantly converts to Catholicism and tended to represent the more "francophile" view in factional Iroquois politics nonetheless created settlements that were distinct from the authority of New France. David Preston urges us to think of Laurentian settlements as a "republic" that could claim its own sovereignty. See David L. Preston, *European and Indian Settler Communities on the Frontiers of Iroquoia, 1667-1783* (Lincoln: University of Nebraska Press, 2009), 53.

battlefield was rerouted to New England's northeastern borderlands because of Iroquois neutrality. Most French attacks centered on New England towns and almost completely avoided the Albany region throughout the war. Albany's good fortune arose not from disloyalty or Dutch economic partnerships with the French but rather from the agreements of Laurentian and League Iroquois peace. When Mohawks eventually decided to take part in an expedition against the French in 1709, they secretly sent messengers to Kahnawake, urging villagers to stay at home and not fight when the Anglo Dutch forces and Mohawk warriors arrived. The League Iroquois even conveyed false messages publicly as a diversion from the true, secret communications they shared with their Laurentian kin. The public messages reassured French observers, "That it was not probably ye govt. of N: York would concern themSelfs in Such an Expedition for they never had medled all this while with ye warr that n: England was So deeply Engag'd in, altho they were their oun Countrymen, yt were murther'd dayly by ye french & their Indians."[26] The false conveyance reflected gossip circulating about Albany—that its leadership cared little for the suffering of New England.

Iroquois neutrality left the French and the English in competition, always hoping to tip the balance to one side or the other. Mistakes of diplomacy and a failure to properly maintain bonds of peace could prove disastrous for the English; diplomatic errors allowed "francophile" Iroquois a rising voice in League politics.[27] Albanians greatly feared a French-Iroquois military alliance and what such an alliance might mean for all frontier settlements in northern Anglo America. In a 1709 letter to Kiliaen van Rensselaer (the lord of the manor of Rensselaerswijck), the governor of New York, John Lovelace, expressed resignation to a policy of neutrality:

> I am sorry that they [the Iroquois] shew soe great a disposition to Treat with the French. . . . I doe not see what service her Majesty can Expect from our Indians as long as they shall entertaine such an Opinion of the power of the French and soe great an Inclination . . . as long as . . . French be masters of Canada, we must Continue to . . . [enter]taine them in Frindship to us, the best we Can.[28]

26   Lawrence H. Leder, ed., *The Livingston Indian Records, 1666-1723* (Gettysburg: Pennsylvania Historical Association, 1956), 212.

27   Richter, *Ordeal of the Longhouse*, 177, 215-18.

28   "[Gov. Lovelace?] to Kiliaen van Rensselaer, New York, ca. March 1709," Van Rensselaer Manor Papers, box 9, folder 26, New York State Library, Albany, NY.

Having witnessed firsthand Iroquois military prowess, no one was eager to be on the wrong side of League diplomacy. For the Iroquois, as with many Eastern Woodlands societies, trade was at the heart of forging and maintaining alliances; trade signified mutuality, and smuggling was a wholly European construct.[29] Staying on the right side of Iroquois diplomacy, then, meant reciprocal gift giving and persistent trade. Some Albany-based traders maintained an illegal trade with Laurentian Mohawks through Kahnawake, which strengthened the city's bonds of peace with all Iroquois peoples. Without the persistence of smuggling, the English faced a very real danger that the Iroquois might break neutrality.[30] Taken in the context of diplomacy, smuggling on the Albany frontier appears less sinister than its opponents made it seem. For those New Englanders who lived among charred buildings and had lost everyone they knew and loved during the imperial wars, the concept of forging inter-ethnic bonds with the Iroquois through smuggling would have offered little comfort, and rumors spread throughout Anglo America that the Dutch at Albany were disloyal at best and, at worst, entirely corrupt.

During Queen Anne's War, elite Dutch Albanians struggled to prove their fidelity to New England and its suffering colonists because their relationship with the Iroquois protected them from wartime violence. Moreover, they traded and prospered throughout the period of hostilities, participating in both elicit trade and smuggling. Instead of filling their canoes with ammunition, as they had symbolically done in King William's War, Albany responded to the suffering of New England by transforming the networks which had once served personal financial interests into highways of information and prisoner exchange. Peter Schuyler, the former Albany mayor, wealthy trader, and commissioner for Indian Affairs, wrote letters to interested parties whenever he heard news or rumors of an imminent attack. In 1704 he promised William Whiting, "assoon as I receive more certain Intelligence shall not be wanting to give you notice thereof."[31] The Albany leadership under Schuyler's direction helped plan an expedition against Canada in 1709, and asked Kiliaen van Rensselaer and Robert Livingston to hire

[29] Tesdahl, "The Price of Empire," 20-22. David Preston argues that the Albany-Montreal trade/smuggling network that depended on Kahnawake intermediaries was an Iroquoian innovation. Without Iroquois carriers to navigate and traverse native spaces, such a trade would have been unfeasible. See Preston, *Texture of Contact*, 54-59.

[30] Tesdahl, "The Price of Empire," 52-54.

[31] Leder, *Livingston Indian Records*, 195.

indigenous spies to travel ahead of New York's forces and gather critical intelligence to aid the expedition.[32]

Even more than information, during wartime, prisoner negotiations became the most valuable use of the riverine highway between Montreal and Albany. In a cordial letter to Kiliaen van Rensselaer, the Canadian governor Philippe de Rigaud Vaudreuil started negotiations for the exchange of many Dutch and English prisoners held in French custody back to their homes with the hope of securing specific French prisoners held throughout New York and New England. He opened the letter by stating, as a gesture of goodwill:

> The War, though never so hotly presented between our Nations, ought not to rob us of Generosity and consideracion towards each others, this is that moves me, to day to give way unto Mr. Barent Staats Madam Schuylers Cousin and two other Dutchmen taken Captive last Summer to repair unto.[33]

His letter demonstrates that even the powerful Schuyler family was not immune to the losses of war. Prisoners came from all English borderlands, including New York. Small-scale French raids occasionally resulted in captivity for Dutch settlers, and larger attacks on villages saw numerous English prisoners—regardless of age, gender, or socioeconomic status—forced to make the trek to Montreal or Quebec, often in the dead of winter.

Survivors of frontier battles were left wondering what had become of their loved ones, and reunions could take decades, if they happened at all. Like many prisoners' families, in the initial years after his daughter was taken captive in the famous Deerfield, Massachusetts, raid of 1704, Reverend John Williams tirelessly explored every possible channel to negotiate for her return. He learned that she was being held in Kahnawake, a common destination for prisoners taken during Queen Anne's War. Indeed, one historian described the Laurentian settlement as a multiethnic space that housed an amalgam of native peoples and colonial prisoners, many of whom never returned from their captivity.[34] Williams began sending messages for his daughter by way of friends and relatives who traveled to Albany to participate in the

---

[32]   Ibid., 202-6.

[33]   "Letter from Canadian Governor the Marquis de Vaudreuil to [Kiliaen van Rensselaer], [ca. late 1709 or 1710?]," Van Rensselaer Manor Papers, box 9, folder 48, New York State Library, Albany, NY.

[34]   Preston, *Texture of Contact*, 39-41.

fur trade. Through Albany he could reach French officials in Montreal, the Jesuits who resided in Kahnawake, and the Laurentian Iroquois who had adopted Eunice Williams. Reverend Williams depended on the fur trade network to connect him to his daughter; Albany was the doorway to reuniting his family.[35]

Queen Anne's War also afforded Albany's traders opportunities to open new commercial networks with France's current and former Indian allies. The leading merchants had long sought to divert France's Great Lakes trade away from Montreal and toward Albany; during wartime, they took advantage of imperial prohibitions on trade with New France and cut off Montreal from its flow of cheap, high quality English goods, like rum and woolens. The situation for the French became quite desperate: they had a glut of high-quality furs with no market and lacked the crucial goods necessary to maintain their side of gift exchanges with their Indian allies.[36] Again, Iroquois neutrality worked to Albany's advantage; like most actions on the Albany frontier, building trade partnerships with the western Indians required the consent of the Iroquois through whose territory all parties would need to travel. For example, before neutrality, during King William's War, Arent Schuyler mistakenly negotiated with a nation then currently at war with the Iroquois, who expressed outrage that New York would trade with such an enemy. Ultimately Peter Schuyler corrected his brother's mistake by bringing Iroquois representatives along to a negotiation among all parties.[37] The Grand Settlement of 1701 created peace among western nations and the Iroquois, who now allowed safe passage for traders to Albany.[38] Iroquois neutrality was a necessary catalyst for Albanian economic warfare against the French.

The French gathered their own intelligence regarding Albanian inroads with the western nations and were indeed quite distressed by the effects on trade. In 1704 Vaudreuil wrote to his superiors in France:

> Five canoes of Indians belonging to Detroit have been this year trading at Orange [Albany], and as they have been cordially welcomed, it is to be feared that they will seek to continue this

---

35 Leder, *Livingston Indian Records*, 201, and John Demos, *The Unredeemed Captive: A Family Story from Early America* (New York: Knopf, 1994), especially 91-92, 131-33, and 167-68.

36 Armour, *Merchants of Albany*, 91-93, 106-7.

37 Leder, *Livingston Indian Records*, 168-69.

38 On peace negotiations and travel through Iroquoia, see Norton, *Fur Trade in New York*, 133-34, and Parmenter, *Edge of the Woods*, 262-63.

trade which cannot be carried on except to the detriment of ours, some of the Detroit Indians being so much attached to the English that in order to ruin that post, one of them set fire to the barn of the fort, which would have been completely burnt, had the fire not been promptly extinguished.[39]

Not only was the trade moving toward Albany, but France's supposed allies were actively trying to destroy the fort at Detroit, a prominent symbol of French military and economic power in the Great Lakes region. Meanwhile, in New York, Robert Livingston proposed to expand Albany's sphere of influence well beyond the Iroquois by building a fort or fortified trading outpost near Detroit. New York governor Richard Coote, Earl of Bellomont, even agreed to sponsor a new fort, although not one so close to the French. Military necessity ultimately stalled these nascent plans, but they were picked up again by Governor Robert Hunter at the end of Queen Anne's War.[40]

Before New York's governors could build forts in the wilderness, they had to provide adequate fortifications for their vulnerable towns, including Albany. When it became obvious that the planned expedition against Canada would not be going forward at the end of 1709, the leaders of the city and county of Albany, the military leadership of the expedition, and the commissioners for Indian Affairs jointly proposed that Albany would need, in lieu of an offensive campaign, extensive defensive measures. Such provisions would include: repairs for its dilapidated fort and city fortifications, payment for two hundred Indian scouts to keep watch all winter, and four hundred troops at the ready in case of a French raid.[41] This request was not the first—nor would it be the last—petition on behalf of Albany's Dutch leaders for an increased military presence within and around the city. Securing the town and its inhabitants was a preoccupation of Albany's leadership during King William's and Queen Anne's wars.[42] The predominance of security concerns and the numerous requests for soldiers, guns, ammunition, engineers, money, and provisions to, as historian Donna Merwick elegantly describes, "clothe increasingly more points on the landscape in military dress," call into question the dichotomy of commerce and settlement and the contention that traders were uninterested

---

[39]   O'Callaghan, *Documents Relative to New-York*, 9:763.
[40]   Norton, *Fur Trade in New York*, 155-58.
[41]   Leder, *Livingston Indian Records*, 213-14.
[42]   For the tension between trade and security during this era and the positions of Albany's leadership, see Norton, *Fur Trade in New York*, 60-78.

in war.[43] In Merwick's view, the military clothing was imposed upon Albany's landscape by English imperialists, but she does not account for the enthusiasm for war with France as expressed by Albany's Dutch leadership. That Anglo Dutch traders supported England's imperial designs demonstrates how the interests of settlement and commerce could complement one another. Certainly, Albany did not fight England's wars in the same way that New England did, but the city willingly contributed in its own distinct, primarily commercial ways to outbursts of warfare.

In the age of imperial war, Albany was a city unlike any other in Anglo America. It was a Dutch town within the English settlements, strategically yet uncomfortably nestled between the Iroquois and French empires. Its unusual location, singular history, and commercial economy all lent it tactical advantages over New England towns that were burned to the ground by the French and their allies. Even though high-ranking Dutch families can be found among the lists of prisoners held captive by the French, and even though Schenectady burned just as Deerfield did, Albany's critics were right to note that Albanians did not suffer the same losses as New Englanders. Imperial loyalty, however, cannot be measured by body counts. During wartime, Albanians opened their commercial networks to exchange information and prisoners, sometimes paying out of pocket to retrieve fellow colonists from the bonds of captivity. Further, they put their economy to imperial use by diverting some of the Great Lakes trade and cutting off Montreal from the goods it needed to sustain alliances. Did these wartime profits make Albany's leadership profiteers, given the strategic aims of such trade? Albany's critics saved their most scathing attacks for smugglers, whom they viewed with the deepest disdain. Cadwallader Colden attributed the actions of smugglers to the Dutch origins of Albany: settled by "the meanest People," the Dutch leadership of Albany served only their pocketbooks and cared little for their town or the other English settlements. Of course these accusations were little more than anti-Dutch, antimerchant propaganda. Even smuggling served crucial economic and diplomatic purposes, especially after the Iroquois Grand Settlement of 1701. In the end, commercial interests and landed interests went hand in hand. Albanians used their pocketbooks to defend their city and English imperial power in the region, ultimately shaping the course of Anglo-American settlement.

---

[43]   Merwick, *Possessing Albany*, 269.

CHAPTER 8

Albany's Commissioners for Indian Affairs in Colonial New York: The Dutch Shaping of Indian Diplomacy in the Larger British Empire, 1691–1755

Andrew T. Stahlhut

A minor diplomatic incident between various Indian and European settlements flashed in the British North American colonial backcountry in January 1723. According to Captain John Scott at Fort Hunter, west of Albany, and not far from areas settled by colonial New Yorkers, a small party of Iroquois Indians had recently arrived from the Virginia hinterlands with a scalp and a native prisoner. This in itself was nothing too notable, since the Iroquois of the area that is now New York and along the St. Lawrence River in Canada had for generations traveled south to make war upon their southern enemies. Both scalps and prisoners were, as always, two of the primary rewards sought in such actions. What was troublesome, however, was the 1722 Iroquois-Virginia peace treaty that had been part of a larger plan to quiet Virginia's backcountry and stem the endemic violence tracing back to the mid-seventeenth century. To make matters worse, the Indian prisoner claimed to be the servant of Virginia's lieutenant governor Alexander Spotswood.[1]

---

[1] *Minutes of the Commission of Indian Affairs in Albany*, 1:6-7, http://ebooks.library. cornell.edu/i/indianaffairs/browse.html. Hereafter cited as *MCIA*.

Fort Hunter sent a letter "by an express" to the New York Commissioners of Indian Affairs in Albany, apprising them of the situation. The commissioners immediately drafted a response on the same day that the message arrived, January 17, 1723. They thanked the captain for his timely message and informed him that they would send Lawrence Claessen, an interpreter, so that "we may inquire further into this affair." "We command you forthwith," they authoritatively instructed Claessen, "to go up to Fort Hunter and desire the Indians who have taken this prisoner forthwith to come hither to us and bring him along." Like any wise diplomats dealing with Indians, they included the cost of "seven hands of wampum" to facilitate matters.[2]

The requested Iroquois visitors arrived in Albany and opened discussions with the officials on January 20.[3] The commissioners berated the Indians, expressing "surprise" that the Iroquois would commit violence near Virginia, given that "a treaty of peace has been so lately concluded between the government of Virginia and the [Five Nations] and so solemnly confirmed by the Five Nations but this last summer" and admonished them that "the same should be kept inviolable on their side." Claiming innocence, these Iroquois claimed that they "were gone out a fighting" before the treaty had gone into effect.[4] Regardless of the truth of this excuse, the commissioners clearly prioritized the return of the prisoner and his safe homecoming to Virginia. Once again, the commissioners utilized the means of Indian diplomacy—this time, offering a belt of wampum to lend strength to their request to have the prisoner released. The Iroquois refused the request—and, presumably, as decorum required, the wampum belt as well—and announced that the prisoner would instead continue home with them. The commissioners would have to deal with "our sachems" to pursue the matter. With no other path available, the commissioners resolved to send a message, again with a belt of wampum, to show their

---

[2]   MCIA, 1:6-7.

[3]   There is some confusion as to the exact date. The first relevant entry in the MCIA is dated the twentieth and notes that the Indians were expected to arrive "tomorrow morning." The following entry that records the actual discussion, however, is dated the nineteenth. Likely one or both of these dates is slightly off due to simple human error.

[4]   The commissioners referred to them as "Canada Indians" because these Mohawks were from Caugnawaga, a "castle" in the St. Lawrence Valley. Although near Montreal, the population maintained its independence from French colonial authority. David L. Preston, *The Texture of Contact: European and Indian Settler Communities on the Frontiers of Iroquoia, 1667-1783* (Lincoln: University of Nebraska Press, 2009), 18.

sincerity and respect, in a longer-term effort to secure the release of the prisoner. The Albany Indian commissioners felt no rush to inform New York's royal governor, William Burnet, of this diplomatic imbroglio. Not until three weeks later, in a letter to Burnet, sending along a copy of their minutes, did they mention the diplomatic drama in an almost offhand manner. The commissioners made clear to Burnet that they had decided not to press the issue with the Iroquois too far with superfluous action, since such pressure might "disoblidge them" from fighting against enemy Indians in the East and "make them embrace the governor of Canada's proposal to war against New England."[5] Such an unfortunate turn of events might cause this relatively minor diplomatic incident to spread violence across multiple colonial settlements.

This incident illustrates the degree of influence and autonomy which the Albany Indian commissioners wielded in a borderlands diplomatic world that spanned much of northeastern North America and shows how intimately involved they were in the issues most fundamental to Britain's continued influence on the continent. Issues of Indian fidelity, the safety of various different British colonies, and the looming threat of French violence all provided the larger context in how this single example played out. Clearly more than just an outpost on the edges of British settlement, Albany served as a focal point for conversations and actions that would define Britain's North American domain over the course of the eighteenth century. In the example above, the commissioners acted swiftly, and on their own authority, to tackle a conflict that started in another colony far to the south. Through experience built upon foundations stretching back into the seventeenth century, they knew that gifts of wampum were needed to add emphasis to their words, and they spent the funds necessary to obtain them. They hired and instructed a colonial interpreter, Lawrence Claessen, on their own authority to implement a course of action they devised themselves. In fact, they sought to inform the provincial governor only three weeks later, in passing, and casually framed themselves as making decisions in the best interests of the empire.

Most importantly, this small group of Dutchmen shaped, in minor and major ways, the larger currents of Indian diplomacy in the British continental empire, and as a result, the British Empire itself. The Albany commissioners often acted on their own authority, regularly made decisions while contemplating an imperial scope, and took action (or inaction) on Indian affairs that related to other colonies. In doing

[5]   *MCIA*, 1:7-8a.

so, they exemplified the important notion that Dutch settlers in and around New Netherland maintained important roles and duties in the functioning of colonial New York and even the larger British Empire.

This essay explores these ideas by pursuing three paths.[6] First, this essay will briefly explore the New Netherland roots of what would eventually become an official colonial institution in New York—the Albany Commissioners for Indian Affairs—and its growth from informal tool of early English governors after 1664 to formal institution in the 1690s. Although this institution received its official authority from British colonial sources, the working knowledge and experience of borderlands Indian diplomacy was rooted in the Dutch period of New Netherland. Second, this essay will provide a brief overview of that body's composition during its existence from the 1690s to the 1750s, noting how much of that Dutch background persisted into the British era. Far from existing as a disjointed group of unrelated Indian officers, the Albany commissioners composed a closely knit web of family and local Albany officials. Last, and perhaps most important, this essay will explore how this small group of provincial Dutch officials projected their influence into the larger British colonial world on the continent. In sum, the overall argument contends that these Dutch commissioners played a critical role not just in their capacity as local Indian officials but also in matters spanning the British Empire and beyond. In essence, historians need to recognize this important contribution of these Dutch settlers to the larger story of British colonial America. Indian diplomacy in northeastern North America, a critical component of the British Empire's existence during the colonial period, was heavily influenced by the words and actions of a small cadre of Albany Dutchmen for half a century.

Dutch exploration, trade, and settlement of New Netherland began in the early seventeenth century. Although a few agriculturally based patroonships dotted New Netherland's landscape, most notably, the uniquely resilient manor of Kiliaen van Rensselaer, the primary impulse behind early Dutch activity in New Netherland, remained trade. Dutch investors formally incorporated the West India Company in 1621. While focused upon South American sugar plantations, the venture also hoped for efficient and profitable extraction of wealth

---

[6] For a much more complete exploration of these topics, see the author's PhD dissertation: Andrew T. Stahlhut, "The Albany Commissioners of Indian Affairs: New York, the Iroquois, and the Borderlands Shaping of Empire, 1691-1755" (PhD diss., Lehigh University, 2016).

in the form of furs acquired from the Indians in and around New Netherland. The company built Fort Orange in 1624, in the upper Hudson Valley, which over time spurred development of a small settlement named Beverwijck.[7] The Dutch pursued some agriculture here, improving land that would make the trading post self-reliant and more flexible in pursuing its economic goals but not as a preface to expansion.[8] Unlike their New England counterparts, early Dutch traders and settlers saw no need to convert or "civilize" nearby indigenous groups.[9] Ideally, company traders would utilize this northern outpost to barter peacefully and in a controlled manner with visiting Indians. Historian Donna Merwick encapsulated this Dutch ideal by coining the term "alongshore" to present the idea that the Dutch held an "animus against colonization" to avoid repeating the violent patterns established by the sixteenth-century Spanish. Instead, the Dutch hoped simply to "lie alongshore," which would grant them the benefits of trade, while avoiding the dangers of deeper entanglement.[10] New Netherland's longest-serving governor, Peter Stuyvesant, evaluated war and peace "through a merchant's eyes," according to Merwick, seeking to avoid violence whenever possible, simply because it would negatively affect trade.[11]

Early Dutch traders and settlers established important relations with the nearby Mohawk Indians, providing the groundwork for a relationship that would last until the mid-eighteenth century and the conversion of Dutch New Netherland into English New York. While Beverwijck's early families were establishing government, churches, and other institutions, they mingled regularly with visitors and traders from the nearby Mohawk Nation who, "although they were not 'official'

---

[7]   For a more detailed account of this evolution, see: Janny Venema, *Beverwijck: A Dutch Village on the American Frontier, 1652-1664* (Hilversum and Albany: Verloren and State University of New York Press, 2003), chs. 1-2; James W. Bradley, *Before Albany: An Archaeology of Native-Dutch Relations in the Capital Region, 1600-1664* (Albany: University of the State of New York, 2007), chs. 2-4.

[8]   Thomas J. Condon, *New York Beginnings: The Commercial Origins of New Netherland* (New York: New York University Press, 1968), 77.

[9]   Matthew Dennis, *Cultivating a Landscape of Peace: Iroquois-European Encounters in Seventeenth-Century America* (Ithaca: Cornell University Press, 1993), 120.

[10]   Donna Merwick, *The Shame and the Sorrow: Dutch-Amerindian Encounters in New Netherland* (Philadelphia: University of Pennsylvania Press, 2006), 35-36. Merwick utilizes this metaphor entirely for Dutch Manhattan, but its implications apply naturally to Beverwijck. Although Beverwijck was an inland settlement, the Hudson stayed wide enough to that point to remain a de facto extension of the ocean for the purposes of trade.

[11]   Merwick, *The Shame and the Sorrow*, 256.

inhabitants . . . were certainly very present in the village."[12] These Mohawks acted as vital conduits for the fur trade and thus the economic prosperity that undergirded Albany during the seventeenth century. As historian Jaap Jacobs notes, by the 1650s, "The trade in beaver pelts could be crucial to individual colonists, making competition fierce" and lead to questionable trading practices on the part of the Dutch.[13] In sum, the growth of Beverwijck as a settlement and a trading nexus was inextricably intertwined with the fur trade and Mohawk Indian presence.

The Dutch traders in and around Beverwijck benefited greatly from their growing relationship with the Iroquois, solidifying the shaky economic ground upon which they built their financial empire. Dutch officials signed their first treaty of "friendship and brotherhood" with Mohawk leaders in 1643, and sixteen years later reaffirmed it with a box of wampum wrapped in an iron chain, the first link in what eventually became the silver Covenant Chain under the English.[14] This special relationship facilitated a steady increase in the number of furs traded over the Dutch period, rising to a high of about forty-six thousand per year in 1656 and 1657.[15] Close relations with the Mohawks also alleviated some of New Netherland's political and military problems with other Indian polities. Company officials often relied upon Mohawk diplomats to mediate disputes with other Indian groups, and sometimes Mohawk warriors enforced Dutch interests in other parts of the borderlands.[16] Mohawk friendship, while avoiding missionizing and other cultural intrusions, made the economic goals of Dutch traders much easier to pursue.

The English takeover of New Netherland in 1664 prompted and paralleled several significant alterations in the shape and character of the province as a whole and more nuanced changes in Beverwijck specifically. Over the three decades between 1664 and 1691, the provincial government shifted several times: from a ducal proprietary (1664-85); to a royal colony (1685-87); to incorporation within the Dominion of New England (1688-89); to control by "an alliance of merchants and disaffected politicians," led by Jacob Leisler (1689-

[12] Venema, *Beverwijck*, 24.

[13] Jaap Jacobs, *The Colony of New Netherland: A Dutch Settlement in Seventeenth-Century America* (Ithaca: Cornell University Press, 2009), 116.

[14] Fenton, *The Great Law of the Longhouse*, 271.

[15] Trelease, *Indian Affairs in Colonial New York*, 131.

[16] Charles T. Gehring and William A Starna, "Dutch and Indians in the Hudson Valley: The Early Period," *The Hudson Valley Regional Review* 9, no. 2 (1992), 18.

91); and finally to re-establishment as a royal colony (1691).[17] Despite these many shapes, English governors maintained a growing awareness of the importance of Albany and Indians and trade between the two in the empire's larger plans for imperial security against the growing Indian and French threats. The continued presence of Dutch traders and settlers smoothed potential uncertainties in Indian diplomacy that may have arisen under so many changes.

Early English governors relied upon a cadre of Albany's traders and magistrates to act as unofficial diplomats and facilitators during the three decades between the English takeover in 1664 and the formal establishment of the Commissioners for Indian Affairs in 1696. These men, motivated by the potential benefits of strong trading ties, maintained the positive trade-based relationship between Anglo and Iroquoian worlds during this transition period and provided the immediate roots for the institution of the Albany commissioners. For example, Andros appointed Robert Livingston clerk of the court of Albany and ex officio secretary of Indian affairs in 1674.[18] Livingston earned wealth and influence through trade, landholding, and by filling multiple offices and established a family whose name intertwined with New York politics and Indian affairs for generations. His fluency in Dutch served him well in connecting the Dutch nature of Indian relations with the new English-speaking regimes, and he further incorporated himself into the local Dutch hierarchy by marrying the widow, Alida van Rensselaer, originally part of the locally prominent Schuyler clan. The growing importance of Indian affairs in these years, coupled with his own personal interest, prompted Livingston to keep and translate Indian records covering mostly the second half of the seventeenth century, an era with an otherwise dearth of sources.[19]

Other lesser-known Albany leaders facilitated Indian diplomacy during these transition decades, and they, like Livingston, shared the common characteristics of holding local office, earning their livelihood through trade, and being part of the local Dutch culture, a continuance from the earlier Dutch period. Johannes Wendell was a perfect example of this continuation. He was born in New Netherland in 1649 and entered the fur trade as a young adult, likely due to influence from his

---

[17] Michael Kammen, *Colonial New York: A History* (New York: Charles Scribner's Sons, 1975), 99. Of course, the colony reverted to Dutch control briefly in 1673 and 1674.

[18] Cynthia A. Kierner, *Traders and Gentlefolk: The Livingstons of New York, 1675-1790* (Ithaca: Cornell University Press, 1992), 15.

[19] Trelease, *Indian Affairs in Colonial New York*, 208.

father. He became justice of the peace in 1684, earned a commission as militia captain in 1685, and became an alderman in 1686.[20] He appears in Livingston's records several times from 1685 to 1687, often recorded as participating in Indian diplomacy specifically due to his position as justice of the peace, militia captain, alderman, and "magistrate" of Albany. For example, in June 1685, Wendell was one of the "Justices of the Peace" who received four Senecas at the Albany courthouse. In another example from September 1685, Wendell and other "magistrates of Albany" met with representatives of "the [Mohakws], Oneidas, Onondagas, Cayugas, and Senecas" to hear their response to petitions made by representatives from Virginia.[21] Gerrit Bancker's life follows a very similar trend. He was born in Holland and arrived in New Netherland around 1655. He became a trader and married into the Van Epps family, one of the "pioneer" families of New Netherland.[22] Livingston's incomplete records list him as active in Indian diplomacy during the mid-1680s, but other sources suggest he was part of these borderlands interactions as early as 1672. Livingston's records often list him as "magistrate" of Albany as well.[23] These two men are examples of the Dutch traders and officials who, along with Robert Livingston and others, oversaw Indian relations in Albany during the decades of shifting English government.

Clearly, the three decades between the English takeover in 1664 and the formal establishment of both royal government and the Commissioners for Indian Affairs in the 1690s served as a critical nexus between the history of the seventeenth century and the coming imperial struggles of the eighteenth century. The Dutch traders of Albany, having transacted diplomatic and economic relations with the Iroquois and other Indians since the 1620s, continued these activities

---

[20]   Stefan Bielinski, Colonial Albany Project biography 2942, http://www.nysm.nysed. gov/albany/bios/w/jowendell2942.html, last modified n/a. Bielinski's People of Colonial Albany project, hosted by the New York State Museum, offers much invaluable biographical information on Albany's colonial denizens, a resource especially helpful for the more obscure individuals. This source will be abbreviated as CAP in future citations.

[21]   Leder, *Livingston Indian Records*, 76, 77, 79, 82, 84, 87, 90, 108, 120. The records of these two specific meetings start on 76 and 87 respectively.

[22]   Bielinski, CAP biography 6467, http://www.nysm.nysed.gov/albany/bios/b/ gebancker6467.html, last modified n/a.

[23]   Leder, *Livingston Indian Records*, 79, 82, 84, 87, 90. For the reference to 1672, see: "Some Old Dutch Families," in *New Amsterdam Gazette: Historical Sketches and Reminiscences of the Dutch Regime of New Amsterdam and the New Netherlands*, ed. Morris Coster (New York: Morris Coster, date n/a), 4:14.

but in an increasingly different context. The new English governments, while varying in form, introduced and sustained an expanded imperial outlook in New York and relied on these Dutch traders to achieve those ends. The opening of King William's War in 1689, the first of four major conflicts with the French and other Indian polities, prompted the need for an even stronger, more organized method of dealing with Indian nations, especially the critically important Iroquois. As a result, Governor Fletcher formally established the Albany Commissioners for Indian Affairs in 1696.

Moving on to the essay's second point, close scrutiny of the Albany commissioners uncovers how thoroughly Dutch the institution remained despite its existence in the British Empire. Albany's Commissioners for Indian Affairs was composed almost entirely of a close web of Dutchmen, linked to each other through marriage and to Albany through history that predated the English conquest. A numerical approach to the commissioner minutes reveals an institution composed of a small group of men serving long terms with little turnover in the core membership. Taken together, fifty-three individual men served as commissioners at Albany during all but the tail end of the institution's lifetime.[24] The data suggest a large spectrum in length of tenure, from the single year of Edward Clarke and John Lindsay, to those whose careers spanned more than two decades of service, such as Evert Bancker and Myndert Schuyler.

This distillation of information provides a launching pad to uncover how a relatively small core of commissioners dominated these years. For those commissioners, fifty-three men served a combined total of 524 years, resulting in an average service of approximately 9.9 years per commissioner. Such a number, however, is misleading, because many of these men served very short tenures. For example, Arent Bradt served only three years. William Dick served for four years, while Edward Clarke served a single year. Removing men who served for three or fewer years raises the average tenure to approximately 12.5 years per commissioner. Ultimately, defining "long-term service" as ten years or more raises the average length of tenure to approximately 16.6 years. This core of twenty-three men serving ten years or more comprised a

---

[24]   The brief period from 1753 to 1755 will not be included in this chapter. The Albany commissioners served then between William Johnson's role as provincial Indian commissioner (1746-53) and his appointment as Indian superintendent for the northern colonies as a whole (1756 onward). Generally speaking, these were new commissioners, and their necessarily short tenures serve only to confuse the data from the previous period of 1696-1745.

group of long-tenured commissioners that provide a starting point for understanding the institution's core membership. Specifically, these data start to uncover a fundamental characteristic of the Albany commissioners: the institution, and by extension New York's Indian diplomacy, remained in the hands of under two dozen men, mostly Dutchmen, for approximately half a century.

One can easily supplement this conclusion regarding tenure length by counting how many meetings each individual commissioner attended, thus providing a better understanding of what members constituted a core group of commissioners.[25] Such a step is critical in understanding the true nature of the core, since a long tenure means nothing if a commissioner rarely attended any meetings. Most men in the core group were very active in their duties as Albany commissioners. One, however, cannot easily calculate a ratio of meetings per years of service. In some cases, an individual commissioner continued to attend meetings long after his commission had expired. For example, Philip Schuyler earned commissions in 1728, 1729, 1732, and 1734. The minutes, however, list him as present at commissioner meetings well into the mid-1740s. Regardless, this long-tenured core was incredibly active over the first half of the eighteenth century. It should be noted, however, that a handful of commissioners who served less than ten years were still notably active. John Collins, for example, served for eight years and attended sixty-nine meetings during that time. Essentially, the exact core membership can shift slightly based on the specific requirements imposed by the researcher.

Recognizing the existence of a long-tenured core of commissioner members is critical in understanding New York's Indian policy in the first half of the eighteenth century. This institution, so critical to imperial safety, was not a weak, shifting body, open to easy change or turnover. The Commissioners for Indian Affairs was a solid institution with a core membership maintaining continuity for over half a century. Thanks to its New Netherland roots, it survived and thrived in an era of English government and imperial conflict. An exploration of the lives

---

[25]   Quantifying the number of meetings that individual commissioners attended requires some interpretation on the part of the researcher. For example, the present dissertation considers every "roll call" a separate meeting, even if they were on the same day. This happened especially during larger conferences, where Indian speakers would often leave to discuss matters before giving a formal answer later that day. Individual commissioners may have arrived or departed between these sessions. Also, in a small number of cases, the minutes are too faded to read some names, meaning that at least some attendances cannot be recorded. As a result, these numbers are close approximations and cannot be exact.

of these core members indicates that this nexus between the British Empire and the Iroquoian borderlands remained remarkably similar in composition to its seventeenth-century Dutch roots.[26]

Brief biograpical sketches of the longest-serving core members highlight the common positions of Dutch trader and Albany officeholder among the formally established Commissioners for Indian Affairs. Myndert Schuyler had an extensive thirty-five-year tenure as Indian commissioner, and his background epitomized the general nature of the commissioners as a whole. Born in New Netherland in 1672, Myndert was the fourth son of David Pieterse Schuyler, a prominent fur trader and local official who traveled west from Holland in the mid-1650s. Myndert served the local government as juror, alderman, and militia captain, and the provincial governor appointed him mayor of Albany in 1719, 1720, and 1723. Myndert earned his wealth through trade and real estate, and his marriage into the Cuyler family provided strong links to another prominent Dutch family.[27] He attended at least 332 commissioner meetings over these decades.

Philip Livingston was born in Albany in 1686, and historian Stefan Bielinki calls Philip's father, Robert Livingston, "the most important person to live in colonial Albany." Robert Livingston's contributions to Albany's early Indian diplomacy are explored above. Philip's mother was Alida Schuyler van Rensselaer Livingston, a woman whose full name indicates a notable pedigree of prominent local families. As a young man, Philip acted as his father's assistant in trade and diplomatic capacities, giving him the necessary background for his twenty-three-year tenure as Albany commissioner. He served as city and county clerk in Albany and as secretary to the commissioners from 1725 onward. His wife, Catharina van Brugh, connected him not just to the prominent Van Brugh family but also to the Cuylers, through Catharina's mother. Philip attended at least 263 commissioner meetings over several decades.[28]

---

26 Albany's commissioners did not draw a salary from the colonial coffers for their service.

27 Bielinski, CAP biography 101, http://www.nysm.nysed.gov/albany/bios/s/mynschuy ler101.html, last modified Oct. 25, 2002; Bielinski, CAP biography 1262, http://www.nysm.nysed.gov/albany/bios/s/dapschuyler1262.html, last modified Sept. 20, 2003.

28 Bielinski, CAP biography 86, http://www.nysm.nysed.gov/albany/bios/l/phliving ston86.html, last modified Dec. 21, 2012; Bielinski, CAP biography 94, http://www.nysm.nysed.gov/albany/bios/l/rlivingston94.html, last modified Apr. 16, 2009; Bielinski, CAP biography 8628, http://www.nysm.nysed.gov/albany/bios/vb/cavbrugh8628.html, last modified n/a.

Peter van Brugh was born in 1666 to a family already involved in the New Netherland fur trade. He married into the Cuyler family in November 1688 and entered the Albany fur trade after moving there from New York City. Over the decades, he served as constable, high constable, assessor, collector, and contractor. The governor appointed him mayor in 1699 and again in 1721. Peter's tenure as commissioner spread across four decades and included his presence in at least 130 meetings.[29]

A brief collective biography of the other core members further supplements this unique legacy of Indian diplomacy in the hands of Dutch traders and local officials. The vast majority of these core members made their living at least partially as merchants and fur traders. Aside from three men whose occupations were unclear, the only exceptions were Edward Collins who practiced law and Henry Holland who commanded the fort at Albany. Even more striking is the comparison between the core membership and local office holding. All of the core members held positions in local government, ranging from sheriff and constable to alderman and mayor. Eleven of these long-tenured commissioners served as mayor at one time or more, covering nineteen of the twenty-seven, or approximately 70 percent, of all mayoral administrations from the Dongan charter of 1686 through 1748. Clearly the same social and economic influence required to earn appointment as mayor also demanded repeated commissions as Albany commissioner.

Family ties further strengthened connections among this small cadre of commissioners. Almost all core members married into a family with at least one member already serving as an Indian commissioner. For example, Dirck ten Broek married Margarita Cuyler in 1714. Margarita was the eldest daughter of Ten Broek's fellow commissioner Abraham Cuyler. Her mother was Catharina Bleeker, making her uncles Albany commissioners Nicholaes and Rutger Bleeker.[30] Thus Dirck ten Broek found himself connected by marriage to both the Cuylers and the Bleekers, families with representation in the ranks of the Albany commissioners. In another example, core commissioner Hendrick van Rensselaer married Catharina van Brugh in 1689. Catharina's brother

[29] Bielinski, CAP biography 5300, http://www.nysm.nysed.gov/albany/bios/vb/pv brugh.html, last modified n/a.

[30] Bielinski, CAP biography 33, http://www.nysm.nysed.gov/albany/bios/t/dtbroeck 33, last modified Feb. 25, 2002; Bielinski, CAP biography 591, http://www.nysm. nysed.gov/albany/bios/c/mgtcuyler591.html, last modified Aug. 15, 2006.

was Peter van Brugh, member of the Albany Indian commissioners for almost three decades.[31] A few core members had mothers who represented those same families. This interrelatedness by marriage further defines the tightly knit character of the core membership. All of the extant data, taken together, clearly shows how a small, intermarried cadre of Dutch men served as Albany's Commissioners for Indian Affairs, continuing a configuration stretching through the transition decades of the 1660s to the 1690s, back into the New Netherland period. These fewer-than-two-dozen men served at the forefront of Indian diplomacy for New York and much of the rest of the empire for half a century.

These commissioners remained culturally Dutch as well. Historian Allen Trelease notes that Albany and its environs "were perhaps less affected by the transition to English rule than any other part of the province," remaining "overwhelmingly Dutch in composition" well into the eighteenth century.[32] Swedish traveler Peter Kalm emphasized this nature on his trip through the British colonies. He noted that the "inhabitants of Albany and its environs are almost all Dutchmen," specifying that they "speak Dutch, have Dutch preachers, and divine service is performed in that language," ultimately concluding that "Their manners are likewise quite Dutch."[33] Dutch culture also persisted in legal arenas. For example, settlers living in and around Albany declared their wills in English at a much lower rate than those living in Manhattan during the first half of the eighteenth century.[34] For all intents and purposes, Albany remained an outpost of Dutch culture, despite its presence within British imperial borders. Dutch culture thus undergirded a continuity between New Netherland and New York that provided stability for Indian diplomacy with the Iroquois Nations and served the imperial ends of a growing British North American realm. In sum, these were Dutchmen at the fore of British Indian affairs in and around New York, and their "Dutchness," while slowly diluting over time, remained a constant and important factor in borderlands life.

---

[31]   Bielinski, CAP biography 5053, http://www.nysm.nysed.gov/albany/bios//vr/hvr5053, last modified May 5, 2006; Bielinski, CAP biography 8627, http://www.nysm.nysed.gov/albany/bios//vb/cavbrugh8627.html, last modified July 2003.

[32]   Trelease, *Indian Affairs in Colonial New York*, 205.

[33]   Peter Kalm, *Travels into North America, Containing Its Natural History, and a Circumstantial Account of Its Plantations and Agriculture in General, with the Civil, Ecclesiastical, and Commercial State of the Country* (London: John Reinhold Forster, 1771), 2:261.

[34]   David E. Narrett, *Inheritance and Family Life in Colonial New York City* (Ithaca and Cooperstown: Cornell University Press and New York State Historical Association, 1992), 21.

Moving into this essay's third point, Albany's commissioners—Dutchmen with British colonial commissions—exerted a significant influence in borderlands Indian diplomacy both in New York and in matters that ranged from New England to Virginia.[35] Looking at the commissioners' relationship with New York's royal governors, one realizes how much the colony's governors relied on these Dutch commissioners in their dealings with the Iroquois and other Indians. For example, when Governor Montgomerie traveled to Albany in May 1731 to make an important proclamation to the assembled Iroquois diplomats, he relied heavily on the assistance of the Albany commissioners. The day before his lengthy speech, Montgomerie "[laid] before this board a draft of a proposition he intends to make to the sachems of the Six Nations for this board to peruse." The commissioners "after making some amendments thereunto have returned the same to his Excellency." At this same series of meetings, the Iroquois visitors requested of Montgomerie a reprieve for a murderer, leading the governor to "desire the opinion of this board whether he should grant it," overall "pleased to ask the opinion of the Commissioners of the Indian Affairs on that subject." Montgomerie "ordered the said Commissioners to attend at his lodgings" to hear their ideas.[36] Clearly governors relied on these experienced experts for the successful completion of their meetings with the Iroquois and other indigenous polities in Albany. As such, although governors sometimes made the trek northward with broad instructions from the Crown to participate in Indian diplomacy themselves, they required the commissioners' help for translation, protocol, and advice on more nuanced issues outside the scope of a governor's broad diplomatic goals.

Most of the time, however, New York's governor stayed safely in New York City, leaving Indian affairs up to the Albany commissioners. Governor visits to Albany to treat with Iroquois leaders served as punctuation to the continuous conversation of New York's Indian affairs, while the steady presence of the commissioners served as the conversation itself.

Albany's commissioners served as vital conduits of intelligence concerning Indian matters. In November 1705, for example, the commissioners received information that Canada's governor had shifted French troop position; "From hence they suggested he

---

[35]   Again, for a significantly fuller analysis, see the author's PhD dissertation (note 6 above).

[36]   *MCIA*, 1:335-37a.

designed some attack upon Albany or the settlements thereabout." They immediately "wrote a letter to the governor desiring he will fall upon proper measures to secure [Albany]."[37] In a similar case, in September 1723, the commissioners drafted a letter to Governor William Burnet, passing along information they had just received from Laurence Claessen, the commissioners' interpreter. Claessen reported the "surprising news that the greatest number of the French Indians were making themselves ready to join with the eastern Indians to go out fighting against New England." The commissioners stated to Burnet in a letter that they, "thought in duty to forward to your Excellency without loss of time," and enclosed a copy of Claessen's letter with theirs. The commissioners maintained these critical connections to the borderlands communications web that allowed them to gather information important to other colonial officials and pass it along as needed.[38]

Albany's commissioners also participated in Indian diplomacy that exceeded the local New York borderlands and influenced events in other parts of the British North American Empire, such as New England and Virginia. Brief examples will serve to represent larger trends. In 1723, for example, the commissioners hosted "one of the sachems of the [Mohawks] and two young Indians of that castle," and they used this opportunity to project their influence into New England Indian affairs. These commissioners told their visitors "that they had received a letter from New England" a few days prior, warning them that "A number of 60 or 80 Indians attacked two small forts at Northfield that morning." The letter noted that the assault had "wounded two men and it's feared three or four are killed," and its author proposed that, "If a number of the Six Nations, together with some of the River Indians, were dispatched immediately, they might probably arrive at the mouth of the Otter Creek before the enemy reach that place and be capable of doing service." The commissioners thus "now demand your opinion in that affair whether it can probably be effected that is proposed in said letter." Refusing to answer concretely, the visiting Mohawks "say

---

37   Peter Wraxall, *An Abridgement of the Indian Affairs: Contained in Four Folio Volumes, Transacted in the Colony of New York, From the Year 1678 to the Year 1751*, ed. Charles Howard McIlwain (New York: Benjamin Blom, 1968), 45.

38   Sometimes the lack of bad news concerning the French would worry the commissioners just as much as firm intelligence. In a letter to Governor Burnet in September 1727, for example, the commissioners worried that they "hear no manner of intelligence from Canada, which makes us uneasy what is hatching there." *MCIA*, 1:204.

that they can't give a direct answer but they are going to their castles and will acquaint their people with what this board told them."[39] While the commissioners were unable to effect immediate action in this case, this scenario still served as an excellent example of how the Albany commissioners involved themselves in New England Indian affairs, especially as important purveyors of information for New England's colonies.

Albany's commissioners also involved themselves in Indian affairs centered on the Chesapeake colony of Virginia in the first half of the eighteenth century. Virginia's Indian affairs bled northward due to the Carolina Road linking the Virginia backcountry with Iroquoia. The commissioners, as the primary link between the British world and the Iroquois war parties that utilized this road, often found themselves making diplomatic decisions that influenced events far to the south. For example, in November 1719, the commissioners met with sachems of the Five Nations to "renew the Covenant Chain with them in behalf of this government & all His Majesty's governments on the continent," including Virginia. At this meeting, Iroquois diplomats agreed that "They renew the Covenant Chain with this government, but as to renewing the Covenant Chain with the governments of the southward, they wonder that is mentioned," insisting that "For that [two] years ago, the governor of Virginia made complaints of some of their people doing mischief in his country." The Iroquois visitors desired that Virginia's governor "would come himself or depute some body to come to Albany with some sachems of the Indians in his Alliance that they might adjust all matters face to face." Responding to their visitors' views, "The Commissioners reply that they desire they would delay their going out a fighting to the southward till next spring, which time they may hear from Virginia."[40] In this case, the commissioners successfully utilized their influence over the Iroquois to preclude any continuing violence between the Iroquois and the Virginia-allied Indians that would bleed over into colonial Virginia itself.

In sum this essay has addressed three issues. First, it has traced the roots of the Albany Commissioners for Indian Affairs back to the New Netherland period, showing how Dutch traders and settlers at Albany gained the expertise in Indian affairs and diplomacy that carried into the British era of New York. Second, this essay has provided a brief analysis of that body as a formal institution in British New York,

[39]   *MCIA*, 1:60a.
[40]   Wraxall, *An Abridgement of the Indian Affairs*, 125-26.

emphasizing how the body had a small core membership of highly active members. More important, this small core was overwhelmingly Dutch and existed as a tightly knit family due to intermarriage among its member families. Last, this essay has shown that this small cadre of Dutchmen were critical agents of Indian diplomacy not just to New York but also to other British colonies and even inserted themselves into imperial level issues regarding the British rivalry with French Canada.

The larger idea to take away is fascinating. Specifically, the Indian diplomacy of the British Empire, a critical crux of its power on the continent, was under the influence of a small group of Dutchmen living in Albany. Two dozen Dutchmen played an enormous role in Indian affairs throughout the colonies, inserting themselves into the affairs of New England and Virginia and concerning themselves with the imperial rivalry between British and French Crowns. As historians are certainly aware, Dutch settlers did not simply disappear as New Netherland became New York, but these Dutch settlers also did not simply quietly exist in a new British world either. The Albany commissioners shaped the colonial world around them, locally and imperially, and deserve to be recognized as notable actors in the British colonial world. Such a recognition blurs traditional lines and borders of empires and opens up new narratives of how the British Empire often relied on non-British peoples for its proper functioning. The Albany commissioners helped bring the Dutch into this imperial story.

Part Four

American Influence on Dutch Communities
and Churches

CHAPTER 9

Slaveholding: The Dutch Reformed Church's Debates of 1855

Earl Wm. Kennedy

In 1855 General Synod of the Reformed Protestant Dutch Church (henceforth RPDC) rejected the application for membership of the German Reformed Classis of North Carolina, some of whose clergy and laity were slaveholders. The classis had recently declared its independence from the German Reformed denomination, located mainly in the North. The proposal of classis was broached and extensively discussed at the June 1855 regular annual meeting of synod and was debated at even greater length and finally turned down in October at the extraordinary session of synod called to consider the issue further. The main stumbling block for union, as appears repeatedly in the religious and secular press, as well as in several RPDC pamphlets written at the time, was slavery. It is therefore surprising that the published minutes of General Synod for 1855 do not say a word about slavery and contain no hint that the South's "peculiar institution" was at the very heart of the synodical deliberations.[1] A review of the course of events may help explain this apparent anomaly.

1   Edward Tanjore Corwin, *A Digest of Constitutional and Synodical Legislation of the Reformed Church in America [Formerly the Ref. Prot. Dutch Church] Prepared by Order*

At first glance, a union of the southern classis with the Dutch denomination in the North would appear to have been a marriage made in heaven, because the German and Dutch Reformed denominations had both been under the oversight of Classis of Amsterdam until 1792-93, and the North Carolina classis and the RPDC had both just recently (1852-53) broken ties with the German Reformed denomination because of the influence in it of the "high church," "Romanizing," Mercersburg theology (and liturgy) of John Williamson Nevin (and Philip Schaff), which had nullified the whirlwind courtship and virtual engagement of the RPDC and German Reformed synods in the early 1840s.[2] Furthermore, there was the recent precedent of an entire classis (the Dutch immigrants of Holland, Michigan) joining the RPDC (1850),[3] not to mention the lure for the RPDC, largely confined to New York and New Jersey, of becoming more of a national church (like the Presbyterians) with a branch in the South.

The June 1855 General Synod: the issue raised and postponed

The 1855 tempest in the RPDC teapot began when Rev. Thornton Butler, representing the newly independent Classis of North Carolina, appeared at the annual June meeting of General Synod with a request

---

of General Synod (New York: Board of Publication of the RCA, 1906), 467-68, 680, in providing context for and summaries of the actions of the June and October 1855 General Synod, confirms the key role slavery played in its deliberations. Rev. Thomas Morris Strong (1797-1861), the Flatbush, Brooklyn, New York, pastor from 1822 until his death, was, for the last thirty-four years of his life, General Synod's stated clerk and thus "author" of the minutes; Edward Tanjore Corwin, *A Manual of the Reformed Church in America . . . 1628-1902*, 4th ed. (New York: Board of Publication of the RCA, 1902), 759-60.

[2]   James I. Good, *History of the Reformed Church in the US in the Nineteenth Century* (New York: Board of Publication of the RCA, 1911), 1-6, 179-82, 188, 222-23, 243-45, 259-63, 298-300, 304-7; Corwin, *Digest*, 386, 584-86; Gregg Mast, "A Decade of Hope and Despair: Mercersburg Theology's Impact on Two Reformed Denominations," in *A Goodly Heritage: Essays in Honor of the Reverend Dr. Elton J. Bruins at Eighty*, ed. Jacob E. Nyenhuis (Grand Rapids: Eerdmans, 2007), 163-80. Additional factors favoring merger include the presence in the North Carolina classis of a few antislavery pastors from Pennsylvania, the relatively benevolent slave policy of the classis, the presence until very recently of slaves in the RPDC, the fact that RPDC General Synod (as well as the German Reformed synods) had not condemned slaveholding, the influence in both denominations of moderate revivalism, and the (unrealistic) hope that the RPDC could supply clergy and money for the North Carolina classis, including support for its infant Catawba College, which had begun as a "low church," local alternative to the German Reformed schools in Pennsylvania.

[3]   Corwin, *Manual*, 129; Corwin, *Digest*, 319.

Rev. Samuel Blanchard How

Samuel B. How

by classis to join the RPDC.[4] This petition was referred to synod's committee on correspondence, chaired by Rev. Samuel Blanchard How, veteran pastor of the large First Reformed Church of New Brunswick, New Jersey, in whose sanctuary the synod happened to be assembled.[5]

How's committee learned from Butler that the North Carolina classis had twenty-four churches scattered over a wide area, but only

[4] Thornton Butler (1820-1870), a North Carolina native whose mother was a Wykoff (presumably of Dutch Reformed extraction), early was a Methodist Episcopal exhorter but soon turned German Reformed, graduating from Marshall College (1846) and Mercersburg Seminary (1848) in Pennsylvania. He suffered from ill health during much of his ministry, which was mostly in North Carolina; Samuel H. Ranck et al., eds., *Franklin and Marshall College Obituary Record* (Lancaster, PA, [1900]), 1:63-65; H. Harbaugh, *The Fathers of the German Reformed Church in Europe and America* (Lancaster, PA: J. M. Westhaeffer, 1872), 4:396-99.

[5] Samuel Blanchard How (1790-1868), born in New Jersey but with North Carolina (and Huguenot) links on his mother's side, was a graduate of the University of Pennsylvania and Princeton Theological Seminary, served three New Jersey Presbyterian churches and one in Georgia (seven years), received a Union College DD degree (1830), and was president of (Presbyterian) Dickinson College, 1830-32, all before he became the longtime pastor (1832-61) of the RPDC congregation in New Brunswick. How was "in all respects . . . an old school man" who "venerated the past"; he was learned, a hard-working pastor, "the perfect gentleman"; Corwin, *Manual*, 530. In 1837 a major revival added many members to How's congregation, ultimately requiring the formation of a second Reformed church in New Brunswick; J. David Muyskens, *"The Town Clock Church": History of the First Reformed Church, New Brunswick, NJ* (New Brunswick: Consistory, 1991), 38-39, 41.

First Reformed Church,
New Brunswick, New Jersey,
erected 1812

eight ministers, and thus needed additional clergymen, and that classis had approached the RPDC because it was deemed to be the denomination closest to it in faith and practice, even if not in geography (e.g., the Presbyterians). The Carolinians said they wished to join the RPDC because they (like the RPDC) disapproved of the Mercersburg innovations in the German Reformed Church. In addition, classis had a "literary institution," Catawba College at Newton, North Carolina, which they hoped to expand significantly.

Since classis (some of whose congregations possessed much land) owned its property as the German Reformed Church, it hoped to be able to keep this name in any union with the RPDC—and thus to be called Classis of the German Reformed Church of the RPDC. In light of all this, the committee foresaw an opening to the South—a vast missionary opportunity—and so recommended that synod look with favor on the North Carolinians' application to become part of the RPDC.[6]

Extensive debate of this recommendation ensued on the floor of synod. Rev. Isaac Newton Wyckoff[7] was happy that God, in his providence, had brought these churches "in our arms," but wondered

---

[6] *The Acts and Proceedings of the General Synod of the Reformed Protestant Dutch Church, . . . June 1855* (New York: Board of Publication of the RPDC, 1855), 535-36.

[7] Isaac Newton Wyckoff (1792-1869) was the longtime pastor (1836-66) of Albany's Second Reformed Church (and a warm friend of the Holland, Michigan, colonists),

Catawba College, Newton, North Carolina, founded 1851

"if the institution of slavery ["a great horrible incubus which rests on the South"] pervades the limits of the North Carolina classis"; "it has caused contention and division in other ecclesiastical bodies"[8]—so if Wyckoff could be satisfied that the reception of the North Carolina classis would not result in that, he would receive it gladly, "for the honorable stand they have taken with regard to another incubus which rests over us, but little less dreadful to contemplate—Popery" (i.e., the Mercersburg theology).[9]

Samuel B. How responded, "I am informed by Mr. Butler that out of the eight ministers within the Classis, only three own slaves, one of which he obtained in this manner: Owing to the death of the master of this slave, his property had to be sold, and the slave, fearing he would have to be sold and taken away from his home, entreated this minister to purchase him. It was not until after repeated entreaties that he listened to the request, and, finally, as a favor to the slave, purchased him. The same minister has also a woman and her child, who take care

8   The Baptists and Methodists had divided between the North and South over the slavery question in 1844-45.
9   *Christian Intelligencer*, 21 June 1855, which also details the course of the debate on the floor of synod for the rest of its June meeting; this is the primary source for the ensuing paragraphs on this session.
10 Two of the three slaveholding pastors, judging from the 1850 federal census, appear to have been Rev. John Lantz (1811-1873), who then had a wife, three small children, and two slaves (a nineteen-year-old male and an eighteen-year-old female) and Rev. Jeremiah Ingold (1816-1893), who had a wife, little daughter, young relative of his wife, and one female slave, aged twenty-three. In the 1860 census, neither of these men had slaves, but Rev. George Boger (1782-1865), long retired

Rev. Isaac Groot Duryee

of his house. Another minister owns two slaves, and another, one.[10] Five own no slaves at all, but they are making noble efforts and are exhibiting a high Christian spirit with reference to the matter. They are taking measures to approach the North Carolina Legislature to procure passage of legislative enactments legalizing the marriage of slaves, to

---

then, did have a single female slave, aged sixty; apparently he had had no slaves in 1850. Did these "slaveholding" ministers, all native North Carolinians, constitute a real and present danger to the RPDC in 1855? One other member of the classis with a "suspect" record was Maryland-born Rev. John H. Crawford (1801-1864), the fundraiser for Catawba College, married and childless, who had one adult female slave (aged 36-54) in the 1840 census (but none in the 1830 and 1850 censuses); in 1860, in Augusta County, Virginia, he had four slaves (two mulatto and two black); www.ancestry.com (1840, 1850, and 1860 censuses). The very few slaves involved in these three or four cases were presumably "household" slaves, to help in and around the parsonage, perhaps as perquisites in the ministerial contract (except for Boger, who was retired from the ministry). It appears, however, that having slaves as part of the "furnishings" of the parsonage was not mandatory; the three "Yankee" (Pennsylvania-born) pastors in the classis (David Crooks, George William Welker, and William Sorber) had no slaves, nor did the other North Carolina native, Thornton Butler. There thus seems to be some correlation between place of birth and slaveholding among the ministers in the classis. Perhaps a much more serious issue from the antislavery viewpoint is the fact that the first members of the board of trustees of Catawba College (founded 1851 to train "sound" ministers for the German Reformed denomination) were mostly "large farmers and probably all owned slaves"; some of these trustees were major slaveholders who provided or raised much of the financial support for the college (they contributed relatively little cash themselves, since their wealth was in land and slaves) and presumably also for the ministers. Jacob Calvin Leonard, *History of Catawba College* (Columbia, MO: Trustees of Catawba College, 1927), 37.

prevent the separation of children under twelve from their parents, and to enforce the education of slaves. They are acting in the spirit of high philanthropy. They are making efforts to put down slavery, and they are beginning just at this point where they ought to begin. If slavery be a sin, it is not our sin; and we might just as well break Christian fellowship with Christians in New Jersey (for there are slaves still held there in the old Dutch families)[11] as attempt to refuse fellowship with these brethren. I will pledge myself, if they be admitted, that the question of slavery will never be introduced by Southern ministers, and, further, if it be introduced, it will be by Northern men."[12]

[11]   New Jersey was the last northern state to end slavery, beginning officially but only gradually in 1846. There were still 235 slaves listed in New Jersey in the 1850 census, many of whose owners had Dutch surnames; www.ancestry.com (1850 census). Some of these slaves were still living with their masters at the time of the 1855 General Synod, as How pointed out, and some may have been old and worn out, so that their "bondage" could even have become for them a limited kind of "social security." Just possibly one or more of synod's delegates were (former) slave owners. See James J. Gigantino II, *The Ragged Road to Abolition: Slavery and Freedom in New Jersey, 1775-1865* (Philadelphia: University of Pennsylvania Press, 2015), for a thorough treatment of the complicated and very slow end of slavery in New Jersey; he may err in asserting that How himself was a slaveholder; ibid., 236. For brief overviews of the RPDC and slavery, see John W. Beardslee III, "The Reformed Church in America and the African American Community," *Reformed Review* 46, no. 2 (winter 1992), 104-8, and Firth Haring Fabend, *Zion on the Hudson: Dutch New York and New Jersey in the Age of Revivals* (New Brunswick, NJ: Rutgers University Press, 2000), 179-86.

[12]   The pro-Union, antislavery, longtime stated clerk of the North Carolina classis, Rev. George William Welker, penned its history late in his life (in the 1880s). He dealt with the subject of "the colored people, slaves and slave-holding," which "must throw a shadow on the history of Classis." He pointed out, however, that several of its official acts indicated its relative enlightenment. In 1838 the classis recommended that, following the example of other southern denominations, room and pews in the church buildings should be provided for the blacks, and also that they should be received into communicant membership when their knowledge and piety allowed, and, if slaves, then with their master's permission. But, Welker reported, the latter regulation did not satisfy a Catawba County elder in 1845, who objected to his minister and consistory baptizing and confirming people of color and admitting them to communion. The classis responded that since, "in the Providence of God, domestic slavery exists in our midst," ministers should explain and enforce "the duties that devolve upon Christian masters and mistresses . . . towards the bodies and souls of their servants." Moreover, the ministers and elders must "give particular attention to the spiritual instruction and training of the servants belonging to the families under their care; that, whenever practical, they have special preaching for their benefit and adapted to their situation," and that violation of that part of the constitution "prohibiting cruelty to servants be met with the appointed penalty." Then, at a meeting of classis in 1848, when the subject of slavery was becoming a subject of "*intense* interest, and even bitterness, the following motion was passed unanimously: 'Whereas, as in the mystery of

At this point, Rev. Isaac Groot Duryee, first pastor of the Second Reformed Church of Schenectady, a longtime, active member of the American Anti-Slavery Society,[13] one of the few out-and-out RPDC abolitionists, took the floor, opposing the admission of the North Carolina classis. "The question of slavery is the great question of this nation, and when the line is to be drawn I shall not be slow to show which side I am on. Sir, I am on the side of liberty—Freedom . . . I can say that my inmost soul shrinks from extending the fellowship of our church to slaveholding churches as I shrink from the touch of the torpedo."[14] Moreover, "I would rather carry Dr. Nevin [the Mercersburg theologian] and all his theology on my back all the rest of my life than to give the slightest seeming endorsement to the crime of slavery, with its attendant host of evils."[15] This speech, which included Luther's "Here I stand" line, was reportedly interrupted once or twice by overt expressions of approval from some in the audience.[16] (Harriet Beecher

---

God's providence, negro slavery exists in our midst, and as many of our members sustain the responsible relation of master and mistress of bond servants, while this Classis has no disposition to interfere in the political or civil relation thus found existing, they would however have a care to see that the religious, relative duties be regarded, therefore, *Resolved*, that in the judgment of this Classis, the relation of Christian master and slave makes them part of one household, and that the master should give his slaves every religious advantage, and discharge toward them the duty of the head of a Christian family, as toward his own children, believing slaves to be part of the master's family, and entitled to its religious privileges; that it be enjoined on the members of our churches to have their slave children baptized as Abraham circumcised his, and that they take particular attention to give them religious instruction, and so to train them up as to make it an eternal blessing to their souls to have been members of a Christian family." George Wm. Welker, *A Historical Sketch of the Classis of North Carolina* (Hickory, NC: A. L. Crouse, Printer, 1895), 19-20; Good, *History of the Reformed Church*, 199.

13   Isaac Groot Duryee (1810-66), converted as a young man (1832), was graduated from Union College (1838) and Andover Theological Seminary (1841, with his middler year [1839-40] spent at the Divinity School of Yale College), joined the American Anti-Slavery Society while in college, cofounded the Union College Anti-Slavery Society (1836), the Schenectady Anti-Slavery Society (1838), and the first black church in that city (1837; now the Duryee Memorial AME Zion Church), and was active in the Underground Railroad in Schenectady, etc.; "Local Abolitionist Isaac Groot Duryee," in Grems-Doolittle Library Collections Blog, 30 January 2014, at http://gremsdoolittlelibrary.blogspot.com/2014/01/local-abolitionist-isaac-groot-duryee.html.

14   *New York Daily Tribune* (no date given), quoted in "Local Abolitionist Isaac Groot Duryee."

15   Quoted in Good, *History of the Reformed Church*, 301.

16   According to the Republican Dutch-language weekly, *De Nieuwsbode* of Sheboygan, Wisconsin, citing the 19 June 1855 *New York Daily Tribune*, this fiery oration called forth, on one or two occasions, openly expressed acclaim (*toejuichen*)—whether from

Uncle Tom's Cabin (1852), title page

UNCLE TOM'S CABIN;

LIFE AMONG THE LOWLY.

BY

HARRIET BEECHER STOWE.

VOL. I.

BOSTON:
JOHN P. JEWETT & COMPANY.
CLEVELAND, OHIO:
JEWETT, PROCTOR & WORTHINGTON.
1852.

Stowe's antislavery *Uncle Tom's Cabin* happened to be at the peak of its popularity at this time.)

But then Rev. George Washington Bethune of Brooklyn, an avowed foe of both slavery and abolitionism,[17] cautioned the assembly

---

the delegates or from the onlookers is not specified; *De Nieuwsbode*, 3 July 1855, at http://zoeken.krantenbankzeeland.nl. Groot's apparent view (and that of other abolitionists) to exclude slaveholders from the Christian church would seem to be similar to that of those later opposed to Freemasonry, that is, to erect an "extra-canonical test for church membership"; Donald J. Bruggink, "Extra-Canonical Tests for Church Membership and Ministry," in *A Goodly Heritage*, ed. Nyenhuis, 50-54; see note 61 below. Another great moral crusade (involving the churches), in addition to abolition, would be the temperance (prohibition) movement.

[17] George Washington Bethune (1805-62), whose well-to-do parents were Scottish immigrants (although his paternal line was earlier Huguenot), was born in New York City and graduated from Dickinson College (1823) and Princeton Theological Seminary (1826), after which he served very briefly as a Presbyterian missionary to sailors and blacks in Savannah, Georgia (1826-27), where he was befriended and mentored by Rev. Samuel B. How, for whose help he remained grateful when both men were in the RPDC. In Savannah, Bethune preached once—not yet ordained—in How's church and also elsewhere to slaves; at this time, he became a strong advocate for the cause of colonization and later promoted the American Colonization Society. How urged him to remain in Savannah, but he soon returned to the North, where he was immediately ordained in the Presbyterian Church and at the same time transferred into the RPDC (all in 1827) because he was attracted to the liturgy and relative harmony of the RPDC, which he deemed preferable to the Presbyterian Church's lack of forms and its internal quarreling (note the impending Old School-New School Presbyterian schism [1837]). From 1827 to 1849, Bethune filled four successive RPDC pulpits, after which he served the Reformed Church on the Heights in Brooklyn, New York, until 1858, when he moved to a New York City RPDC congregation (his last, from which he retired for reasons of health). A powerful, popular preacher, with a natural gift of eloquence, he was awarded an honorary DD

Rev. George Washington Bethune

against making a hasty decision in this matter; he had positive words to say about the North Carolina classis, and he averred that he would rather die than exclude anyone from Christian fellowship because he owned slaves.

How spoke once again a couple of times. He insisted that he did not wish to add fuel to the fire by increasing the animosity of contention. How related that his nearest relatives lived in North Carolina and that his grandfather, a Revolutionary War soldier,[18] was a North Carolinian (Carolinians have "the purest patriotism"). How went on to claim that "when Negroes are emancipated, they sink into a state of degradation below that of any slaves. They become robbers and plunderers." This

---

degree relatively early in his career (1838) by the University of Pennsylvania (when he had a Philadelphia pastorate). Preferring to remain in the pastorate, Bethune declined offers to be chaplain of the US Military Academy, chancellor of New York University, and provost of the University of Pennsylvania. He was an outspoken Democrat, opposed to both slavery and abolitionism, and supported the Union when the Civil War broke out. Probably his most unusual characteristics were his secret (because presumably unbecoming for a minister) devotion to fishing, in theory and in practice (he edited, anonymously, the first American edition of Izaak Walton's *The Compleat Angler*), as well as his deep interest in the humanities (e.g., philosophy, theology, classical and modern languages, poetry, music, painting, and sculpture). He published his own poems (including hymns) in addition to a volume on the poetry of British female poets. Many of his sermons, addresses, and articles also appeared in print. Corwin, *Manual*, 318-21; A. R. Van Nest, *Memoir of Rev. George W. Bethune, DD* (New York: Sheldon and Company, 1867), 63, 65, 68-70; "George Washington Bethune," in Dickinson College Archives and Special Collections, at http://archives.dickinson.edu/people/george-washington-bethune-1805-1862.

[18]   How's maternal grandfather, Andrew Blanchard (1728-87), born in New Jersey, of Huguenot ancestry, moved to North Carolina before the Revolution, participated in the war against the British, and became an affluent (state) printer and pioneer newspaper publisher; "Blanchard, Andrew," in *Dictionary of North Carolina Biography*, vol. 1, ed. William S. Powell (Chapel Hill: University of North Carolina Press, 1979), at http://ncpedia.org/biography/blanchard-andrew; Walt Howe, "Howe Genealogy," at http://www.howegenealogy.org/index.php.

had compelled southern legislatures "to enact laws to prevent the emancipation of slaves." He next told about one of his elders when he had pastored the Independent Presbyterian Church of Savannah, Georgia (1823-30). The man, who owned many slaves, became deeply convicted about slavery, prayed, sought advice, and "his conscience and judgment led him to feel that it was the greatest possible evil to emancipate his slaves," that it was his "duty to retain their possession—instruct them, care for their souls and bodies." Accordingly, the elder's wife asked How for books to instruct their slaves and thereby "slowly proceed to emancipation."[19]

Sensing which way the wind was blowing, Rev. Thornton Butler requested and was granted the opportunity to address synod: "We [i.e., the German classis] would rather remain as we are and fight alone in the cause of our Master than to throw a brand into your house. I therefore desire most respectfully to withdraw our application for admission into the Synod. I shall return to my Brethren in the South." Butler maintained that he would leave with "no unkind feelings" toward synod. The president of synod responded that the classis' extreme distance would have made care by the RPDC difficult and the relation merely nominal.

Following Butler's statement, a committee of five was appointed (three ministers, including Bethune, and two elders) "to prepare resolutions expressive of the views of this Synod." The committee quickly produced three resolutions: (1) gratitude to God for the classis' "noble stand . . . in defense of the great essential truths of the Reformation against the errors of the Mercersburg theology"; (2) kind feelings for Butler and sympathy for the brethren in their "efforts to maintain and spread the Gospel" and "establish their struggling seminary of learning"; and (3) commendation of "these brethren to the material aid of our Churches" and to assure them that their "pious youth" were always very welcome at the RPDC's New Brunswick Theological Seminary.[20]

[19] Horace Greeley's Republican *New York Daily Tribune* of 19 June 1855, as translated in *De Nieuwsbode* of Sheboygan, 3 July 1855, commented that How's speech was noteworthy, not as a well-reasoned defense of slavery, but as an example of the chatter (*gekal*) used fifteen years previous by slavery defenders in narrow-minded circles, and that How must have been sleeping all this time. Incidentally, in New Brunswick, blacks (slave and free) constituted ten percent of How's First Reformed Church's membership when he began his ministry there (1832); during his pastorate, they had their own separate Sunday school class and cemetery; Muyskens, *"The Town Clock Church,"* 35-36, 42-43.

[20] A glance at New Brunswick Seminary's students 1850-69 reveals that no one from the North Carolina classis (or probably from the German Reformed denomination)

Next, the synod, by a majority vote, requested Butler to reconsider his withdrawal of the papers applying for membership in the RPDC and to leave them with synod until a special meeting in October.[21] This he proceeded to do.

At this juncture, a member of the minority in the previous vote, Rev. Hervey Doddridge Ganse, pastor of the Freehold, New Jersey, Reformed Church,[22] responded that he and others had not agreed with the previous speakers. He thought that "elders and Christians in the church" needed to discuss "any great moral question which God in his providence should bring into this body." It should be discussed "fully and frankly," and many on the floor agreed with him and said so. Ganse would return to this important theme—whether or not slavery was sin—at the October meeting of General Synod.[23]

The summer of 1855: the issue simmering in the classes East and Midwest

After the adjournment of the June General Synod, during the summer and early fall, virtually nothing on this topic appeared in the pages of the RPDC's weekly newspaper, the *Christian Intelligencer*, whose anti-abolitionist outlook was apparently close to How's.[24] An exception

availed himself of this "generous" offer, although there were a surprising number of German-born students attending during these years; John Howard Raven, compiler, *Biographical Record Theological Seminary New Brunswick, New Jersey 1784-1934* (New Brunswick: n.p., 1934), 94-129. The author of this friendly report of the five-man committee was the well-connected and much published Rev. William James Romeyn Taylor (1823-91), pastor of the Third Reformed Church of Philadelphia, later recipient of a Rutgers College DD degree (1860), president of General Synod (1871), and the *Christian Intelligencer* editor (1872-76); Corwin, *Manual*, 775-79.

21   *Acts and Proceedings, June 1855*, 531-32.
22   Hervey Doddridge Ganse (1822-91), a graduate of New Brunswick Theological Seminary (1843) was in his first charge, soon (1856) to be left for a twenty-year pastorate in New York City, before he departed the Reformed Church for the Presbyterian Church. He was gifted with a very keen mind and was a fine preacher and a talented General Synod debater; Corwin, *Manual*, 482-84.
23   Almost all of the details of the foregoing debate at the June General Synod are taken from the pages of the *Christian Intelligencer*, 21 June 1855.
24   The *Christian Intelligencer*'s editor (1852-68) was Rev. Elbert Stothoff Porter (1820-88), who denied that his weekly and (consequently) the RPDC as a whole were proslavery, or at best "lukewarm" (cf. Rev. 3:16), as some alleged, simply because they were not abolitionists. Such accusations were lodged, for example, in 1860, by the pastor of the Sixth United Presbyterian Church of Philadelphia; Thomas H. Beveridge, "Pro-Slavery and the *Christian Intelligencer*," in the *Evangelical Repository* 19, no. 7 (December 1860), 398-99; Beveridge was the editor of this periodical of the newly created (1858) United Presbyterian Church of North America, which was on record as excluding slaveholders, as was the True Reformed Dutch Church (begun

to this apparent editorial blackout was the paper's publication in the early fall of a few classes' annual reports with opinions on the matter.[25] Outside the press, also, storm clouds were forming. For instance, Rev. Theodore Ledyard Cuyler,[26] abolitionist pastor of a New York City RPDC congregation, sent a letter to How dated 16 June 1855, the day after synod ended (Cuyler had not been a delegate to synod), in which he expressed the "fear that admitting 'the handful of slaveholders from Carolina' would 'rend my own church into fragments' because his congregation had 'many New England people and many who are firmly opposed to slavery.'"[27]

Not only did abolitionist and antislavery sentiment seep into the RPDC from New England Congregationalism,[28] but at least some

---

1822), which had already in 1829 put a policy in place barring slaveholders and slave dealers from membership; Monroe N. Work, ed., *Negro Year Book: An Annual Encyclopedia of the Negro 1921-1922* (Tuskegee, AL: Negro Year Book Publishing Co., 1922), 159. The *Christian Intelligencer*, which tried to keep to the middle of the road, was criticized not only from the antislavery *New York Daily Tribune* but also the proslavery (or at least tolerant of slavery) *New York Observer*. Already in an 1850 sermon, Porter had denounced slavery as a great evil (which should end) but argued that abolitionism (which would ignore the law) was an even greater evil. He was speaking out here, in the aftermath of the "bruising struggle" over the Compromise of 1850, against "the blind and bigoted and passionate rage of party spirit"; Elbert S. Porter, *The Perils and the Security of Our Country. A Sermon, Delivered in The Ref. Prot. Dutch Church, of Williamsburgh, L.I., on Thanksgiving Day, Dec. 12, 1850* (Williamsburgh, Long Island: Joseph C. Gandar, 1850). Even so, Porter himself engaged in a bit of "party spirit" on a different front when he attacked Mercersburg theology in the pages of the *Christian Intelligencer* in the 1840s and 1850s; James W. Van Hoeven, "Dort and Albany: Reformed Theology Engages a New Culture," in *Word and World: Reformed Theology in America*, ed. James W. Van Hoeven (Grand Rapids: Eerdmans, 1986), 25, 27, 145. As soon as the Civil War began, Porter and the *Christian Intelligencer* supported the Union enthusiastically and were soon very highly "patriotic"; Dennis N. Voskuil, "Piety and Patriotism: Reformed Theology and Civil Religion," in Van Hoeven, *Word and World*, 129-31, 146.

25   *Christian Intelligencer*, 4, 11, and 18 October 1855.

26   Theodore Ledyard Cuyler (1822-1909) was a graduate of the College of New Jersey (now Princeton University) and Princeton Theological Seminary (1846); the former institution would grant him two honorary doctorates (DD in 1866 and LLD in 1897). He served two Presbyterian congregations until 1853 when he went to the Market Street RPDC in New York City, after which he spent thirty years in Brooklyn as pastor until 1890 of what then became the largest Presbyterian church in the nation. Cuyler was not only a widely hailed, eloquent pulpiteer but also a prolific author of religious articles and books; he knew and corresponded with an amazing array of prominent American and British people. Corwin, *Manual*, 400-401; "Theodore L. Cuyler," at https://en.wikipedia.org/wiki/Theodore_L._Cuyler.

27   Gigantino, *The Ragged Road to Abolition*, 236, 304.

28   Van Hoeven, "Dort and Albany," in *Word and World*, 21-22, 27, points out the difference between the more "open" RPDC around Albany (nearer to New England)

of the recent immigrants from the Netherlands, members of the new Classes of Holland and Wisconsin, were interested, from afar, in the whole debate, especially after the events of the June General Synod.[29] Some of the newcomers were Democrats, like the editor of *De* [or *The*] *Hollander*, Hermanus Doesburg, of Holland, Michigan, and some

---

and the more "ethnocentric" (Dutch) RPDC in the area of New York City and New Jersey, represented by the *Christian Intelligencer*. Note that the abolitionist, Isaac G. Duryee, an adherent of the American Anti-Slavery Society, was from Upstate New York (Schenectady). Welker, *Classis of North Carolina*, 30, speaks of a "New England abolition element" then in the RPDC, in contrast to "almost all the original Dutch" who favored receiving the NC classis into the RPDC. It should not be forgotten that Negro slavery had existed in the eighteenth century in the North and had only recently been abolished in New York (1827) and was still dying out in New Jersey (ca. 1850); slaveholding was thus a living memory in the Eastern RPDC. The Dutch West India Company (founded 1621) had transported many slaves from West Africa to the plantations of South America and the West Indies but also, on a smaller scale, to the colonial Dutch of New York and New Jersey; the early directors of the West India Company discussed this topic; Janny Venema, *Kiliaen van Rensselaer (1586-1643): Designing a New World* (Hilversum: Verloren, 2010), 281-83; P. C. Emmer, *The Dutch Slave Trade 1500-1850* (Oxford: Berghahn, 2006).

29 Although the recently arrived Dutch Reformed immigrants in the Midwest were mostly well removed geographically from the slave states and owned no slaves themselves, and although most of them were too busy eking out a living farming to be much involved in politics, they nevertheless had access to the news through newspapers like *De* [*The*] *Hollander*, the Sheboygan *Nieuwsbode*; Christine Jacobs, "The Western Michigan Dutch During the American Civil War: A Question of Loyalties," a paper for Prof. E. Van Kley, 19 November 1988, typescript at History Department, Calvin College; Jacobs questions a too "patriotic" (pro-Union) portrayal of the immigrants. They were of course aware of the slavery question since it was discussed in their homeland. King William I (pressured by the British and the Congress of Vienna) had abolished the slave trade in the entire Dutch colonial empire in 1814-15, while slavery itself would continue (but with growing public opposition in the 1840s and 1850s, stimulated by the publication of *Uncle Tom's Cabin* in Dutch in 1853) in the East Indies until 1859 and in the West Indies until 1863; G. J. Schutte, "Slavernij," in *Christelijke Encyclopedie*, ed. George Harinck et al. (Kok, 2005), 1647; "Slavernij: Protest in Nederland," at http://www.slavernijenjij. nl/de-afschaffing/nederlands-protest-tegen-slavernij. The leaders of the Dutch *Réveil* (like their evangelical counterparts in England, such as William Wilberforce) had been prominent in urging these reforms, but the *Afscheiding* men like Anthony Brummelkamp, Hendrik P. Scholte, and A. C. van Raalte also shared their abhorrence of slavery; M. Elisabeth Kluit, *Het Protestantse Réveil in Nederland en daarbuiten 1815-1865* (Amsterdam: H. J. Paris n.v., 1970), 433-35, 471-72; Melis te Velde, *Anthony Brummelkamp (1811-1888)* (Barneveld: Uitgeverij De Vuurbaak, 1988), 447-48. The 1857 Synod of the Christian Seceded Reformed Church judged that it was not necessary to petition King William III to abolish slavery (in the colonies), since that matter was already pending before the government; *Handelingen van de Synode . . . 1857 te Leijden [sic]*, Art. 158, p. 73, in *Handelingen en verslagen van de Algemene Synoden van de Christelijk Afgescheidene Gereformeerde Kerk (1836-1869)* (Houten/Utrecht: Den Hertog b.v., 1984), 719.

were Republicans, like Jacob Quintus, the editor of the *Nieuwsbode* of Sheboygan, Wisconsin.[30] These weeklies republished, usually in Dutch translation, articles from New York newspapers on this subject.[31] Also, in late September 1855, Rev. Albertus C. van Raalte and Classis of Holland in Michigan sent a letter urging the October General Synod, for the peace of the church, to exclude Classis of North Carolina,[32]

[30]   Robert P. Swierenga, *Holland Michigan: From Dutch Colony to Dynamic City* (Grand Rapids: Eerdmans, 2014), 2:1677-78; Hans Krabbendam, "Jacob Quintus and the *Sheboygan Nieuwsbode*," *Origins* 30, no. 1 (2012), 7-8, tells how Quintus alternated in the 1850s between the Republican and the Democratic Parties. Michael J. Douma addresses the subject of the attitudes of the immigrant Dutch about slavery in "A Dutch Confederate: Defending Slavery in a Transnational Context," a paper delivered at a conference of the New Netherland Institute and the Association for the Advancement of Dutch American Studies, "The Dutch in America Across the Centuries: Connections and Comparisons," Albany, NY, 18 September 2015; this article is awaiting publication in BMGN-*Low Countries Historical Review*, 2016.

[31]   As noted earlier (notes 16 and 19), the Republican *De Nieuwsbode* of Sheboygan, Wisconsin, published the *New York Daily Tribune*'s report of the June 1855 General Synod meeting in New Brunswick. The following spring, *De Nieuwsbode*, 15 April 1856, published a long article from a Dutch-born, twenty-nine-year-old Holland Academy (forerunner of Hope College) student, Hendrik Wilhelmus Brandt (1827-94), who would graduate from New Brunswick Seminary (1862), serve briefly in the Union Army, and become a minister in Belgium, South Africa, and the Netherlands, where he died. Brandt's piece was a strong refutation of Samuel B. How's address to the October 1855 General Synod. This speech was first published in the *Christian Intelligencer* and then appeared as a pamphlet as *Slaveholding not Sinful* (see below); the newspaper version had been translated into Dutch and published in installments with favorable editorial comment in Hermanus Doesburg's *De Hollander*, 12 March and 9 and 16 April 1856. Brandt's article was a response to Doesburg, as well as to How. Raven, *Biographical Record Theological Seminary New Brunswick*, 112; *First Catalogue and Circular of Hope College . . . with a Catalogue and Circular of the Holland Academy, 1865-66*, 38; www.wiewaswie.nl.

[32]   Among the Midwestern Dutch immigrant churches, the question appears to have come to the fore largely in the wake of the June 1855 General Synod. Thus the consistory of the First Reformed Church of Holland, Michigan, at its regular meeting held 26 August 1855, Rev. A. C. van Raalte, president, requested the Classis of Holland to convey to General Synod its view that the "peace" (rest) of the church would be promoted by not receiving the slaveholding congregations of South Carolina [*sic*] (Art. 6); Clerk van Raalte, mistakenly wrote "South" instead of "North" Carolina. Then, nine days later, at the 5 September 1855 regular classis meeting, Rev. Cornelis van der Meulen, one of the two members of the classis at the June General Synod in New Jersey, told the classis that the Holland consistory had reported "that there are eight [*sic*] churches in South [*sic*] Carolina that consist chiefly [*sic*] of slaveholders, and wish to unite with the Dutch Reformed Church, with regard to which, they [the consistory] had feared that they [the slaveholders] would be accepted." He went on to shed (eyewitness) light on what had transpired at General Synod. "Many brethren at the synod were earnestly opposed to it [the admission of the North Carolina classis], but the matter was postponed to the adjourned session of the synod, which is to take place in October. The reverend [Van

while the infant Classis of Wisconsin asked synod to receive the classis, provided the gospel was preached to the slaves there.[33]

The October 1855 General Synod: the issue decided and dodged

In this tense context, the RPDC General Synod met again for four days, from 23 to 26 October 1855 (Tuesday to Friday), with somewhat fewer, but mostly the same, delegates as had attended the ten-day June session. This time the venue was the Ninth Street Reformed Dutch Church in Manhattan, New York City.[34] Some miscellaneous business

der Meulen] proposes that this assembly send a humble and friendly disapproving voice [*stem*] to the synod. The assembly decides accordingly and that this letter shall be written by the corresponding secretary, Rev. van Raalte" (absent); Classis of Holland minutes, 5 September 1855, Art. 8. The assumption (a correct one, as it turned out), was that no classis delegate would be sent to October General Synod, presumably due to lack of funds. In fact, none of the four western classes (Holland, Wisconsin, Michigan, and Illinois) of the future (1856) Particular Synod of Chicago appeared at the October meeting.

Therefore a separate letter "in the name of the Classis of Holland" was penned in (almost) perfect English (but not in Van Raalte's hand), dated 20 September 1855 (over two weeks after the classis had met), Holland, Michigan, to the president of General Synod, signed by Van Raalte and Van der Meulen, stating that it would be impossible for the (June) delegates from the classis (Van der Meulen and Elder Jannes van de Luijster) to attend the extra General Synod meeting in October. The classis did, however, "most heartily concur with those who think that such application [of the North Carolina classis to join the RPDC] ought *not* to be granted. We cannot but think it would be inexpedient and highly improper to admit into our number churches which would perhaps bring among us such an element of discord as the slavery question. We think it far better, now that we are free from any difficulties on this subject, to use every endeavor to keep clear of this exciting matter. May the God of all wisdom direct the reverend body . . . to proper decisions on this," etc. Original in the papers of General Synod of the Reformed Church in America in the archives of the RCA; photocopy in the Van Raalte files at the A. C. Van Raalte Institute. The position of the Classis of Holland was thus that the admission of the North Carolina classis would bring discord to the denomination, not necessarily that slaveholding was per se sinful, although some may have believed that as well.

[33] The request of Classis of Wisconsin to General Synod appears to have had its birth at the first (recorded) consistory meeting of the Alto, Wisconsin, Reformed Church, when a congregational member (Jan William Sleijster), who asked whether slaveholders were not obligated to instruct their slaves in the way of salvation, was delegated to formulate an overture about this to the classis; consistory minutes, Alto Reformed Church, 22 September 1855, at Joint Archives of Holland; Classis of Wisconsin minutes, 26 September 1855, Art. 5, typescript copy at the Van Raalte Institute.

[34] Later (1858) this church would be a noon site of the interdenominational, business men's, prayer meeting revival; it was built in 1831 and was part of Manhattan's Collegiate Church system, 1836-55, after which it continued as a separate congregation, the Central Reformed Dutch Church, until it closed in 1861; Corwin, *Manual*, 997, 1005.

was on the agenda, but the main purpose of the adjourned session was to deal with the hot topic of Classis of North Carolina's application for membership in the RPDC. In this regard, the sentiments of several classes (and a group in one congregation) were noted.[35]

In any case, once again, a properly credentialed "commissioner" from Classis of North Carolina, namely, its stated clerk, the Pennsylvania-born Rev. George William Welker,[36] appeared in synod "for the purpose of effecting an ecclesiastical *relation* with General Synod of the Reformed Protestant Dutch Church," and he "was heard." Rev. Samuel B. How introduced him on the first day of synod, Tuesday.

The next day, Wednesday, the report of the committee on correspondence (still chaired by How), which had been *accepted* (but not

[35] For instance, synod minutes reported that "the remonstrance from certain individuals belonging to the [newly formed (1850)] Church of Hastings-on-Hudson," strongly opposed to the admission of the NC classis, claimed that "cruelty is inseparable from slavery," which is "pernicious and demoralizing" to slaveholders and slaves alike, making the former unfit for "the right hand of fellowship"; thus at least some abolitionists would presumably excommunicate slaveholders. The first pastor of the rapidly growing Hastings church at this time (1850-59), evidently *not* an abolitionist (the congregation was apparently split on slavery), was Rev. Philip Phelps Jr. (1826-86), future principal of Holland Academy and first president of Hope College; he was a delegate at both the June and October 1855 sessions of General Synod and voted at the latter for admission of the North Carolina classis; see notes 40, 41, 61, and 62 below. In addition, two classes were reported as already on record (in their minutes) in favor and one opposed to the application; the positions of the Classes of Holland and Wisconsin were also noted. See notes 32 and 33 above. These reports, as well as the subsequent discussions and decisions on the floor of General Synod summarized in the present article, are all recorded in the pages of the *Christian Intelligencer*, 1 November 1855.

[36] George William Welker (1817-94), quite likely the architect of the plan for the North Carolina classis to join the RPDC, had, for family reasons, been unable to represent the classis at the June General Synod. Of German ancestry, he was educated in Pennsylvania at Marshall College and Mercersburg Theological Seminary (whose theology he later opposed) before going in 1842 to be pastor of a yoked parish in North Carolina. Welker, who had only one eye and early fought a difficult but ultimately successful battle to rid his parish of whiskey stills, was also counter-cultural in opposing slavery in a slave state. One of his congregations received seven adult slaves on profession of their faith (October 1854); moreover, he himself preached special funeral sermons for slaves. Welker married three times and fathered fifteen children over a period of thirty-seven years, the last one when he was sixty-four. He spent his whole ministry in the same place and was classis clerk for most of that time; www.findagrave.com. Samuel H. Ranck et al., *Obituary Record. A Record of the Lives of the Deceased Alumni of Marshall College and of Franklin and Marshall College* (Lancaster, PA: Franklin and Marshall Alumni Association, 1897), 1:14-16; William Herman Gehrke, "Negro Slavery among the Germans in North Carolina," *North Carolina Historical Review* 14, no. 4 (October 1937), 316-17 (this article contains the data on Welker's ministry to slaves).

Rev. George William Welker

adopted) at the last meeting, was taken up; it had "resolved" that Classis of North Carolina be incorporated into the RPDC. It was moved and seconded that this motion be *adopted*, but with the amendment that "German Reformed" be "stricken out from the name."

How led off the main part of the debate on the admission of the North Carolina classis by reading a long speech. He complained that he had been blindsided by the presence of abolitionists at synod. He explained his position that slavery, although an evil as it then existed, was not sinful per se, since it was never declared to be such in scripture; it was "a result of the fall," and its "remedy was the preaching of the gospel." He supported his argument with much material from the Old and New Testaments. This oration would soon be edited and published, thereby beginning a brief pamphlet debate in the RPDC about slavery.[37] How's speech is seen as a "classic" example of a Northern defense of slavery, very similar to that of Charles Hodge of the Old School Presbyterians at Princeton Theological Seminary[38]

---

[37]   The literary controversy surrounding How's pamphlet will be dealt with later.

[38]   James H. Moorhead, *Princeton Seminary in American Religion and Culture* (Grand Rapids: Eerdmans, 2012), 149-61; 172-79; W. Andrew Hoffecker, *Charles Hodge: The Pride of Princeton* (Phillipsburg, NJ: P & R Publishing, 2011), 167-77 (about the situation in NJ, the Princeton theologians' theory and practice in regard to slaveholding, and Hodge's views on slavery in his 1836 article and later). See also Allen C. Guelzo, "Charles Hodge's Antislavery Moment," in *Charles Hodge Revisited: A Critical Appraisal of His Life and Work*, ed. John W. Stewart and James H.

But this is to get ahead of the story of the events at synod. Rev. George W. Bethune responded to How that he completely agreed with his arguments but had questions about the legality of the way in which classis had applied to enter the RPDC and especially about the injury to the conscience of abolitionists if the request of classis were to be allowed. Bethune therefore moved that the whole matter be indefinitely postponed, which motion was lost.

As the discussion continued, Rev. Hervey Doddridge Ganse announced that he would not vote to admit classis unless General Synod made "a broad declaration that slavery was sin. . . . Let these brethren [of North Carolina] declare . . . that slavery is a monster evil, but we are ready to sympathize with those who (not by choice) find themselves in the midst of it" (because of the laws of North Carolina). Accordingly, Ganse introduced a preamble to the motion to admit the classis, "Whereas, This Synod, while it cannot to any degree sympathize with the system of American slavery, but must regard it as embodying the most serious injustice, does yet sympathize sincerely with such Christian men as, finding themselves in the midst of that system, are slaveholders, not by preference, but by the necessities of the case, and with a Christian regard to the true temporal and eternal interests of the slaves themselves." How objected to this motion, at which point the day's session ended.

The next morning (Thursday) the discussion of Ganse's preamble continued.[39] How countered that, if slavery is an injustice, then it is sin, and "immediate emancipation would be the highest injustice," and that "slavery had been a blessing to the African because it brought civilization and Christianity." Another pastor, opposing Ganse's

Moorhead (Grand Rapids: Eerdmans, 2002), 299-325, esp. 300-302; Molly Oshatz, *Slavery and Sin: The Fight against Slavery and the Rise of Liberal Protestantism* (Oxford: Oxford University Press, 2012), 51, 68, 79, 93-94. Both How and Hodge were New Jersey men and graduates of Princeton Seminary there. New Jersey, as RPDC Congressman John Van Dyke pointed out in 1850, was essentially a border state, positioned midway between South and North (straddling the Mason-Dixon Line; see note 47 below); Gigantino, *The Ragged Road to Abolition*, 216, 222. How may have been implicitly defending some of his own parishioners, who had, at least until the very recent past, been slaveholders themselves.

39 All sorts of opinions and arguments for and against the proposal to admit the classis were expressed by various delegates on the floor of synod; for example, "white men are not naturally heathens," and "black men are not naturally Christians"; slavery is an evil that "could be a blessing"; abolitionists are "infidels"; if slavery is permissible, why not polygamy (note the new Mormon practice, then hotly condemned), since both occur in the Old Testament?

preamble condemning slavery, thought that General Synod had "a rule not to legislate on abstract principles." An amendment softening Ganse's preamble condemning slavery was defeated. Then Bethune, arguing that receiving the North Carolina classis would, inter alia, bring discord into the RPDC, moved to table the question—which passed narrowly by fifty to forty-seven on a crucial roll-call vote.[40]

The following morning (Friday), the debate about Ganse's motion resumed, but by this time, he had expanded it (incorporating the prudential considerations he had been hearing at synod) into a gentle but firm rejection of the North Carolinians' application. He explained that he had voted against the previous day's motion to table, because he wanted a direct General Synod vote on his (new, developed) "minute and resolution": "American slavery" embodies "the most serious injustice" and leads to "the most serious social evils." Yet General Synod can "fraternize with such Christian men who find themselves in the midst of that system," who are "slaveholders not by choice but by the necessity of their position" and who are giving "Christian attention" to the physical and spiritual well-being of their slaves, with "wise Christian efforts to their ultimate enfranchisement" (this last phrase goes beyond his initial preamble of Tuesday). But since the admission of classis would threaten to disturb the peace of the RPDC (without any compensating benefit), and "since the classis can find adequate ecclesiastical relations elsewhere, . . . Resolved That the Synod is unwilling to affect the Union proposed." Ganse's main aim was to get General Synod to go on public record as opposed in principle to slavery, while at the same time declining, for reasons of expediency (the peace of the RPDC), to receive the admittedly Christian brethren (including slaveholders) of the North Carolina classis into the denomination. (The RPDC had never condemned slavery as sinful.)

A delegate then reported that he had heard that abolitionists in the New York City streets were saying that the RPDC was afraid to take a stand on this issue and that he, the delegate, could believe this, with synod now contemplating a compromise. Ganse insisted that the RPDC face up to "a great moral question," but synod, by a forty-seven-

[40]   The names of those voting aye and nay were recorded in the minutes; defenders and opponents of admitting the North Carolina classis were on both sides: those voting with the majority included Bethune, Wyckoff, and Duryee, and with the minority How, Ganse, Phelps, and Taylor; *Acts and Proceedings . . . Convened, Pursuant to Adjournment, at the City of New York, October 23, 1855* (New York: Board of Publication of the RPDC, 1855), 13.

to-eighteen vote, adopted Bethune's substitute for Ganse's proposal, which would subsequently become the RPDC's final, "prudent," word on the subject. It had dodged Ganse's slavery bullet. Finally, by a roll-call vote of fifty-five to thirty-four, synod passed the following resolution: "Whereas, it is evident from the opinions expressed on the floor that the Synod cannot unite cordially in receiving the Classis of North Carolina within the limits of our Church; and whereas the Synod desire [*sic*] to treat the Classis of North Carolina with the courtesy and kindness due to respected Christian brethren, therefore 1. Resolved that the North Carolina commissioner be requested to withdraw his papers, and 2. Resolved that a certified copy of the above preamble and resolution with the action of the Synod, as recorded on page 531 of the Minutes, be sent to the Classis of North Carolina."[41]

Thus the RPDC's last "word" on the issue of slavery itself before the Civil War was total silence. This helps explain why the official minutes of General Synod's 1855 gatherings say nothing about it either, although these minutes of the *Acts and Proceedings* of synod do, as a rule, include a limited amount of explanatory detail ("proceedings") and not merely a bare record of motions made and accepted or rejected ("acts"). It probably reflects the viewpoint sometimes assumed—if not asserted—at synod that the church should stay out of politics—the so-called "spiritual doctrine of the church," especially popular then (and later) in the South. Christian slaveholders who treated their slaves properly could be accepted as "brethren" in the church, even though Christians as individual citizens could work in society to end the slave system.[42] Only in June 1864, a year and a half after the Emancipation

---

[41]   Those voting with the majority were, predictably (this time), Duryee, Ganse, Bethune, and Wyckoff; presumably the first two voted on the basis of "principle," while the latter were led by "prudence"; Taylor (who authored the June committee report) and Phelps (see notes 35 and 39 above) voted with the minority. *Acts and Proceedings, October 1855*, 14. How abstained from voting because he had promised that to Welker, who had seen the handwriting on the wall with the fifty to forty-seven vote to table the motion and had withdrawn from the sessions, requesting How to do nothing more on the matter at synod. Samuel B. How, *Slaveholding not Sinful. An Argument before the General Synod of the Reformed Protestant Dutch Church, October 1855* (New York: John A. Gray, 1855), 4-5. The *Christian Intelligencer*, 1 November 1855, is the primary source for the foregoing account of the General Synod discussions of October 1855.

[42]   In hindsight, General Synod thereby missed a golden opportunity to have gone publicly on record as opposed to slavery, prior to the great conflict; it could have done this with very little harm to itself, because it had no southern constituency. It found itself unable to be thus "prophetic," since the exegesis of Samuel B. How (and his cohorts) stood firmly in the way by virtually equating biblical and American

Proclamation, did General Synod reverse its silence about slavery, hoping that since God's providence has opened a "prospect . . . for the ultimate and entire removal of that system which embodies so much of moral and social evil," which would then open the way for Christian labors throughout the land.[43]

Coda 1: the pamphlet debate

Samuel B. How's October 1855 General Synod address was published by him as a twenty-seven-page pamphlet (with a brief introduction added), *Slaveholding not Sinful*, before the end of the year. It elicited two major pamphlet rejoinders early in 1856. The first one (eighty-five pages long) came from the temperate, nuanced pen of Rev. Hervey D. Ganse (as noted above, a key participant at the October synod): *Bible Slaveholding not Sinful: A Reply to* [How's] *"Slaveholding not Sinful."* [44]

Ganse's point, as implied in the title, was that, although slaveholding in biblical days may not have been (called) sinful, it was never given apostolic approbation as a system; furthermore, slaveholding as it was currently practiced in the South was indeed sinful, and How's learned arguments had largely dealt with biblical slavery, which would not exonerate American slavery, which How had termed (merely) "an evil [not a sin] much to be lamented." Although Ganse was against immediate abolition (and radical "abolitionists"), since Africans ("ignorant and vicious men") were as yet unfit for emancipation, he

---

slavery. In addition, the so-called spiritual doctrine of the church (a Reformed counterpart to the Lutheran doctrine of the Two Kingdoms; cf. Abraham Kuyper's "sphere sovereignty"), as enunciated most forcefully by James Henley Thornwell (1812-62), a southern Presbyterian theologian (who saw slavery more as a positive good, if not a "divine right"), had adherents north of the Mason-Dixon line, for example, Charles Hodge, who embraced a slightly weaker version of this doctrine. D. G. Hart, "The Spirituality of the Church, the Westminster Standards, and Nineteenth-Century Presbyterianism," in *Calvin Studies*, 106-18, a paper given at the Colloquium on Calvin Studies, Davidson College, 1996, at http://www.foundationrt.org/documents/Hart_Spirituality_Church.pdf. Mark A. Noll, *The Civil War as a Theological Crisis* (Chapel Hill, NC: University of North Carolina Press, 2006), 62-63.

43   Oddly, the reason given for the General Synod's previous silence was that American slavery "existed in regions beyond the bounds of our Church," not because of a spiritual doctrine of the church. *Acts and Proceedings . . . June 1864* (New York: Board of the Publication of the RPDC, 1864), 504.

44   H. D. Ganse, *Bible Slaveholding not Sinful: A Reply to "Slaveholding not Sinful, by Samuel B. Howe, D.D.,"* (New York: R. & R. Brinkerhoff, 1856); How's name was misspelled (as "Howe") throughout the pamphlet.

H. D. Ganse,
Bible Slaveholding not Sinful,
1856

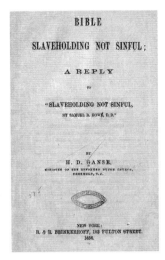

urged the gradual end to the slave system by legislation and, in the meantime, the ending of its worst abuses, such as separating families, violating women, ruthless beatings, denial of education, and exclusion from church membership—but at the same time, he would not bar masters (caught in the system) who treated their slaves in a Christian (i.e., New Testament) way.[45] Ganse's pamphlet called forth a rejoinder from How, reiterating his position.[46]

[45] Ganse, *Bible Slaveholding not Sinful,* 27, 51, 57, 73-76. Ganse related that he had very recently overheard, "in the saloon of one of our most frequented steamers, a gray-headed man, whose dress and language indicated education and wealth—and who was called by name by some of those about him—assert, with a grossness of expression which it pollutes the page to hint at, his own paternity of many of the slaves of his plantation and his absolute power over the victims of his lust"; Ganse went on to concede that "the flippant boast of power which this wretch made" was not typical of Southern slaveholders, "but the law that admits of even one such instance, admits of ten thousand"; ibid., 74-75. Ganse, trying desperately to hold a middle ground, opposed the "monomania" of "single-minded radicals" on both sides—of those who would dissolve the Union were slavery allowed to spread or those who would do so were it *not* allowed to spread; ibid., 80-81.

[46] How produced a second edition of his *Slaveholding not Sinful* early in 1856, with a subtitle (new) and an erudite appendix (its first two-thirds supplementing his earlier arguments and the last third replying to Ganse), that was sixty percent larger than his original published speech; Samuel B. How, *Slaveholding Not Sinful. Slavery, The Punishment of Man's Sin, Its Remedy, The Gospel of Christ,* 2nd ed. (New Brunswick: J. Terhune's Press, 1856); the long subtitle mitigates the starkness of the bare title; certainly How never took the radical proslavery stance that the South's "peculiar institution" was anything like a positive good. Space does not permit further summarizing of the arguments in these pamphlets; a fine, short summary by John Osborne of How's second edition appears on the website of the Dickinson College Archives and Special Collections, at http://archives.dickinson.edu/sites/all/files/files_digitized_resources/How_About_Book_Slaveholding.pdf.

SLAVEHOLDING NOT SINFUL.

SLAVERY,

The Punishment of Man's Sin,

ITS REMEDY,

THE GOSPEL OF CHRIST.

AN ARGUMENT BEFORE THE GENERAL SYNOD OF THE
REFORMED PROTESTANT DUTCH CHURCH,
OCTOBER, 1855.

BY SAMUEL B. HOW, D. D.

PASTOR OF THE FIRST REFORMED DUTCH CHURCH, NEW-BRUNSWICK, N. J.

SECOND EDITION.

New-Brunswick, N. J.:
JOHN TERHUNE, 81 ALBANY STREET;
NEW-YORK : R. & R. BRINKERHOFF, 103 FULTON STREET.
J. TERHUNE'S PRESS, NEW-BRUNSWICK.
1856.

Samuel B. How,
Slaveholding not Sinful,
2nd edition, 1856

The second pamphlet to reply to How's published speech came from John Van Dyke, a New Jersey Republican, Reformed Church elder (of South Branch, New Jersey), lawyer, and former United States Whig congressman,[47] who argued in a sixteen-page pamphlet (with powerful,

---

[47]   John Van Dyke (1807-78), a New Jersey native, was admitted to the bar in 1836 when he began the practice of law in New Brunswick. He gained fame five years later as the prosecuting attorney of Middlesex County, New Jersey, in the trial of Peter Robinson for the murder of Abraham Suydam. Soon thereafter he became president of a New Brunswick bank and mayor of that city. He then served two terms (1847-51) as a Whig in the United States House of Representatives, after which he chose to return to practicing law. One of the founders of the Republican Party in New Jersey, he was a delegate to the 1856 Republican National Convention. Van Dyke was a judge on the New Jersey Supreme Court, 1859-66, retiring in 1868 to Minnesota, where he served a year in its state house of representatives and was a judge of its third judicial district for a year before retiring. "Van Dyke, John," in *Biographical Directory of the United States Congress*, at http://bioguide.congress.gov; "Van Dyke, John," in *Appleton's Cyclopedia of American Biography*, at http://famousamerican.net/ johnvandyke; "John Van Dyke," at http://www.minnesotalegalhistoryproject.org. As for Van Dyke's views on slavery, he took a moderate position in an important address in the House of Representatives on 4 March 1850. At that time he espoused gradual, not immediate, emancipation in the debate about admitting California to the Union, in connection with the Compromise [about slavery] of 1850; he rejected Southern charges of Northern aggression and supported the Fugitive Slave Law; in discussing whether New Jersey was a Northern or a Southern state, he observed that "one thing is pretty certain, that neither she nor any of her representatives

John Van Dyke's 1850 House of
Representatives slavery speech

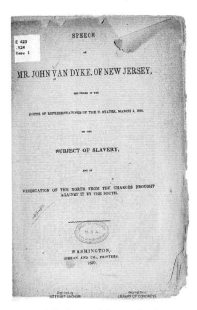

lawyerly rhetoric, sharper in tone than Ganse's)[48] that, although slavery might be humane in certain cases (e.g., caring for the old slaves in New Jersey), this was not generally the case in the South.[49]

Van Dyke looked at the realities and cruelty of slavery as it was then widely practiced (backed by the slave laws of the various states), involving "man-stealing" (condemned in the Old Testament), separating spouses, practicing adultery and fornication, depriving slaves of the gospel by prohibiting reading, and exercising the power of life and death;[50] this catalogue sounds similar to that of Ganse and doubtless many others. Van Dyke made three main points: the Golden Rule was opposed to slaveholding;[51] the slavery permitted in the Old

are very *fanatical* on the subject of slavery." Gigantino, *The Ragged Road to Abolition*, 222. John Van Dyke, *Speech of Mr. John Van Dyke of New Jersey, delivered in the House of Representatives of the U. States, March 4, 1850, on the subject of slavery, and in vindication of the North from the charges brought against it by the South* (Washington: Gideon and Co., Printers, 1850). By the time of his response to How in 1856, however, Van Dyke had witnessed the abuses of slavery in the South firsthand and was no longer lukewarm on the subject, having become a passionate opponent of the system, although, even then, he did not enter into the subject of immediate emancipation or the politics of the matter.

48 John Van Dyke, *"Slaveholding not Sinful:" A Reply to the Argument of Rev. Dr. How* (New Brunswick: Fredonian and Daily New-Brunswicker Office, 1856).

49 Ibid. 5.

50 Ibid., 6-7.

51 Ibid. 8-9; Van Dyke uses some powerful rhetoric in support of this application of the Golden Rule.

Testament (e.g., that practiced by Abraham)[52] was not Southern, Negro slavery;[53] and the slavery known in New Testament times was never positively endorsed by Paul.[54] Van Dyke argued that "the only slavery in question" was "American Slavery, but to defend this, I presume, seemed too Herculean an undertaking to attempt directly, and so you [How] carefully threw over it the flimsy mantles of Abraham and Paul, and coolly transferred the scene of the conflict from the cotton fields and rice swamps, the slave pens, the auction blocks and shipping posts of the South, where it properly belonged, to the land of the olive and the vine, where the great ruler of the Universe, for reasons of his own, granted privileges to and tolerated practices, among his peculiar and chosen people, not sanctioned anywhere else, before or since."[55] Van Dyke had recently been an eyewitness to the inhumanity of slavery in the South, how at "the auction-block . . . parents and children [were] sold like *other* beasts of burden to the highest bidder . . . to be subjected without restraint to whatever hardship and cruelty his whim or malice might suggest or invent."[56] Van Dyke suggested that How, when he was a pastor in the South, may have been kept from witnessing such crimes because he was a minister.[57] That Van Dyke had once been a county prosecutor (and also not one of How's flock) may be detected in his sharp pamphlet, which was very soon answered even more sharply by How's own son.[58]

[52]   Van Dyke explains that this was allowed by God for reasons of his own, as may also have been polygamy, annihilation of evil nations, and Abraham's illegitimate child by Hagar; ibid., 10-11.

[53]   Ibid. 9.

[54]   Ibid., 11-12.

[55]   Ibid., 4.

[56]   Ibid., 16.

[57]   "You are doubtless aware that . . . we all lay aside our vices and crimes and put on our best behavior in the presence of 'the dominie.' So in the South, no man ever carried his slave in your presence to be lashed, or to have the thumb-screw applied—no one ever bared the striped back of his slave for your inspection. None voluntarily made you a witness to the ruthless separation of husbands and wives, parents and children, brothers and sisters, to meet again, never! No one ever carried you to the negro nursery where human chattels are reared for the market, like horses and cattle and swine. The fact, therefore, that you never saw any of these things, should not lead you to conclude that they do not exist." Van Dyke, *Reply to How*, 15. See Gigantino, *The Ragged Road to Abolition*, 215-16, 222, 236-37. For an extended summary of Van Dyke's pamphlet, see Noel Leo Erskine, *Black People and the Reformed Church in America* (New York: Reformed Church Press, 1978), 50-53.

[58]   A thirty-four-page response to Van Dyke's pamphlet, dated 8 March 1856, was published by Samuel B. How's only (surviving) son, then a thirty-year-old bachelor, Henry Kollock How (1825-75), who was also a member of his father's congregation. The younger How, born in Savannah, Georgia (when his father was serving there

Coda 2: subsequent General Synods

The last mention of the matter at General Synod came the following year (June 1856), when an extract from the minutes of classis of North Carolina containing resolutions regarding the action taken by the October 1855 General Synod was received. Synod chose not to act upon these resolutions (whose content was not recorded in the synod's minutes), because its previous action regarding the classis, sent to that body by the clerk, was "in its tenor final," yet "respectful and courteous."[59]

---

as the successor to Rev. Henry Kollock), was an alumnus of Rutgers College (1842) and attended New Brunswick Theological Seminary 1848-50 but never graduated (because of ill health); he worked as a "pharmacist" in the 1850s, married in 1857, fathered two children, and appears in the 1860 and 1870 censuses as a well-to-do farmer in North Brunswick Township, Middlesex County, New Jersey; in politics he was a Democrat (as befitted his anti-abolitionism); www.ancestry.com; www.findagrave.com; Raven, *Biographical Record Theological Seminary New Brunswick*, 97; "Henry K. How," in *History of Union and Middlesex Counties, New Jersey, with Biographical Sketches*, ed. W. Woodford Clayton (Philadelphia: Everts & Peck, 1882), 756-57. Henry K. How, a loyal son, began writing a defense of his father's position as soon as he received Van Dyke's pamphlet. His response (twice the length of the piece it was answering) was predictable, competent, and meticulous, if not tedious in its sharp, point-by-point rejoinders to Van Dyke's arguments and assertions, conceding little if anything to the former congressman. In addition to numerous other things, the younger How argued that southern slavery, such as that of North Carolina, was not so different from the benign form of that institution (e.g., caring for old and decrepit slaves) only then ending in New Jersey; Gigantino, *The Ragged Road to Abolition*, 237. He wound up the pamphlet with a very brief reiteration of his responses to a few of Van Dyke's main points—and a parting insult: "The way you make assertions without proof is appalling; the manner in which you misconstrue Dr. How, and the illogical conclusions you draw, and your modest assurance have afforded me much amusement and laughter. Indeed, all the good that can be derived from your pamphlet is to enjoy a laugh over and at it; and that it is useful to have something to laugh at was acknowledged as far back as the time of the flood . . ., for it is said that Noah was about to exclude the peacock from the ark because he would take up too much room on account of his great strutting and tail-spreading propensities, but his scruples were at length overcome, and the Peacock admitted at the solicitation of the Owl, who said that if the Peacock was good for nothing else, he would do for a laughing stock for the rest of the animals." After this adolescent impertinence, young How had the gall to end his piece with "Yours respectfully" preceding his own name. Henry K. How, *Slaveholding not Sinful: An Answer to John Van Dyke, Esq.'s Reply to the Argument of Rev. Dr. How* (New Brunswick: Fredonian and Daily New-Brunswicker Office, 1856), 33-34. Incidentally, the rhetoric in these pamphlets is doubtless relatively kind in comparison with private remarks, for example, those penciled, probably by a Reformed minister many years later, in the margins of the Samuel B. How entry in my copy of the 1879 (3rd) edition of Corwin's *Manual*: "He no doubt now whips slaves before the Great White Throne."

59   *Acts and Proceedings . . . June 1856* (New York: Board of Publication of the RPDC, 1856), 54.

With regard to the slavery question, General Synod had nothing more to say until after the Emancipation Proclamation (January 1863), although in June 1861, just after the outbreak of the war, it issued a statement giving full backing to the United States government and "the integrity of the Union" in the spirit of the Dutch "fathers" who had fought for liberty three centuries earlier. Nevertheless "we deeply lament" the national and individual sins "which have justly provoked the Most High to visit us with this direful calamity" of civil war, and harbor "no feelings of bitterness, wrath, or hatred towards those who are unhappily arrayed against us, and utterly repudiate the spirit of retaliation and revenge." Moreover, "we remember our brethren of all sections in our prayers."[60] These resolutions on "the present condition of our national affairs" were eventually adopted almost unanimously by General Synod after an attempt was defeated by a margin of more than two to one (on a roll-call vote) to postpone their consideration indefinitely. No reason for the motion to postpone is given in the minutes,[61] but the *Christian Intelligencer*'s account of synod's deliberations makes it clear that the majority wished to make a patriotic political statement supporting the Union, while the minority believed that the church as church should stay out of politics, although virtually all of them, as individuals, largely approved the sentiments expressed in the resolutions (which had tried

---

[60] *Acts and Proceedings . . . June 1861* (New York: Board of Publication of the RPDC, 1861), 101. Nothing was said about slavery. These words sound somewhat like precursors of Lincoln's second inaugural address in 1865: "With malice toward none, with charity for all."

[61] The vote was seventy-one to thirty-four. Voting with the minority were five of the six delegates from the young Particular Synod of Chicago (including the two from the Classis of Holland, Revs. Philip Phelps [of the Holland Academy, now Van Raalte's colleague and friend] and Pieter Jan Oggel [Van Raalte's son-in-law]). Van Raalte's benefactor and friend, elder Samuel B. Schieffelin, one of the three-man committee that produced the report, voted for postponement. The abolitionist Isaac Duryee voted with the majority. What was the issue here? *Acts and Proceedings, 1861*, 100. Van Raalte, a Democrat turned Republican shortly before the war, was an early, enthusiastic supporter of the Union and its war effort; moreover, in August 1863, he preached in Holland, Michigan, against American slavery ("grounded upon breeding men" and its "atrocities," as "*absolutely* forbidden in the Bible"), which he sharply distinguished (unlike Samuel B. How in 1855) from Old Testament slavery ("allowed in the present state of sin, and restricted, guided and softened" through God's mercy); Michael Douma, "Rev. A. C. van Raalte on Slavery," *Origins* 31, no. 2 (2013), 40-41; for Van Raalte's support of the Union, see his letter to Philip Phelps Jr., dated Holland, Michigan, 24 August 1862, in Elton J. Bruins and Karen G. Schakel, eds., *Envisioning Hope College: Letters Written by Albertus C. Van Raalte to Philip Phelps Jr., 1857 to 1875* (Holland, MI: Van Raalte Press; Grand Rapids: Eerdmans, 2011), 93-95. See notes 35 above and 62 below.

to harmonize opposing views) and heartily supported the cause of the Union. The minority appealed to the Constitution of the RPDC, which (following the Church Order of Dort) stated that in ecclesiastical "assemblies, *ecclesiastical matters* only shall be transacted, and that in an ecclesiastical manner."[62] Rev. Isaac G. Duryee, ever the abolitionist, put the case in favor of the resolutions thus: "As a nation we have been guilty of Sabbath-breaking and intemperance, and since the foundation of the Government we have been guilty of oppression."[63]

At the end of the Civil War, the RPDC envisioned for a short time a ministry to the freedmen.[64] In 1871-72 there was a flurry of General Synod interest in reconsidering union with the North Carolina classis, but this was quickly dropped because that body had already rejoined its mother denomination. A final courtship between the German and Dutch Reformed churches ended fruitlessly when a federal (not organic)

---

[62] This sounds like the spiritual doctrine of the church; see note 42 above. One delegate recommended that, to avoid trouble, synod should take the path of "expediency," as it had in dealing with the North Carolina classis. Philip Phelps of Holland, Michigan, doubted that it was the church's duty to "bear testimony" on the nation's troubles (as a delegate had just urged), since "much of these troubles had been brought on by this 'bearing of testimony'"; in 1870 Phelps was on a General Synod committee that (similarly) opposed establishing a denominational policy excluding Freemasons (an "extra-canonical test"); Bruggink, "Extra-Canonical Tests," in *A Goodly Heritage*, ed. Nyenhuis, 52; see notes 16, 35, and 61 above. Another delegate complained that a pastor had "desecrated" his pulpit by placing a flag behind it (note American "civil religion"), while yet another observed that, unfortunately, some ministers were so patriotic that they really ought to leave their pulpits and join the army. Several delegates pointed out that the church should proclaim the gospel of peace and not be warlike. All these—and other—arguments for postponement were in vain in the midst of the patriotic fervor then sweeping the North. The motion to postpone dealing with the resolutions because they were unconstitutional was made by Rev. Thomas Campbell Strong, the oldest of four ministerial sons of the longtime stated clerk of General Synod, Thomas Morris Strong, who died during the 1861 General Synod. Corwin, *Digest*, 756-60; *Christian Intelligencer*, 20 June 1861. Constitution of the RPDC (1833), chapter 2, article 1, section 2, in Edward Tanjore Corwin, ed., *A Digest of Constitutional and Synodical Legislation of the Reformed Church in America* (New York: The Board of Publication of the RCA, 1906), xxxv.

[63] Duryee held that "God was pouring out his wrath upon us. If ever there was a time when the ministers of Christ should stand between the porch and the altar in defense of the right, it is now." He reminded the assembly that General Synod of 1812 ordered a day of prayer and fasting for the state of the country (the War of 1812). Another delegate noted that General Synod's hearing representatives of the American Colonization Society was ipso facto a further precedent for its involvement in nonecclesiastical matters; *Christian Intelligencer*, 20 June 1861. Synod backed this society and its "solution" to slavery from 1820 until well into the 1860s; Corwin, *Digest*, 20-21.

[64] Corwin, *Digest*, 302.

union proposal was rejected by the latter in 1893, largely because it was opposed by the western (immigrant) classes.[65]

Coda 3: the later years of the principals of the 1855 synod

Samuel B. How, elected president of General Synod in 1859, retired in 1861 at age seventy-one, due to the infirmities of age; he died in 1868. George W. Bethune gave a passionate pro-Union address in New York City at the start of the Civil War, just before leaving for Florence (he loved art) for his health, where he died of a stroke the next year (1862). Isaac G. Duryee died in 1866 of an intestinal ailment contracted when he was a Union Army chaplain (1862-65). Hervey D. Ganse declined (as against the spirit of the gospel) Rutgers College's offer of a DD degree in 1861, was elected president of General Synod in 1866, and was editor of the *Christian Intelligencer* from 1871 to 1875, concluding his ministry in the Northern Presbyterian Church.[66] John Van Dyke went from practicing law to becoming a justice of the New Jersey Supreme Court during the Civil War, after which he was briefly a legislator and then a judge in Minnesota. The two North Carolina pastors both suffered the privations of living in the Confederacy during the Civil War and endured hostility from some of their parishioners for their Union sympathies. Thornton Butler, long fighting tuberculosis, left the South in 1868 for a church in Illinois, where he died two years later.[67] George W. Welker, postbellum, became active in North Carolina

---

[65]   Herman Harmelink III, *Ecumenism and the Reformed Church* (Grand Rapids: Eerdmans, 1968), 38-52. One of the arguments used by the Dutch Reformed against the proposed union was that the German Reformed subscribed only to the Heidelberg Catechism and not also to the Belgic Confession and the Canons of Dort; ibid., 41, 50. Curiously, this line of reasoning, as an objection to admitting the North Carolina classis in 1855, does not seem to have been heard in the debates on the floor of General Synod then, presumably because of the all-consuming preoccupation with slaveholding.

[66]   His grandson, Rev. Hervey Ganse Little (1904-90), a 1929 Princeton Theological Seminary graduate, was pastor of the Pasadena Presbyterian Church, 1952-69, moderator of the General Assembly of the Presbyterian Church in the United States in 1966, and, after initial hostility in the 1950s to his young, "divisive," Pasadena neighbor, Fuller Theological Seminary, helped reconcile it and the Presbytery of Los Angeles in 1964; www.ancestry.com (1870 census); www.findagrave.com; George M. Marsden, *Reforming Fundamentalism: Fuller Seminary and the New Evangelicalism* (Grand Rapids: Eerdmans, 1987), 107-8, 255; the author's knowledge in situ ca. 1955.

[67]   Sources for the foregoing data on the later years of the major participants in the debates of 1855 may generally be found in the footnotes attached to the initial appearances of these men in this article.

Republican politics (a "scalawag"), received two honorary doctorates, and continued his pastoral work in Guilford County until 1893 (having served there for fifty-one years); he also remained the stated clerk (for a total of forty-seven years) of Classis of North Carolina, which reunited with the German Reformed Church in 1866, and whose history he wrote late in life, dying in 1894, the last survivor of the major participants at the turbulent RPDC Synod of 1855.[68]

Conclusion

The debates in 1855 surrounding slaveholding are instructive in laying bare some perennial issues, such as the relative weight to be given to letter and spirit in biblical interpretation, the institutional church's involvement in extra-ecclesiastical matters (e.g., social issues), the relation between God and country (Christ and Caesar), and the criteria of congregational membership.

Whether General Synod "did the right thing," whether it was cowardly or wise, in its decisions regarding Classis of North Carolina, may still be in the eye of the beholder.

---

[68] A minority of Welker's Guilford County, North Carolina, parishioners objected to his "abolitionist" convictions, caused a "slight skirmish" at one of his churches, and lodged a complaint about him to the governor of the state in August 1861; Gehrke, "Negro Slavery among the Germans in North Carolina," *The North Carolina Historical Review* (1937), 316-17, 324. Writing a couple of decades after the end of the Civil War, Welker mentioned that that conflict had brought about "animosities" within the classis and between individuals ("wounds not yet heald" [*sic*]); Welker, *Classis of North Carolina*, 28. Although he and his congregations suffered along with others in the area during the war, he emerged afterward as a leader in the state's Republican Party and as one of the framers of a new constitution for North Carolina in the late 1860s, all the while continuing his long ministry at the local level. A clear indication of Welker's pro-Union sentiments is contained in his history of the German Reformed in North Carolina, where he calls the Civil War "the War of the Rebellion"; Welker, *Classis of North Carolina*, 28. Welker was granted honorary doctorates of divinity from the University of North Carolina (1870) and from Heidelberg College (now University) in Ohio (1871); Ranck, *Obituary Record of Marshall College (1897)*, 15.

CHAPTER 10

Of Men and Words: A Holland Debating Society

Nella Kennedy

Eloquence, the selectest boon which Heaven has bestowed on man.[1]

A hefty volume recently came to light; it contains the Dutch-language minutes of a virtually unknown debating society founded in Holland, Michigan, in 1872. Hitherto only passing references to this society had appeared in two newspapers, in 1874 and 1907.[2] Although its existence was relatively early in Holland's history, it was by no means the first debating society. The Union Debating Society was established in Holland not even ten years after the *kolonie* was settled in 1847, with the ostensible goal to discuss "weighty questions and matters."[3] Its

---

[1]   Epes Sargent, "Oratory, Ancient and Modern," in *The Handbook of Oratory: A Cyclopedia*, ed. William Vincent Byars (St. Louis: Ferd. P. Kaiser, 1901), 272.

[2]   Frederick Jan Van Lente's obituary in the *Holland City News* on 14 February 1874 named his pallbearers as members of the *"landelijke vereeniging,* a rural literary society." The other, in the *Grand Rapids Herald* of 7 September 1907, referred briefly to a former "debating school" in Holland. Randall P. Vande Water, *Holland Happenings, Heroes and Hot Shots* (Grand Rapids: published by author, 1997), 4:25.

[3]   Robert Swierenga, *Holland Michigan: From Dutch Colony to Dynamic City* (Holland, MI: Van Raalte Press; Grand Rapids: Eerdmans, 2014), 3:2025.

membership was comprised mostly of young single males, although it did include some married men. Three other Holland-based literary societies existed (and ended!) in the 1870s: the Holland Literary Association, the Shakespearean Club, and the Young People's Literary Society.[4]

Dutch Americans "settling in"

When our Holland debating society, the Landelijke Vereniging (henceforth LV), was formed in 1872, the community of Holland was less than thirty years old. It is remarkable that the Dutch American settlement, still processing the ways of a very different nation and people, already included these organizations or societies. Several branches of the national veteran organization were founded after the Civil War. That conflict had made patriots of Dutch Americans and had aided the Americanization process,[5] just as had happened with the Eastern Dutch during and after the Revolutionary War (discounting a Loyalist minority) and was to happen during and after WWI. Not all American organizations, however, found favor: some were excoriated by most of these devout Hollanders, such as dancing clubs and, even more egregiously, Freemason lodges.

Whether the organizations had national connections or were locally organized, the language spoken depended on the membership since many non-Dutch resided in Holland in the 1870s. For decades, however, Dutch was to remain the lingua franca for the majority of Holland inhabitants, mostly because it continued to be used in church and in the home. For the seven or more years that the LV existed, it is therefore not surprising that the minutes were written in Dutch, which, although generally passable, was sprinkled with frequent Anglicisms. The offspring of the first immigrants were educated in English-speaking schools and had become comfortably bilingual.

The Landelijke Vereniging: unique or common?

Founded by a group of neighbors meeting in a home, the LV deviated from the traditional setting for a debating society. In the eighteenth century, European and American debating societies were almost always found within universities. Although this pattern continued in the nineteenth century—especially in the first half—grass-

[4]   Swierenga, *Holland, Michigan*, 3:2026.
[5]   Ibid.

roots organizations with the same intent began to spring up in the United States alongside the academic world.

Our particular nonacademic debating society was therefore not unusual. They were part and parcel of the ubiquitous self-improvement organizations in America, which were especially numerous in the latter half of the nineteenth century.[6] It was commonly held that civility lay dormant in every human being and that even a working man could reach a gentleman's status by educating himself.[7] Grass-roots societies, like the one set up by these Dutch Americans, differed from those inaugurated less than a century earlier in their former homeland. Steeped in Enlightenment ideals, benevolent members of the upper and middle classes provided free instruction in a variety of theoretical subjects for the working "common man."[8] The LV, although aspiring to similar ideals of advancement, was uniquely American in that it was created for and led by "common men."

It is highly unlikely that the first members of the Holland debating society were aware of the ultimate goal of the enlightened Dutch benefactors, that is, that the education of the laboring classes would have a useful effect on society. It was argued that this would create order and stability. The intent expressed at the LV's first meeting shared at least one of the objectives expressed decades earlier, for they wished to spend the "long winter evenings in a *useful* manner." The word *useful*, however, did not embody some grand societal transformation but had as a goal the "practice of eloquence together."[9] No doubt in this they were part of the American dream to make something of themselves in a society where this was possible and even encouraged.

The LV membership was undoubtedly well acquainted with an older society in Holland which practiced rhetoric. The Meliphone Literary Society had already been founded at the Holland Academy in 1857. The students aimed at learning to speak well and correctly while dealing with "great questions and themes," and to acquire "knowledge

---

6   Richard L. Bushman, *Refinement of America: Persons, Houses, Cities* (New York: Vintage Books: Random House, 1993), 421. Beginning early in the nineteenth century, the American populace could attend lectures organized by the Lyceum. A more varied approach to adult education was the long-lasting and hugely popular Chautauqua movement which began a few decades later.

7   The saying by America's influential educator, Horace Mann, that "a human being is not attaining his full heights until he is educated," confirms this sentiment.

8   Mostly conducted during the evenings.

9   The scribe actually writes *welspreekheid* instead of the correct *welsprekendheid*, which means literally "speaking well."

about parliamentary law."[10] It is likely that they were aided by one or more of the many "elocution primers" available to secondary schools, colleges, and debating societies. The publications served as technical guides for speaking more effectively and learning declamatory stances.[11] It is possible—assuming such primers were not available to LV members—that the periodic public demonstrations of the students' oratorical skills at the Hope Academy inspired and informed other aspiring debaters. The minutes of the LV reveal that the members favored extemporaneous speaking, although they did allow at least once, and somewhat reluctantly, one of the members to read his position. This way of presenting, of course, would limit the declamatory poses so prized in the nineteenth century.

Landelijke Vereniging minutes, 1872-77

The minutes, while providing the reader with an interesting and sometimes amusing tale, furnish rich fodder, worthy of a closer analysis. How successful were the members of the debating society in their quest to become "eloquent," and what led them to pursue that skill? What methods were used to attain this? Were the topics for debate "weighty," and did they reflect the debaters' ethnic origin and their process of Americanization? Who were these men, and how much were they in touch with other such groups, directly or indirectly? What do the minutes reveal (or conceal) about the members, their relationship to each other, and to American ideals?

The title on the first page, *Notulen der Landelijke Vereeniging, Opgerigd Nov. 5, 1872*[12] (Minutes of the Rural Society, founded on 5 November 1872) needs explanation. The word *landelijk* (rural) is significant, for the 1876 *Atlas of Ottawa County* reveals that most, if not all, of the members lived near each other, that is, directly east and southeast of Holland's city boundaries at that time.[13] The close proximity of its members

---

10   *The Milestone Annual* (1905), 46-47, Joint Archives of Holland (JAH); *The Anchor* 3, no. 10 (July 1890), JAH; *De Hollander*, 30 December 1857. Initially only "the oldest students" could join this debating society, which was led by principal Rev. J. Van Vleck, but later both the preparatory school and the college had such a society at various class levels.

11   For example, *Charles W. Sanders' School Speaker: A Comprehensive Course of Instruction in the Principles of Oratory; with numerous exercises for practice in declamation* (New York: Ivison and Phinney; Chicago: S. C. Griggs & Co, 1857).

12   The writer spells *opgericht* (founded) with the archaic spelling *opgerigd*.

13   *Illustrated Historical Atlas of the Counties of Ottawa and Kent* (Chicago: H. Belden and Co., 1876), xx, xxi. The organizational meeting was at the house of one of the farms in the neighborhood, that of the widow Jantje Hekhuis. A son of her first marriage,

makes sense, given the winter weather, the poor roads, and limited conveyances. The acronym LV for Landelijke Vereeniging was used by the scribes after a while.[14]

Structurally the LV conformed to the many organizations that were springing up all over the United States and—significantly—reflected democracy in action. Members could organize these groups, vote, and speak out. Especially the older members of the LV must have compared the lack of restriction in doing so to constrictions in the Netherlands; prior to the 1850s, government approval was needed to organize a society.[15] Although conviviality was an important element, the society, nevertheless, was constitutionally bound to self-imposed rules. One entry in the LV's minutes records that the new president had promised that he would abide by these rules and not "add novelties" (38).[16] The LV, like virtually all other American organizations at that time, had strict guidelines about attendance and punctuality,[17] with fines meted out to transgressors.[18] Not only were the essential rituals (taking attendance, the reading of minutes, etc.) at each meeting meticulously chronicled, but the minutes also frequently show corrections made by members at the next gathering. It was clearly important to have the possibility of input at all times.

The rules laid out in the constitution, however, were constantly under scrutiny. Many a meeting was filled with suggesting revisions

---

Hendrik Hidding (Dutch born), and sons of her third marriage, Lambertus and Gerrit J. Hekhuis (both US born and ministers later), were members. Gerrit J. joined in 1877 when he was twenty. Jantje's real estate in Holland Township in 1870 was worth $2,000, not an insignificant amount then. *Dutch Households in US Population Censuses 1850, 1860, 1870*, comp. Robert P. Swierenga (Wilmington, DE: Scholarly Resources, 1987), 1:423.

14   In the early minutes, the scribe wrote *Landelijke Ver Eeniging*, dividing the correct spelling *vereeniging* into two words. He and a subsequent scribe therefore used the acronym L.V.E. But the acronym L.V. was used soon thereafter and is also used in this article.

15   *Nederlands Wetboek van Strafrecht*, Article 291, refers to government authorization of organizations. It was used widely by the Dutch government during the first two decades or so to prevent seceders from the national Reformed Church to meet in groups exceeding twenty.

16   Parenthetical page numbers cited in this article follow those in the manuscript.

17   Ordinary workers could afford factory-produced watches by the early 1860s. Keeping time became very important in the nineteenth century. In the early years of the LV, "gate keepers" were appointed to see to it that the meetings were conducted "orderly and on time."

18   David Potter, "The Literary Society," in *History of Speech Education in America: Background Studies*, ed. Karl R. Wallace (New York: Appleton-Century-Crofts, 1954), 238-58.

or additions. The constitution, unfortunately, is not extant, but the minutes do occasionally mention specific articles. For example, Article 13 (98) apparently stated that the executive committee should provide wood for the stove (which they had neglected one time). Article 7 pertained to the swearing in of new members and officers, a ceremony that evidently deserved more pomp and circumstance. Furthermore, the constitution must have stipulated that meetings be opened and closed with prayer, for this was always practiced.

Topics

Once the functions and duties were laid down by the fledgling society, members would establish two categories for debate: biblical topics and the natural world. Specific themes within the classification of the natural world covered moral, political, and social questions, quasi-philosophical opinions, and contemporary issues. Biblical topics were of a doctrinal, interpretive, and ethical nature and also included church practices. The fact that one half of the subjects to be debated comprised biblical and theological themes is noteworthy. Although student debates in the United States in the eighteenth century regularly covered religious material, in the nineteenth century, these were mostly superseded by more political and social topics. This may have been true in nonacademic debating societies as well. The men in the LV, however, belonged to congregations which differed very little from the church they had left in the Netherlands, where doctrine was important and discussed freely. The LV's program would have been unusual in their new homeland—a mix of a church's men's society and a debating club.

Religion: theological and practical

The rotation was maintained throughout the LV's history, beginning with the very first topic: "Resolved that the fall of Adam was more for the glorification of God than if he had remained without sin" (8, 10). The vote indicated that the two men who favored that view had spoken best.[19] The topics never dealt with any kind of biblical criticism, but questions about orthodoxy probably had boundaries. It was, however, acceptable to raise questions and give opinions about the moral actions of Old Testament characters. The behavior of the heroes

---

[19]   The length of time given to each speaker was five minutes, and a later resolution specified that the speakers themselves could not vote. The president would often break the tie.

of faith were mostly approved (however violent they were), but there were some exceptions. Two examples suffice: the society resolved that David did *not* sin in "behaving outrageously [*zich razend aan te stellen*] in front of Achas [*sic*]"[20] (106), but on the other hand, the society excoriated Jacob's cunning in cheating his brother (157).

Topics having to do with religious practices came up, such as whether insurance was permitted (16) and whether it was appropriate for worshippers (presumably women) to dress ostentatiously. It most likely referred to the bustles, ruffles, and elaborately draped material of the 1870s (157).[21] In theological discussions, orthodoxy seems to have carried the day; to name two perennials: the LV was in favor of predestination and infant baptism. One topic for discussion concerned hymnody (30 March 1874). Should evangelical hymns be allowed in church (181)? It was a timely debate. Although a majority of pastors and especially elders in the Classis of Holland were in favor of compiling "a collection of spiritual songs" for congregational use, the proposal ultimately was tabled indefinitely in the 1870s. Roelof Pieters, successor to colony founder Rev. A. C. Van Raalte at Pillar Church, opposed it.[22] More than half of the debating society belonged to this church, so it is not surprising that each opening exercise began by singing a Psalm verse. In this the presiding leader followed a pattern which continued in all official Dutch American church meetings.

Surprisingly, members of the LV who belonged to this congregation, as well as those who did not, seemed to be at odds with their own congregation with regard to foreign missions. Most LV

---

[20]   "Achas" is written quite clearly in the minutes, but the name, in every possible alternative spelling, does not make sense. The scribe could have meant Asaph, who was involved in the return of the ark. It does, however, no doubt refer to King David's wife, Michal, who did not approve of David's "uncovered" dancing in front of the ark (I Chron. 13:29).

[21]   This was a result of conspicuous consumption in these post-Civil War days and the extensive use of the sewing machine in the 1860s.

[22]   Earl Wm. Kennedy, *A Commentary on the Minutes of the Classis of Holland, 1848-1876* (forthcoming 2017), 1831-32, 1853-54, 1897. See Art. 48, 2 April 1874 and Art. 16, 9 September 1874. It was tabled permanently on 8 April 1875, Art. 28. Rev. Roelof Pieters was Van Raalte's successor, but the latter had always been more inclined to use hymns during the worship service. Elton J. Bruins, *The Americanization of a Congregation*, 2nd ed. (Grand Rapids, MI: Eerdmans, 1995), 22, 23. Demonstrating that the prohibition of the singing of hymns only pertained to the worship service, the minutes of Pillar Church of 28 November 1872, on the other hand, approve a collection for the "Van Lente Gezelschap" (i.e., the Van Lente choir). Two years later, on 6 October 1874, the consistory also allowed the *zanggezelschap* (singing society) to practice in the consistory room.

members belonged to Pillar Church—a congregation of the mission-minded Reformed Church in America—which in 1851 already had allocated 15 percent of church income to support foreign missions.[23] Yet the question to be debated (25 January 1874) was whether or not it was desirable to send missionaries to other countries, given that there were so many heathens in the United States (111). The minutes report only that the debaters in the affirmative had answered the question best and had been the most articulate. That the question had aroused strong feelings is shown in the "widespread participation" during the free discussion a week later (114).

After every debate, the membership had to decide which of the speakers had spoken or dealt with the subject matter best. The votes were hardly ever unanimous, but most of the time, the minutes record only the debating victory, without describing the content of the debates. As the society's purpose specified, "eloquence" seems to have mattered most in the early years of the LV. By 1875, however, the debates were followed by a membership discussion, after which, another vote was taken. Frequently this vote diverged from the earlier one, so the discussion could apparently change the opinions of some about an issue. The minutes only occasionally report the content of such a post-debate discussion.

The natural world: women

The first topic pertaining to the natural world was: "Do present-day women have more influence than men?" (11). The role and nature of women was not an uncommon topic in many debating societies in the nation, and the LV was no exception. In the early and mid-nineteenth century, the roles of American men and women were divided into public and private spheres, respectively. The home was the sphere of women, where feminine virtues would instill moral behavior in husband and children. Men operated in the public sphere, where, increasingly, specialists began to eliminate women's tasks. Nursing, for example, was relegated to the home, and urban physicians often replaced midwives. An ever-more-prosperous middle class had made this "cult of domesticity" possible. By the 1870s, the decade in which the LV operated, the various topics pertaining to women indicate that the members began to be faced with, and perhaps threatened by,

---

[23]   Henry S. Lucas, *Netherlanders in America: Dutch Immigration to the United States and Canada, 1789-1950* (Ann Arbor: University of Michigan Press, 1955), 521.

growing women's self-assertion movements. In 1873, for example, the Young People's Literary Society of Holland finally allowed women to join, after two earlier votes to admit them had failed. Some apparently availed themselves of the opportunity.[24] On the whole, home and church seem to have been the main spheres for women in Holland, and the LV remained staunchly male.

The resolution that women did not have the right to vote in the political arena was endorsed on 13 January 1873, with one of the speakers making "the members believe that ladies were incapable to vote" (20).[25] It was brought up again a year later (97), but the phrasing in the minutes was ambiguous about the outcome. Votes at an 1876 meeting determined that the members did not think that the teaching of "domestic and technical science" should be opened to women, although the vote was close (152, 153). Five women had graduated from Holland High School three years earlier, but Hope's Female Seminary, after years of faculty opposition, had just begun in 1876.[26] Had the latter been an issue among the Holland population? A question about women's potential power was raised on 30 December 1837: "Were liquor or women stronger?" The men had not been able to decide, but a year later, they excoriated heartily the "foolishness of women . . . as they do in the gin war [*genever oorlog*]" (84). The topic of debate had referred to the Ohio women who were going into the bars to pray.[27] No doubt the men saw this as an inappropriate intrusion into the male public sphere.

The natural world: social rituals

It is likely that the consumption of beer in the Dutch colony was not yet regarded as destructive in the early 1870s. Drinking beer was common, for the water in Michigan was often as unsafe as the rivers in the Netherlands, and several breweries flourished in Holland.[28]

---

[24] Swierenga, *Holland, Michigan*, 3:2037. That two earlier votes had failed indicates that there was persistent interest in and resistance to female membership.

[25] The South Caroline College's Clariosophic Society had ruled in 1847 that the female mind was naturally inferior. B. Evelyn Westbrook, University of Texas "Debating Both Sides. What Nineteenth-Century College Literary Societies Can Teach Us about Critical Pedagogies," *Rhetoric Review* 21, no. 4 (2002), 339-55.

[26] Swierenga, *Holland, Michigan*, 1:391, 500. It lasted only four years.

[27] Women in Hillsboro, Ohio, began the "Woman's Crusade" in 1873 by going into bars to pray. They continued this action throughout 1874, and this ultimately led to the founding of the Women's Christian Temperance Union.

[28] Reportedly Van Raalte received a free keg of beer from one of them weekly. Vande Water, *Holland Happenings*, 2:38.

Nevertheless, voices for abstinence were increasingly heard, and they had affected at least one member. The minutes of 26 June 1873 clarify this. The LV and the Singing Society had made plans to celebrate the Fourth of July together with a *basket pigniek*. The president (Cornelis Rot) objected to the subscription list for beer and lemonade, although it is likely that it was the buying and serving of beer and not the lemonade that was at issue. The heated discussion that followed indicates that probably most men did not oppose the consumption of beer. Rot was given a week to cool off, but that did not change his mind. Ultimately, since the Singing Society had proposed the subscription list, the members felt it was out of their hands (46-49).[29]

The lemonade and beer hullabaloo of 1873 still demonstrated, however, a clash of Dutch and American values with regard to alcoholic beverages. Feelings about the misuse of alcohol (especially hard liquor) were city wide, and the *City News* of that same year had commented disapprovingly about the visible effects of the consumption of "poison" at the "the grove."[30] It is noteworthy that the LV discussed alcohol and drunkenness with greater frequency than any other topic. The members evidently began to share the town's increasing sympathy for the cause of temperance.[31] The last recorded minutes, 30 November 1877, may be another indication of the success of the temperance movement in the United States by the late 1870s. The leading question for the following meeting was: "Resolved that a man cannot stop drinking liquor except than through the grace of God." The phrasing of the question leaves little doubt about the outcome of the vote.

Beside alcohol, the LV discussed other potentially harmful or non-Christian pursuits. It was resolved that tobacco was detrimental to one's health (105), although in the discussion following, it was noted that "several opinions were expressed" (106). No doubt for some of the members it was a difficult habit to break, for as the saying goes: "Take away a Dutchman's pipe and you might as well take away his nose."

---

[29] It was merely passing the buck, for Rot was also a member of the Singing Society!

[30] The article in the *City News* of 12 July 1873 did not specify the location of the "grove," but it could possibly have been Macatawa Park Grove or Scott's Macatawa Grove on the south side of Black Lake (later Lake Macatawa). Lois Jesiek Kayes, *Jenison Electric Park: Holland, Michigan's Beloved Resort and Amusement Park* (In-Depth Editions, 2014), 19.

[31] An ad in the *Holland City News* of 1 July 1876 made clear that no "spirituous liquors" were to be sold at the "Refreshment Stand" at the "Celebration Grounds." The incongruity of the many ads next to it advertising remedies with an alcoholic base can hardly be missed.

Worldly amusements, however that may have been interpreted, was another topic. The vote after the debate shows that Christians could enjoy those, but after the discussion, some killjoys determined by vote that, indeed, they could not (34, 35). Only a few examples of what these amusements might entail appear in some subsequent debates. Dancing was allowed in moderation (133), although a later debate pronounced that, if music was to be played to arouse a desire to dance, it should not be permitted (142). One would expect that the reading of romances would be seen as dangerous, but the brethren condoned that, although the discussion afterward was recorded to have been lively (107). Acting, however, was another matter. *Comedi spelen* (acting) was harmful and would not build up society (117, 119). Local theater groups abounded in the Netherlands in the nineteenth century, and the plays produced were often coarse and the actors considered immoral. Orthodox immigrants-to-be would not have attended, so their rejection is not surprising.

Political issues: race

Race and slavery were other moral issues tackled by the LV, although each subject came up only once. A Civil War veteran selected at the meeting of 25 November 1873 to debate "What is better for the African race: freedom or slavery?" was so outraged by the topic that he refused to participate, for "the question was totally against his conscience and politics."[32] The dubious resultant vote was that the negative side (for freedom or for slavery?) had been voted best. The vote by the members after the discussion, however, was clear. It affirmed the freedom of the "negroes."

A year later, on 4 November 1874, a vote concerning the subject of whether "Indians are the lawful owners of America and have not been treated justly by white people" showed—surprisingly—that the membership thought this was indeed so. The subject of the debate implied criticism also of recent congressional legislation. Three years earlier, Congress had ended the practice of treating Indian tribes as sovereign nations, which had actually resulted in greater control over Indian lands. The LV vote implied sympathy to past and recent unjust treatment of Native Americans. They did encounter few of them in their daily lives and seemed to be intrigued by these early Michiganders.

---

[32] Although unnamed, it was most surely Civil War veteran John Van Lente.

One of the members, during that same meeting in 1874, gave a report concerning an "Indian Lecture," perhaps referring to a *Holland City News* column a month earlier in which a son of Ottawa chief Medewis had expressed a willingness to give a talk on Indian habits and customs.[33] It is, however, unclear why the Native Americans who were living in or near Ottawa County were not included in Holland's grand centennial parade in 1876 but were instead personified by local—presumably "Dutch"—citizens.[34] A change of heart occurred in 1897 when at the semicentennial parade of 1897, twenty-five Native Americans followed Phinney's US band, and their chief gave an inspiring address.[35]

Political issues: democracy and economics

Several topics concerning American political and economic life were selected. It is noteworthy that the society steered clear of topics that pertained to the Netherlands, in spite of the use of (intermittently faulty) Dutch during the debates and in the minutes. Although news from the Netherlands appeared regularly in the local Dutch newspapers, it was too remote from their lives now. Events and issues in the United States had become primary for the members. The Netherlands was perhaps alluded to once with the question whether "a king would be better for the United States than a president." The membership voted that a president was much better (101, 102). Lingering negative memories among the older members may have further influenced the vote. Even in the 1870s, during King William III's reign, only 12 percent of the Dutch population was eligible to vote.[36]

Another question was posed on 15 February 1875 with regard to the American presidency. "What was better for the country: a soldier or a politician" (115) clearly referred to the sitting president Grant. Unfortunately, the outcome of the vote was not clear (116). It may have expressed their feelings about the embattled Grant administration at that time. Many of the topics concerning contemporary political and economic life make clear that the members considered themselves citizens of the United States. This is also conveyed, for example, in

---

[33] *Holland City News*, 4 November 1874.
[34] *Holland City News*, 1 July 1876.
[35] Vande Water, *Holland Happenings*, 3:59.
[36] Information from James C. Kennedy, 6 August 2015. Only 2.5 percent of the Dutch population was able to vote in midcentury. Michael Douma, *How Dutch Americans Stayed Dutch: An Historical Perspective on Ethnic Identities* (Amsterdam: Amsterdam University Press, 2014), 6.

the use of the possessive pronoun "ours": "a republic such as *ours*" (158). On 21 December 1874, a debate regarding high tariffs on imported goods concluded that it was a blessing for *our* country.[37] The subsequent discussion on tariffs elicited a lot of response. No doubt the membership was comprised mostly of Republicans who favored high tariffs.[38]

A vital topic during the Financial Panic of 1873, and in the years following, was the question of paper money. On 6 September 1875, the brethren decided that the exchange of specie into paper money was *not* advantageous for the country.[39]

Religious issues in the United States

A debate question was raised whether the presence of lawyers presented a pernicious element in the United States. Lawyers were indeed ubiquitous in new territories because of the necessity of legal proof of ownership or to settle contested claims and so forth. The profession was lucrative. The discussion which took place on 9 May 1875 concluded that the presence of lawyers was indeed pernicious. The opinion, which was shared by other orthodox Dutch Americans, was based on St. Paul's first letter to the Corinthian church, in which he expounds that the faithful needed to settle disputes among themselves and not among unbelievers (I. Cor. 6:1-8). How lawyer member Cornelis Rot may have felt about the vote is not recorded. In 1875 he and one other man were the only Dutch lawyers, but there were non-Dutch lawyers as well.[40]

Other religious issues in the United States occupied Dutch American debaters in Holland. The Mormon practice of bigamy became

---

[37] Acquiring strong patriotic feelings was one of the byproducts of a debating society. It was believed that the acquisition of eloquence fostered love for one's country and promoted a sense of right and wrong. Frank Moore, "American Eloquence: A Collection of Speeches and Addresses by the Most Eminent Orators of America," in *The United States Democratic Review*, Frank Moore, compiler, 86, no. 179 (New York: D. Appleton & Comp., 1857).

[38] Swierenga, *Holland, Michigan*, 2:1213-43. The vote for Republican candidates spiraled from 74 percent in 1872 to 46-56 percent in the next thirty years due to economic depressions. Republicans won only because the Democrats were split into various parties. Swierenga, *Holland, Michigan*, 2:1704-5.

[39] The debater for the affirmative side—that the exchange of specie into paper money was *advantageous* for the country—had actually been voted the winner just before the discussion ensued. The Specie Redemption Act had passed in 1875, resulting in a return to the gold standard.

[40] Swierenga, *Holland, Michigan*, 2:1204-5.

a big concern in the 1870s when increasingly more non-Mormons began entering Utah. Although the Morrill Anti-Bigamy Act was passed in 1862 during the Lincoln administration, it was not enforced until the Supreme Court upheld it in 1879. It was clear where the brethren stood on polygamy (*veelwijveri*); they soundly condemned it (126).

The Landelijke Vereniging: language

The LV demonstrated in its choice of topics its engagement in American political and social affairs in the 1870s, but even so, virtually all church services in Dutch Reformed denominations were conducted in the worshippers' native language. Dutch continued to be spoken in most homes also, although the settlers did encounter English in the market place and the larger community. The often misspelled Dutch in the LV's minutes are therefore not surprisingly sprinkled with Anglicisms. English words for certain terms are translated into Dutch incorrectly. For example, an officer in an organization is not called an *officier* (misspelled *ofersier*) in the Netherlands but should be *bestuurslid* (member of the board). English words are frequently given a Dutch conjugation; plastered becomes *geplastered*. The Dutch-language minutes often betray the minimal education of most of the secretaries. The occasional odd usage may also reflect regional dialects.[41] But the tide was turning. Toward the end of the LV's existence, it was resolved that one of every four meetings be conducted in English (26 November 1877), perhaps to attract more members and add to its prestige.

The minutes also show that the scribes had an interest in employing more sophisticated words at times. One member, having been invited to share his thoughts, did so "ecclesiastically." Hyperbole was frequently employed, such as the "brilliant [and] highly colored speech" of one, while the speeches of some of the debaters were considered "eloquent" and "brilliant," or excuses were "generously granted." Some remarks were clearly facetious: debaters on the negative side of an issue were comforted in "their heavy defeat." The minutes show internal comraderie and playfulness, in spite of frequent bickering about constitutional interpretations or dwelling on trivial issues which sometimes led to threats to quit. Disputes, however, were always settled amicably.

---

[41]   *Sikretaaris* should be written *secretaris* (secretary). Coffee is spelled *coffy* (*koffie*), and *vacation* becomes *vicansi* (*vacantie*). The last name *Deur* is spelled *Düer*, with a German umlaut ü; clearly this betrays the writer's origin close to the German border.

In the occasional use of some difficult words, the members were true to their intent to become "eloquent." Hearing lyceum orators, long wordy sermons and political speeches no doubt affected the debaters' value of words. Speaking well was praised, so it is not surprising that eloquence was an aspiration held by many. Whether the Holland debaters were successful in their quest is hard to ascertain.

It seems, since the content of the debates are hardly ever spelled out, that oratory and the contest between opposing positions often took primary place. The inauguration of a debate after the debate later in the LV's existence demonstrates that active participation of the topic could alter the previous vote. Good and convincing content, although mostly not spelled out, was definitely an important factor in the debate. The topics themselves had become a bit more challenging over the years, however, such as the topic discussed on 30 November, 1877: "Are the present so-called oppressive times in our land causes to healthy solid progress of the same?"[42] Perhaps new and younger members (some of whom had been to a secondary school) contributed to that change.

Membership of the LV

Since the names of the members of the LV did not generally appear on the list of prominent businessmen and educators of Holland, can it be assumed that they represented the lower rung of Holland's society? A number of them owned large sections of land in the southeast section of Holland. The "abstinence man," Cornelis Rot, was Holland's first lawyer, while Jan Kerkhof Sr. was one of the first elders at Third Reformed Church, retaining that position for nine years.[43] F. J. Van Lente had begun the Van Lente choir, which was taken over by his son John (also a member). Some of the younger members—educated in American schools—later became leading citizens in Holland, and two became clergymen (see footnote 12).

It is clear that some members were appointed to debate more frequently than others or were requested to fill in for a no-show during a meeting. Each year a committee was appointed to select the topics to be discussed,[44] but one member protested that some of these were too

---

[42] The affirmative vote is seven, with seven nays.

[43] Bruins, *Americanization*, 12, 150.

[44] Carolyn Eastman, *A Nation of Speechifiers: Making an American Public after the Revolution* (Chicago: University of Chicago Press, 2009), 255n20. Although the topics chosen by debating societies were often copied fromfrom each other, they were given the peculiar make-up of the LV, that is, Dutch American with an orthodox religious outlook; there could not have been too great a dependence on such borrowed topics.

challenging and should be reviewed by everybody before being finalized. The minutes registered his complaint: "A dumb [*dom*] person should also be able to say something" (33). He must have felt satisfied with the debate: "This earth rests on pillars, and she does not turn" (135). The membership concluded that "this earth turns."

Although there evidently were differences in intellectual ability and education, these qualities were not the deciding factor in founding the LV. Primary was their proximity to each other. Furthermore, many were related or had another kind of relationship. Quite a few members were related to each other through marriage; the LV included a number of brothers-in-law.[45] This was not unusual since it fit the pattern of many other societies in the United States in which members were professionally or kin related.[46] There is even another connection. This group of "self-improving" neighbors was also bound together by their love of singing. More than half of the membership also belonged to the Van Lente *gezelschap* (literal translation is "society," but it was a choir).[47] Several of the altos and sopranos were sisters or wives of LV members.

That these two intertwined societies celebrated the Fourth of July together in 1873 has already been mentioned. The desire to commemorate this event festively shows how much the members had Americanized, especially since the three papers in Holland (two in Dutch, one in English)[48] mention that there was no city-wide celebration and that most people stayed home. The celebration in 1876, however, drew more city-wide attention, and many committees were appointed to organize a grand affair.[49] The LV also appointed a committee to schedule a July 4 celebration "in this neighborhood."

While celebrating the founding of the United States in 1876, the LV seemed to be on its last legs. The members did not meet from 10 June until 20 November 1876, when the membership actually discussed whether they should continue (160). The LV had begun with twelve members and, over the span of five years, had added fifteen more, although some of these rarely attended. Many attempts were made to recruit new members and retain old ones, although, strangely enough, new members were rarely voted in unanimously. One president even

---

[45]   Several families had come to the United States together and bought land near each other. *Illustrated Historical Atlas*, xx, xxi.

[46]   Furthermore, many men were or became business associates. Eastman, 257n33.

[47]   The choir's constitution—not extant—seems to have had the same strict rules with regard to attendance and prompt arrival, with fines levied for transgressions.

[48]   *De Grondwet, De Hollander*, and *City News*, July 1873.

[49]   *City News*, 1 July 1876.

suggested drolly that the membership employ the aggressive recruiting methods of the Mormons.[50] Irregular attendance and frequent absences were chronic, and time after time, two members were nominated to visit an errant member to "really shake him awake" (55).[51] Occasional fractious relationships may have contributed to absences.

The problem with absenteeism was that these malingering members did not own up to their financial obligations. Dues were not paid regularly. This money was needed to pay for simple expenses: purchases of a minute book, scratch paper, ink, oil, kindling and firewood, and pens and pencils. The members presumably also paid for the trees that they planted on "the church square" in the spring of 1875 (122-25). A major financial obligation was to pay for the construction of the LV's own "hall," built together with the Singing Society. It had been constructed on the land of member Frederick J. Van Lente, father of members John and Henry, who lived in the neighborhood (corner of Land [Lincoln] and 16th Streets). The minutes of 1873 were filled with proposals and counterproposals about the log construction of the hall, what labor needed to be outsourced, and what could be done by members themselves.[52] The proceedings of 2 January 1877 indicate that this modest structure was to be moved—no reason given—and a committee was appointed to provide ropes and a chain. Since the LV continued to meet for another eleven months, this must mean that the move was only a matter of a change of location.

A modest debt of $20.55 remained after the construction, but demand for its payment filled many lines of the subsequent minutes. This was not a small thing in those financially worrisome 1870s. One member had been repeatedly admonished to pay his subscription promise. He asked to speak at the 22 March 1875 meeting and told the members that "he finds himself in dire circumstances to pay his debt" (120, 121). Like him, there were others who had also left the LV without paying their debts.

The minutes of 30 November 1877 were followed by others, but oddly enough, these were cut off at the margins. The writing on the remaining stubs of the subsequent twenty-seven cut pages proves a

---

[50] 13 May 1873.

[51] That is, "*om die eens goed wakker te schudde[n],*" 4 November 1873.

[52] It measured 32-by-18 feet and had one door and at least two windows. The interior furnishings included chairs, a stove, and lamps. The members helped to saw and transport the logs, plaster the outside, and nail floorboards "firmly" and planned to be in it before winter set in (minutes of 9 September 1873).

continuation—or perhaps a lingering—of the LV for another year or so. The LV's demise could not be attributed to the language question. The use of English had already been accepted—at least intermittently. Was the LV too "inbred" and therefore occasionally fractious? Were the bonds of family ultimately too restrictive and wider horizons needed? Absenteeism had always been high, and perhaps competition with "American" organizations, such as the YMCA and the Shakespearean Club, was a reason for its slow growth and ultimate decline. Was the financial strain a cause? The end of Holland's Young People's Literary Club in 1875 was attributed by the secretary not only to financial difficulties but also to a decline in membership and lack of interest.[53] Could these reasons also have contributed to the LV's demise? The content of the subsequent minutes could perhaps have provided answers, but for the reader today it must remain a mystery.

---

[53]   Swierenga, *Holland, Michigan*, 3:2037.

Part Five

Rekindling Affection for the Netherlands

CHAPTER 11

Remembering the Knickerbockers: A Lifetime of Scholarship on the Dutch American Atlantic

Peter D. Van Cleave

Francis Adrian van der Kemp has largely been remembered for his attempt to translate the records of New Netherland. The official records of the Dutch colony constitute over twelve thousand pieces, including council minutes, deeds, and correspondence, which are today housed at the New York State Archives. Van der Kemp doggedly worked from 1818 to 1822 to translate as many documents from Dutch to English as he could. In the end, he translated twenty-four volumes and over ten thousand pages of text. The Albany Records, the shorthand name for the twenty-four-volume collection, was the most significant and extensive translation of New Netherland documents up to that point. As such, scholars of the Dutch colony heavily relied on the Albany Records in the years after their completion. But in 1911, all but a few of Van der Kemp's volumes met a fiery demise in the Capitol Fire.[1]

[1] Fortunately, the original Dutch documents survived. A stack of English colonial records had been placed on top of the New Netherland documents and burned first, preserving the Dutch records for future generations. For information about the Dutch records, see the New Netherland Institute, newnetherlandinstitute.org; for the fire, see Paul Mercer and Vicki Weiss, *The New York State Capitol and the Great Fire of 1911* (New York: Arcadia Publishing, 2011).

Yet, like the fire, history has not been kind to Van der Kemp or the Albany Records. Despite their use from contemporary historians, later scholars deemed the Albany Records an exceedingly bad reconstruction of the Dutch colonial records—and for good reason. E. B. O'Callaghan and A. J. F. Van Laer, state translators who were able to view the translations before they burned, relayed that they were incomplete and often inaccurate. Van der Kemp omitted some sections entirely and inserted language not in the original text. The legacy of the Albany Records was so bad that some historians suggested that the failure of the records reflected the shortcomings of the man. For contemporary historians of New Netherland, the Albany Records, and by extension Van der Kemp himself, are notorious for their poor quality and known only for their disappointment.[2]

Van der Kemp's efforts and the legacy of the Albany Records, however, are much more than a failed act of translation. Although the Albany Records are by far the most prominent and well known of Van der Kemp's contributions, they are a poor representation of a life dedicated to scholarship on Dutch American history. First, the Albany Records themselves have been erroneously understood; they should not be viewed as translations but rather as a history of New Netherland. Viewing the records as Van der Kemp's history of New

---

[2]   Scholars who have seen Van der Kemp's records confirm the issues with the manuscripts. See Arnold Johan Ferdinand Van Laer, "The Translation and Publication of the Manuscript Dutch Records of New Netherland: With an Account of Previous Attempts at Translation," *Education Department Bulletin: New York State Library Bibliography* 46, no. 462 (January 1, 1910), 5-28; E. B. O'Callaghan, ed., *Calendar of Historical Manuscripts in the Office of the Secretary of State, Albany, NY: Part I: Dutch Manuscripts, 1630-1664*, New York State Library (Albany: Weed, Parsons, and Co., 1865). For more background on O'Callaghan, see Stephen McErleane, "The Radical Archivist," *New York Archives* 14, no. 4 (Spring 2015): 16-19. Van Laer referred to the records as "absolutely worthless for critical historical work." Russell Shorto describes the records as "worse than worthless," and deems the 1911 fire a blessing for history, see *The Island at the Center of the World: The Epic Story of Dutch Manhattan and the Forgotten Colony that Shaped America* (New York: Vintage, 2004), 322. The most aggressive and dismissive comments of the records and of Van der Kemp come from Jan Willem Schulte Nordholt. Schulte Nordholt wrote, "This ultimate futility seems somehow characteristic of Van der Kemp's lifework. There is, in his life, when all is said and done, superficiality and sketchiness, much fire and little warmth, much glitter and little light." See, *The Dutch Republic and American Independence*, trans. Herbert H. Rowen (Chapel Hill: University of North Carolina Press, 1982), 303. In a conversation with Dr. Charles Gehring, the director of the New Netherland Research Center, he informed me that all of the Van der Kemp translations did not burn in the 1911 fire but that the volumes that remained were indeed as poor as everyone had thought. Dr. Charles Gehring, email message to author, 11 November 2013.

Netherland not only helps to explain why the records were such poor translations—he never intended a word-for-word reproduction—but it is also a more accurate reflection of how Van der Kemp viewed his own work. His primary goal was accessibility and to bring the history of New Netherland into the nineteenth century.[3]

The specific history of the Albany Records and a reassessment of their construction have been covered elsewhere, but the use of the records as the sole framework for understanding Van der Kemp is the second way historians have obscured his life and contributions.[4] By focusing on the years of production from 1818 to 1822, those assessments necessarily miss a much longer and richer history of scholarship on the Dutch American Atlantic. Instead of the beginning of a monumental failure, the Albany Records were the culmination of a life spent vigorously and passionately defending the importance of Dutch American history. An examination of his earlier works provides a much better framework for properly contextualizing the Albany Records and for better understanding Van der Kemp's role in portraying the connections between the Dutch and Americans.

Concurrently, the history that led to the records attests to the continued influence of the Dutch during the Early American Republic. In general, scholarship on the Dutch in America focuses on two periods: New Netherland and Dutch immigration to the Midwest in the late nineteenth century. Even in the works that survey Dutch Americans, the Early American Republic receives passing attention.[5] In fact, much of the attention paid to Dutch American history in the Early American Republic revolves around figures such as John Adams, John Quincy Adams, Washington Irving, and John Lothrop Motley. Examining Van der Kemp reinserts the Dutch back in Dutch American and provides a link between the two dominant traditions in Dutch American studies.

When placed in the larger context of his life and his scholarly work, it becomes clear that the Albany Records were but a continuation

3   Peter D. Van Cleave, "Rescuing the Albany Records from the Fire: Redeeming Francis Adrian van der Kemp's Notorious Attempt to Translate the Records of New Netherland," *New York History* 96, no. 3-4 (Summer/Fall 2015): 354-73.

4   Ibid. See also, Peter D. Van Cleave, "A Successful Failure: A History of the Albany Records," *New York Archives* 16, no. 1 (Summer 2016): 36-37.

5   See Gerald De Jong, *The Dutch in America, 1609-1974* (Boston: Twayne Publishers, 1975); Henry Lucas, *Netherlanders in America: Dutch Immigration to the United States and Canada, 1789-1950* (Ann Arbor: University of Michigan Press, 1955); Jacob Van Hinte, *Netherlanders in America: A Study of Emigration and Settlement in the 19th and 20th Centuries in the United States of America*, ed. Robert P. Swierenga, trans. Adriaan de Wit (Grand Rapids, MI: Baker Book House, 1985).

of Van der Kemp's scholarship, and to judge him solely on their quality is a disservice to his position within Dutch American history. Exploring the long road before the Albany Records shifts Van der Kemp's legacy from that of a worthless translator to an important voice in the history of Dutch America.

The Dutch Republic and a vision of America

Francis Adrian van der Kemp was born in Kampen, Overijssel, the Netherlands, on 4 May 1752. On the same day, thirty-six years later, Van der Kemp, his wife, and their three children arrived in the New York harbor, exiles from their homeland. Those intervening years tell the story of Van der Kemp's involvement in the political developments occurring throughout the Dutch Republic and his rise as a figure of some stature. Those early years in the Netherlands exposed Van der Kemp to the broader Atlantic world and to conversations of revolution and natural rights. More importantly, he was introduced to the cause of the American people.

In the Netherlands, the American Revolution was a catalyzing event. For many, the fight for American independence became a proxy battle for struggles against the growing power of the Stadholder, William V, Prince of Orange. Similar to the Revolution, the Revolt was largely about popular sovereignty and the proper allocation of representation within a confederated political system.[6] Embryonic during the early 1770s, those misgivings gained traction during the debate in 1775 over whether to grant William V's request to allow King George III to use Dutch troops in his fight against the rebelling Americans. Opposition within the States General was enough to deny the request, but the future divisions were clearly drawn between the Orangists who supported William V and the British and the patriots who sought to help the Americans.[7]

---

[6]   Simon Schama, *Patriots and Liberators: Revolution in the Netherlands, 1780-1813* (New York: Vintage, 1977); Wayne Ph. Te Brake, *Regents and Rebels: The Revolutionary World of an Eighteenth-Century Dutch City* (Cambridge, MA: Blackwell Publishing, 1989); Margaret C. Jacob and Wijnand W. Mijnhardt, eds., *The Dutch Republic in the Eighteenth Century: Decline, Enlightenment, and Revolution* (Ithaca: Cornell University Press, 1992).

[7]   The two best overviews of the relationship between the Dutch Republic and the American Revolution are Schulte Nordholt, *The Dutch Republic*; Friedrich Elder, *The Dutch Republic and the American Revolution*, John Hopkins University Studies in Historical and Political Science, 29, no. 2 (Baltimore: Johns Hopkins University Press, 1911).

Though never receiving the same status as France or even Spain, the Netherlands was a crucial participant in the American Revolution. From the start, the Dutch supplied the American rebels with money, goods, and gunpowder in addition to vocal and written support. The Caribbean island of St. Eustatius became a hub of commercial activity. The Dutch officials on the island became the first to salute the American flag, offering implicit if not official acknowledgment of independence. The Dutch Caribbean would later be critical for American success at Yorktown in 1782.[8] It was the promise of further Dutch contributions that compelled John Adams to travel from Paris to Amsterdam in an effort to secure a substantial loan and legitimize Dutch efforts.

Before Adams made his way to the Netherlands, Van der Kemp had been rising in the Patriot ranks. Active throughout the late 1770s writing pamphlets and treatises, he wrote exclusively on Dutch topics, such as the Union of Utrecht and the forced-labor system in the province of Overijssel.[9] As he told his son, "My bosom glowed with the Sacred fire of Patriotism" and he devoted himself to helping the people of the Netherlands "recover a real influence in the choice of their Representatives."[10] His efforts gained him the attention of the leading patriots of the time, including Johan Derk van der Capellen. His writings also caught the attention of the Orangists, which led to a tribunal in Leiden in 1780. Ironically, the piece the Leiden officials charged to Van der Kemp was not of his hand, but rather of Pieter Vreede, his colleague. In order to protect Vreede, Van der Kemp took

---

[8]   Schulte Nordholt, *The Dutch Republic*, 29-41; Wayne Ph. Te Brake, "The Dutch Republic and the Creation of the United States," in *Four Centuries of Dutch-American Relations*, ed. Hans Krabbendam, Cornelis A. Van Minnen, and Giles Scott-Smith (Albany: State University of New York Press, 2009), 204-15; Wim Klooster, "An Overview of Dutch Trade with the Americas, 1600-1800," in *Riches from Atlantic Commerce: Dutch Transatlantic Trade and Shipping, 1585-1817*, ed. Johannes Postma and Victor Enthoven (Leiden: Brill, 2003), 365-83. For a look at how the activity on St. Eustatius directly affected the execution of war in North America, see Andrew Jackson O'Shaughnessy, *An Empire Divided: The American Revolution and the British Caribbean* (Philadelphia: University of Pennsylvania Press, 2000), 213-37.

[9]   Francis Adrian van der Kemp, *Aenmerkingen over de Verklaering der Unie van Utrecht, door P. Paulus, in drie Brieven* (Leiden: L. Herdingh, 1783); Francis Adrian van der Kemp, *Derde Brief over de Drostendiensten in Overyssel, door een Heer uit Twenthe, etc* (Amsterdam: Conradi en Doll, 1779). For a broader contextualization of the pamphlets, see Leonard I. Leeb, *The Ideological Origins of the Batavian Revolution: History and Politics in the Dutch Republic, 1747-1800* (The Hague: Martinus Nijhoff, 1973), 119-20; Te Brake, *Regents*, 43-47.

[10] Francis Adrian van der Kemp, *Autobiography*, Buffalo and Erie County Historical Society Archives, A69-66, Francis Adrian Van Der Kemp Papers, His Autobiography, 1:12, 13.

ownership and faced the charges. Despite pleadings from his friends and the promise of safe passage to France offered by Van der Capellen, Van der Kemp sustained nearly two years of hearings and interrogations until even Orangists called for an end to the tribunal. In celebration, Van der Kemp "published the whole legal process till its conclusion, with a preface and the Ode to prove its innocence."[11]

As the proceedings carried on, Van der Kemp continued his studies and writings, but by 1781, his focus had taken a decided turn. On 17 April 1781, Van der Kemp, along with others, met with John Adams in Leiden to discuss the American Revolution. It was the connection between the Dutch and the Americans, embodied by his own growing friendship with Adams, which framed Van der Kemp's writings for the rest of the 1780s. He wrote Adams shortly after the meeting, "I would be delighted to be of service, to demonstrate the simple fact of my interest in the humanitarian cause in America."[12] As Van der Kemp studied the American Revolution, he came to see the Revolution and the Revolt as inextricably linked, as twin revolutions against hierarchy and the usurpation of power from the people. He unleashed the same combination of passion, vigor, and invective that brought him before the Leiden tribunal in his writings in favor of the American cause.

Whereas his earlier writings analyzed the failings of the Dutch past, his new work utilized the contemporary United States as a projection of a possible Dutch future. In order to promote the cause of the American Revolution, Van der Kemp began gathering documents he eventually published as *Verzameling van Stukken tot de Dertien Vereenigde Staeten van Noord-America Betrekkelijk* (Collection of papers related to the thirteen United States of North America).[13] Following a brief preface, the *Verzameling van Stukken* is entirely a collection of American documents. Van der Kemp included letters between Van der Capellen and Governor Jonathan Trumbull of Connecticut, letters between Van der Capellen and Governor William Livingston of New Jersey, the Articles of Confederation, the Constitution of Massachusetts, and a speech from John Hancock. In the preface, Van der Kemp defended the cause of the Americans, their reasons for revolution, and the promise of their success. He denounced the limited support of the Dutch,

---

[11] Van der Kemp, *Autobiography*, quote 21, 17-21.

[12] Francis Adrian van der Kemp to John Adams, 5 June 1781, microfilm edition of the Adams Family Papers, reel 355, Massachusetts Historical Society.

[13] Francis Adrian van der Kemp, *Verzameling van Stukken tot de Dertien Vereenigde Staeten van Noord-America Betrekkelijk* (Leiden: L. Herdingh, 1781), Van der Kemp Collection, New York Historical Society.

especially when the two countries had so much in common and the Dutch prided themselves on the same opposition to tyranny and love of liberty claimed by the Americans.[14] He asserted in the preface that the United States, in taking up arms and fighting for liberty, had surpassed the Dutch. For Van der Kemp, the Dutch Republic would benefit from following the example of the American republic.[15]

No one embodied the connections between the Dutch patriots and the American Revolution better than Van der Kemp. He even began to adopt rhetoric similar to the American pamphlets he collected. For instance, he framed the Dutch patriots as fighting against their enslavement, writing, "I glowed with indignation when I became convinced, that in the fetters prepared for the Americans, the Slavery of my own country was a chief ingredient." The juxtaposition of slavery and liberty was commonplace in Revolutionary pamphlets.[16] While other patriots used the American Revolution as a foil against the Orangists, no one expressed it as fervently and as completely as Van der Kemp. Moreover, his turn to the American Revolution and the progress of the United States came right at the beginning of the Patriot Revolt. For the entirety of the conflict, Van der Kemp thought of the Dutch rebellion in American terms, a connection he would maintain the rest of his life.

The Dutch Patriot Revolt emerged from the call to arms issued in the influential pamphlet, *Aan het Volk van Nederland* (To the people of the Netherlands). Written by Johan Derk van der Capellen, the leading Patriot figure, and distributed by Van der Kemp in the fall of 1781, the pamphlet urged the Dutch to take the example of America and take back power from the Stadholder and his Orangist allies. The Revolt capitalized on the growing dissatisfaction with William V, especially in the wake of the disastrous showing in the Fourth Anglo-Dutch War (1780-84) against the British. Adams's dogged efforts at The Hague were also beginning to bear fruit. Supported by failure in the Fourth Anglo-Dutch War and the ever-expanding coalition of patriots in favor of the American Revolution, Adams received recognition as the American minister plenipotentiary. Then on 19 April 1782, the anniversary of

---

14   Van der Kemp, *Verzameling*.

15   Francis Adrian van der Kemp, *Memoir on the Use of Copper by the Greeks*, 1803, Buffalo and Erie County Historical Society Archives, A69-66, Francis Adrian Van der Kemp Papers: Memoir on the Use of Copper by the Greeks, 5:7.

16   Van der Kemp, *Autobiography*, 14. For American reliance on slavery as a frame of reference, see Bernard Bailyn, *The Ideological Origins of the American Revolution* (Cambridge, MA: Harvard University Press, 1967, reprint, 1992), 232-33.

Lexington and Concord, the Dutch officially recognized the United States as an independent nation.[17]

The patriots capitalized on the successful campaign to override William V, followed the example of the United States, and expanded the revolt throughout the provinces. By 1784 the movement experienced a series of victories, including removing the Stadholder from The Hague. But internal division threatened future success, and Van der Kemp became concerned. Having already suffered through a tribunal, his prominence in the movement and his decision to lead the militia unit at Wijk bij Duurstede gave him little hope that he would escape unscathed. By 1785 Van der Kemp was in communication with Adams about living in the United States.

Those letters to Adams and fear about the negative effect of his writings proved prescient. In 1787 William V used foreign alliances and Prussian troops to soundly defeat the patriots.[18] As Orangists' troops following in the wake of the Prussian forces made their way into Wijk bij Duurstede, they arrested and jailed Van der Kemp for his previous actions against the Stadholder. As one Orangist commander informed him, "'You sir! with your delicate pen! . . . You reap now the fruits.'" Imprisoned for twenty-four weeks, the Orangists charged him with a fine of 45,000 florins "for the losses incurred by the public during our usurpation." After a wealthy friend paid the fine, Van der Kemp, like many patriots, resolved to flee the country. In reality he did not have much of a choice, since he was banned from the province of Utrecht, and had he gone to Holland, he would have been jailed once again.[19]

Whereas the overwhelming majority of patriots had fled the country for France, Van der Kemp knew exactly where he would end up. In 1788 he gathered his belongings and his family, and with the help of Adams secured passage out of the Netherlands. Armed with letters of introduction to the leading figures in the United States, he set off for his new home. As he wrote Adams early in 1781, "America wil [sic] be my asylum."[20]

---

[17] For Adams, see John Ferling, *John Adams: A Life* (Knoxville: University of Tennessee Press, 1992), 228-42; David McCullough, *John Adams* (New York: Simon and Schuster, 2001), 242-73. For Dutch developments, see Schulte Nordholt, *The Dutch Republic*; Te Brake, "The Dutch Republic."

[18] Schama, *Patriots and Liberators*, 105-32; Israel, *The Dutch Republic*, 1107-14; Te Brake, "The Dutch Republic," 212.

[19] Van der Kemp, *Autobiography*, quotes, 31, 21-33.

[20] Francis Adrian van der Kemp to John Adams, 26 November 1781, microfilm edition of the Adams Family Papers, reel 355, Massachusetts Historical Society.

Life in Old New Netherland

Van der Kemp and his family reached New York in 1788 on his thirty-sixth birthday. From that year forward, he celebrated dual anniversaries on 4 May: his birth in Kampen and his rebirth as an American. By 1825 Van der Kemp had lived longer in the United States than he had in the Netherlands. Yet the life that Van der Kemp forged in New York was not one bereft of Dutch influence or the impact of Dutch history. The Dutch Republic continued to shape Van der Kemp's perspective as he adapted to life on the other side of the Atlantic.

Even before he left for the United States, Van der Kemp was making decisions based on America's relationship to Dutch culture. Although Adams was Van der Kemp's most intimate American friend, and he had other connections to Massachusetts, both he and Adams decided that the Van der Kemps would find the best fit "among the Dutch People in New York."[21] The choice paid immediate dividends. The first few years in the United States marked a zenith for Van der Kemp and his Dutchness. When he presented his letters of introduction to Governor George Clinton and Alexander Hamilton, the Clintons and the Hamiltons welcomed the immigrants in their native language. It was a gift that "was unexpected and enhanced yet further the high value of their numerous favours," but it was also a reflection that the Dutch language was still a common tongue throughout the state.[22]

But even more reassuring was Van der Kemp's visit to George Washington at Mount Vernon. The Dutchman revered Washington, and his admiration only grew when Washington expressed the same relationship between the Dutch Patriot Revolt and the American Revolution—and between the Dutch and the American people—that Van der Kemp had been writing about for years. Washington welcomed other Dutch patriots to immigrate to the United States since they shared similar characteristics and would be beneficial to the country

[21] John Adams to Francis Adrian van der Kemp, 6 January 1788, Francis Adrian Van der Kemp Collection, 1781-1829: Letters of John Adams and John Quincy Adams, 1781-1829, Historical Society of Pennsylvania.

[22] Van der Kemp, *Autobiography*, 38. For the use of Dutch in New York, see Charles Gehring, "The Survival of the Dutch Language in New York and New Jersey" *De Halve Maen* 58, no. 3 (1984): 7-9, 24. The Clintons and Hamiltons had their own personal connections to the Dutch colonial period, The Clintons were descendants of early Dutch settler, Tjerck Claessen de Witt, and Elizabeth Hamilton had her own deep connections to New Netherland through Schuylers, Van Cortlandts, and Van Rensselaers. Brief biographies can be found at http://www.newnetherlandinstitute.org/history-and-heritage/dutch_americans/.

in its infancy.[23] It was praise for the Dutch and an articulation of the Dutch American Atlantic that Van der Kemp could not have written better himself.

Those early years in New York continued to remind Van der Kemp of the deep connections between the Dutch and Americans and how much he benefited from them. When Van der Kemp fled the Netherlands, he was forced to leave behind a substantial amount of wealth. Van der Kemp found various ways to stay solvent, but central to his success was the kindness of friends and his oldest son, John Jacob (J. J.), who secured a well-paid job that allowed him to send his father money. The kindness and money from J. J. often originated from the same source: Holland Land Company. In 1792 six Dutch financiers joined together to form the company, and purchased over 5 million acres of land, 3.3 million of which was located in upstate New York. The company brought in several Dutch agents, including John Lincklaen, Gerrit Boon, and Adam Mappa, to superintend the land, each of whom Van der Kemp knew personally. From 1793 to 1797, the Van der Kemps farmed a tract of land around Oneida Lake in the Scriba Patent. Isolated and lonely, the decision was made to move to one of the new Holland Land Company developments being overseen by Mappa, a fellow Dutch patriot. Lacking the funds to purchase a new tract, Mappa and Boon, who overlapped as agents, simply gifted the land to Van der Kemp.[24] J. J. began working for the company and eventually became the highest-ranking company official in the United States.

To make matters even more Dutch, the village Van der Kemp lived in was named Oldenbarneveld. Oldenbarneveld was a name instantly recognizable to anyone from the Netherlands. Johan van Oldenbarnevelt was a famous Dutch politician and religious dissenter. At seventy-two years of age, he was beheaded for his opposition to the

[23]   George Washington to Francis Adrian van der Kemp, 28 May 1788; Van der Kemp to Washington, 15 May 1788, 16 July 1788, 24 March 1789, and 9 January 1790, Van der Kemp Collection, New York Historical Society.

[24]   John F. Seymour, *Centennial Address, Delivered at Trenton, N.Y., July 4, 1876, with Letters from Francis Adrian Van der Kemp, Written in 1792, and Other Documents Relating to the First Settlement of Trenton and Central New York* (Utica, NY: White and Floyd, Book and Job Printers, 1876), Town of Trenton Municipal Building, Barneveld City Hall; Charles G. Girelius, "The Settlement," in *Barneveld Sketches* (Barneveld, 1952), Town of Trenton Municipal Building, Barneveld City Hall; George Scriba Papers, New York State Library, Manuscripts and Special Collections, SC10521, NYSL, Albany, NY; Paul D. Evans, *The Holland Land Company* (Fairfield, NJ: Augustus M. Kelley, 1924, reprint, 1979); Charles E. Brooks, *Frontier Settlement and Market Revolution: The Holland Land Purchase* (Ithaca: Cornell University Press, 1996).

current stadholder and Reformed Church.[25] For many Netherlanders, Oldenbarnevelt was a martyr, and he became one the most prominent Dutch symbols for opposition to religious and political oppression. In addition to Van der Kemp's history of political antagonism in the Netherlands, Oldenbarnevelt had built an equal reputation for religious dissention. The Dutch Republic did not have an officially established church, but the Reformed Church performed many of the functions of a state church and made Calvinism the public faith of the Netherlands, forcing non-Calvinist religious expression into private spaces.[26] Van der Kemp's explicitly rejected Calvinist doctrine, and his public opposition toward the Reformed Church resulted in his expulsion from the University of Groningen in 1773. Undeterred, he became a Mennonite minister in Leiden, and for a brief period during the Patriot Revolt, he occupied the role of both minister and soldier, preaching in the morning and drilling in the afternoon.[27] With Van der Kemp's own long history of religious and political dissension, the name of the village was simultaneously a direct invocation of his life in the Netherlands and an inspiration for the political and religious freedom he expected in the United States. It was also, of course, yet another reminder of his Dutchness. By roughly 1797, Van der Kemp lived in the state that was the former Dutch colony, on a tract of land in America owned by a Dutch company, in a village named after a prominent figure in Dutch history, in an area of New York dominated by Holland Land Company purchases, all of which were superintended by Dutch employees, who also happened to be his friends and neighbors.

The erasure of the Dutch in America

Even as Van der Kemp encountered daily reminders of the Dutch impact on the United States, it became increasingly clear that he had

---

[25]   Israel, *The Dutch Republic*, 433-59.

[26]   The unique arrangement in the Dutch Republic of a public faith but no state church did inspire a significant amount of religious tolerance and creative adaptations to maintaining peace during and after the Reformation. See Benjamin J. Kaplan, *Divided By Faith: Religious Conflict and the Practice of Toleration in Early Modern Europe* (Cambridge, MA: Harvard University Press, 2007); Willem Frijhoff, *Embodied Belief: Ten Essays on Religious Culture in Dutch History* (Hilversum: Uitgeverij Verloren, 2002).

[27]   Van der Kemp's dual role as preacher and soldier became the subject of an anti-Patriot cartoon that depicted him in the pulpit, half-solider, half-preacher. "Explanation of the liberty-print of the present Cantzelhuzaaren," in F. Muller, *Nederlandsche geschiedenis in platen*, vol. 2 (1867). The cartoon was sent in a letter from Arend H. Huussen Jr. to Harry F. Jackson on 26 April 1965. The letter is located in the Oneida County Historical Society, Manuscript Division, box 19-1986: mss.1; VDK.1 Van Der Kemp, F.A.; WAL.5-Walcott, W.D.; WAS.2- Washington, George, folder: mss.1 VDK.1 Van der Kemp, F. A.-Miscellaneous: mis.1.1/mis.1.5.

been insulated from larger developments which had led most of his fellow New Yorkers to forget their Dutch past. America underwent immense changes in the post-Revolutionary period, New York especially. By 1818, when Van der Kemp began translating the New Netherland records, the constant remembrances of the Dutch in America that had marked the 1790s were greatly reduced.

Although Van der Kemp might not have recognized it from Oldenbarneveld, forgetting the Dutch was a process long in the making. It dated back to the first English conquest of New Netherland in 1664. The burgeoning success of New Netherland threatened the expansionist visions of the English in North America, which set off a quick succession of Anglo-Dutch Wars. New Netherland permanently became part of the English empire in 1674.[28] New York may have started out as a Dutch colony, but it had been an English one longer, and its English history was much more recent. It was also much more prominent in the minds of New Yorkers. In the buildup to the American Revolution, the nature of the colonial protest overemphasized the British features of North America. With the locus of resistance aimed at Parliament and King George III and grounded in Whig ideology, the unique influence of settlements such as New Netherland gave way to hyper-British identities.[29]

Compounding the issue was the fact that the Dutch did not come to North America or the United States in overwhelming numbers. There was not a stream of people that continually reinvigorated Dutch culture and Dutch customs. Immigration was the exception not the norm. Tellingly, people from the Netherlands were barely a majority in the Dutch colony.[30] Yet even with minimal contact with the Netherlands, the Dutch who remained in New York found ways to preserve their identity, mainly through language and the Reformed Church. In the

---

[28] Jaap Jacobs, *The Colony of New Netherland: A Dutch Settlement in Seventeenth-Century America* (Ithaca: Cornell University Press, 2009); Gehring, "Survival," 8.

[29] Jon Butler, *Becoming America: the Revolution Before 1776* (Cambridge, MA: Harvard University Press, 2000), 233-34; Bailyn, *Ideological Origins*; Gordon S. Wood, *The Radicalism of the American Revolution* (New York, Vintage, 1991), 95-109.

[30] David Steven Cohen, "How Dutch Were the Dutch of New Netherland?" *New York History* 62, no. 1 (January 1981): 43-60. For a broader look at Dutch immigration, the work of Robert P. Swierenga is invaluable, see "Exodus Netherlands, Promised Land America: Dutch Immigration and Settlement in the United States," in *A Bilateral Bicentennial: A History of Dutch-American Relations, 1782-1982*, ed. J. W. Schulte Nordholt and Robert P. Swierenga (Amsterdam: Meulenhoff, 1982); Swierenga, ed., *The Dutch in America: Immigration, Settlement, and Cultural Change* (New Brunswick: Rutgers University Press, 1985).

face of English conquest, the disparate population that had made up New Netherland coalesced around their connection to Dutch culture and customs, building an entrenched minority and a persistent Dutch identity.[31]

The persistence of Dutch identity is an impressive story of ethnic survival that was met with an equally impressive level of disdain from the English. Colonial literature abounds with English references to the inferiority of Dutch culture in New York. These diatribes are evidence of both of the Atlantic wars between the Dutch and the English, as well as longstanding antagonisms that existed between English and Dutch settlers.[32] But as Joyce Goodfriend notes, "The New Netherland Dutch surrendered not only their colony, but the power to control the telling of their story."[33] With the story in English hands, it is little wonder that, by the time of the Revolution, the history of the Dutch colony and its influence was a little known chapter in New York history.

Post-Revolutionary America was not much better for the historical memory of New Netherland. Anti-Dutch sentiments were still prevalent and reached peak form with the mass migration of New Englanders into New York. Beginning to reach upstate New York in the late 1790s, the constant stream of Yankees put increased pressure on Dutch cultural survival.[34] Further, most Dutch households and churches in New York adopted English as their primary language. The receding of language was joined by the removal of other distinctive features such as architecture in the effacement of Dutch culture in New York.[35]

[31] Gehring, "Survival"; Joyce D. Goodfriend, The Dutch Colonial Legacy: 'Not Hasty to Change Old habits for New,'" De Halve Maen 65, no. 1 (1992): 5-9. For other accounts of Dutch persistence see Joyce D. Goodfriend, *Before the Melting Pot: Society and Culture in Colonial New York City, 1664-1730* (Princeton: Princeton University Press, 1992); Patricia U. Bonomi, *A Factious People: Politics and Society in Colonial New York* (New York: Columbia University Press, 1971); Firth Haring Fabend, *A Dutch Family in the Middle Colonies, 1660-1800* (New Brunswick, NJ: Rutgers University Press, 1991); Randall H. Balmer, *A Perfect Babel of Confusion: Dutch Religion and English Culture in the Middle Colonies* (New York: Oxford University Press, 2002).

[32] Dixon Ryan Fox, *Yankees and Yorkers* (New York: New York University Press, 1940).

[33] Goodfriend, "Dutch Colonial Legacy," 6.

[34] James W. Darlington, "Peopling the Post-Revolutionary New York Frontier," *New York History* 74, no. 4 (1993): 340-81; David M. Ellis, "Yankee-Dutch Confrontation in the Albany Area," *New England Quarterly* 45, no. 2 (June 1972): 262-70; Fox, *Yankees and Yorkers*.

[35] Elizabeth M. Covart, "Collision on the Hudson: Identity, Migration, and the Improvement of Albany, New York, 1750-1830." Dissertation, University of California, Davis, 2011, ch. 5; Gehring, "Survival"; Joseph Manca, "Erasing the Dutch: The Critical Reception of Hudson Valley Dutch Architecture, 1670-1840," in *Going Dutch: The Dutch Presence in America, 1609-2009*, ed. Joyce D. Goodfriend, Benjamin Schmidt, and Annette Stott (Leiden: Brill, 2008).

The unmooring of the Dutch from the New York landscape made their history malleable and, therefore, often turned into American folklore and legend. The upstate region had continually been subject to immense change, and those rapid transformations created tenuous attachments that undermined the historical permanence of Dutch settlement. The lack of cultural continuity added to the inherent strangeness of the Dutch for nineteenth-century east coast Americans and fictionalized New Netherlanders as myth and legend. Judith Richardson has coined this process as "ghosting" and marks the Hudson Valley as particularly haunted.[36] By the early nineteenth century, the Dutch became figures in many of the stories that emanated from upstate New York. They seemed so distant and, importantly, so different from Americans that they existed as antiquarian relics of a bygone age. In the newness of the American republic, it was not exactly that citizens did not know the Dutch existed but that they believed the Dutch existed so long ago as not to affect the present.

By the early 1800s, Van der Kemp began to notice the negative conceptions of the Dutch in broader New York culture, but it was the War of 1812 that marked a critical juncture in his involvement with the American portrait of Dutch America. His writings and letters in the wake of the war revealed a sharp difference from the halcyon days of the 1790s. As he realized the lack of awareness of Dutch history in America, lamentation became a dominant tone. Yet Van der Kemp also saw opportunity in this vacuum of information. His labors hearkened back to the Dutch Patriot Revolt and his portrayal of the Netherlands and the United States as irretrievably joined. He set about utilizing his longstanding studies of the Dutch American Atlantic for an American audience.

Two particular developments from the War of 1812 fueled Van der Kemp's renewed efforts, and both were related to the processes that led to forgetting the Dutch. One of the prominent features of the War of 1812 is that it was a call to defend American honor.[37] Honor provided

[36]   Judith Richardson, *Possessions: The History and Uses of Haunting in the Hudson Valley* (Cambridge, MA: Harvard University Press, 2003). See also Judith Richardson, "The Ghosting of the Hudson Valley Dutch," in *Going Dutch: The Dutch Presence in America, 1609-2009*, ed. Joyce D. Goodfriend, Benjamin Schmidt, and Annette Stott (Leiden: Brill, 2008).

[37]   Donald R. Hickey, *The War of 1812: A Forgotten Conflict* (Urbana: University of Illinois Press, 1989); Alan Taylor, *The Civil War of 1812: American Citizens, British Subjects, Irish Rebels, and Indian Allies* (New York: Vintage, 2011); Walter R. Borneman, *1812: The War that Forged a Nation* (New York: HarperCollins, 2004).

a crucial unifying element during the war and afterward promoted a sense of nationalism strong enough to downplay the significant sectional discord the war exposed.[38] American postwar nationalism also emphasized a forward-looking vision for the country, one that again made it more difficult for those stressing the importance of the Dutch past.

The other development was the Dutch battle for independence in the 1810s. In 1795 exiled patriots, with help from the French, launched another revolutionary movement in the Netherlands and successfully installed the Batavian Republic. Shortly thereafter, it became clear that the Batavian Republic was contingent upon the support of France, and once Napoleon declared himself Emperor in 1804, it was the end of the Republic. Napoleon installed his brother Louis Bonaparte as monarch in 1806 but eventually annexed all of the Netherlands into the French Empire in 1810. During the greater European war that paralleled the War of 1812, the Dutch rose up against Napoleon and successfully gained their independence. In so doing, they did not reconstitute the Dutch Republic but instead created the Kingdom of the Netherlands in 1814 and installed the Prince of Orange as King William I.[39] Given his stringent opposition to the Orange family during the Patriot Revolt, one would expect Van der Kemp to be wary of William I and of monarchs in general. But there were some important developments during the Batavian period that propelled many Patriot reforms forward, and King William I was installed as a constitutional monarch; more than anything, however, William I was not Napoleon. As Van der Kemp informed John and Abigail Adams, "I would prefer *any* monarchical form of Government, did I reside there, than to remain a Subject of the French empire."[40]

The regained independence of the Netherlands reminded Van der Kemp how close the histories of the two countries remained.

---

[38] Taylor, *The Internal Enemy: Slavery and War in Virginia, 1772-1832* (New York: Norton, 2013); David Waldstreicher, *In the Midst of Perpetual Fetes: The Making of American Nationalism, 1776-1820* (Chapel Hill: University of North Carolina Press, 1997); Amanda Porterfield, *Conceived in Doubt: Religion and Politics in the New American Nation* (Chicago: University of Chicago Press); Gordon S. Wood, *Empire of Liberty: A History of the Early Republic, 1789-1815* (New York: Oxford University Press, 2009).

[39] Schama, *Patriots and Liberators*, 622-47; Israel, *The Dutch Republic*, 1122-30.

[40] Francis Adrian van der Kemp to Abigail Adams, 15 March 1814, Francis Adrian Van der Kemp Collection, 1781-1829: Letters of John Adams and John Quincy Adams, 1781-1829, Historical Society of Pennsylvania. He expressed a similar sentiment to John Adams in a 1 March 1814 letter, Francis Adrian Van der Kemp Collection, 1781-1829: Letters of John Adams and John Quincy Adams, 1781-1829, Historical Society of Pennsylvania.

Although the American war continued, inspired by events in the Netherlands, Van der Kemp wrote and delivered a speech to a gathered crowd in Utica, New York, in March 1814. The oration was less a speech than an extensive history of the Netherlands. In its printed form, it exceeded thirty pages. Van der Kemp tracked the original independence from the Spanish, through the Republic, the Dutch Patriot Revolt and its grievances, to renewed independence and new life as the Kingdom of the Netherlands.[41] It was clearly a lesson for the gathered crowd, but as it was printed, it also became a portable primer on Dutch history.

While the stated purpose was to celebrate the Dutch and their long history as a liberty-seeking people, Van der Kemp's ulterior motive was to unite the histories of the Netherlands and America. Oftentimes, he did so specifically through the history of New Netherland. In a passage where he covered the official independence of the Dutch Republic in 1648, he noted that this was also the period of Dutch expansion and settlement in North America, informing the audience, "*New-Amsterdam*, our New York city, built by Dutchmen, and settlements made on the Hudson at Esopus and at Albany, then *Fort Orange*" were all part of this period. Settlements, he noted at the end of the passage, that were "taken from the Dutch, in time of peace" by the English.[42] He carried the New Netherland connection even further when he covered the loss of independence to the French. He implored the audience to learn the lessons of their ancestors, noting that there were many names in the crowd and in New York that had ties to the Netherlands. "I see here," he announced, "some of the Dutch descendants among my hearers, and recollect the names of others whose forefathers emigrated to this country, of whose families' lateral branches are yet remaining in the United Provinces and their vicinity."[43]

Van der Kemp's explicit citation of the Netherlands as "the country of your fathers" to the crowd exposed his growing worry that New Yorkers did not know about any of these associations. Importantly, he delivered the speech in Utica, as opposed to Oldenbarneveld, where he would have been preaching to the converted. This public oration demonstrated that he began to feel the forces that had been erasing the

---

[41] Francis Adrian van der Kemp, *Oration, Delivered on the 11th of March, 1814, at the Presbyterian Church in the Village of Utica, Commemorative of the Glorious Event of the Emancipation of the Dutch from French Tyranny* (Utica: Merrell & Camp, 1814), New York State Library Manuscripts and Special Collections, New York State Library.

[42] Van der Kemp, *Oration* 19, original emphasis.

[43] Van der Kemp, *Oration* 24.

Dutch in New York and set to turn the tide. At the end of the *Oration*, with the French defeated and Dutch independence once again secured, Van der Kemp returned to the subject of the Dutch American Atlantic and the shared histories of the United States and the Netherlands. He cited the lengths to which the patriots went to support the American Revolution and the honor John Adams held amongst the Dutch people. He beseeched that, with the rebirth of Dutch independence, "May the connection between American and the Dutch be renewed" and hoped that the Kingdom of the Netherlands would be celebrated and appreciated "by Columbia's sons on this side of the Atlantic."[44]

The balance of hope and frustration in Van der Kemp's closing note was similarly manifested in his subsequent work. In his communication with John Adams about the legacy of the Dutch in America, Van der Kemp was reminded that some Americans did know this history and valued the Dutch contributions. Adams consistently placed his time in the Netherlands among the most important events in his life, writing Van der Kemp, "[I]f my name ever did deserve to be remembered," he had no issue if it was for his "Negotiations in Holland in 1780, 1781, and 1782."[45] Adams was also quick to highlight the same commitment to political and religious liberty in the history of the Netherlands that could be found in the United States.[46] As both Van der Kemp and Adams articulated the sustained connections between the two countries, they also worried about the future. The deaths of mutual friends caused them to pause and wonder how a generation fully removed from the Revolution would look at the late eighteenth century.[47] For his part, Van der Kemp outlined an extensive history of the Age of Revolutions to preserve his image of the Dutch American Atlantic for posterity. He entitled it, "Moral and Physical Causes of the Revolutionary Spirit, in part of the 18th Century, with their probable

---

[44]   Van der Kemp, *Oration*, 31, 32.

[45]   John Adams to Francis Adrian van der Kemp, 2 May 1814, Francis Adrian Van der Kemp Collection, 1781-1829: Letters of John Adams and John Quincy Adams, 1781-1829, Historical Society of Pennsylvania; John Adams to Francis Adrian van der Kemp, 29 May 1814, Francis Adrian Van der Kemp Collection, 1781-1829: Letters of John Adams and John Quincy Adams, 1781-1829, Historical Society of Pennsylvania

[46]   John Adams to Francis Adrian van der Kemp, 22 August 1818, Francis Adrian Van der Kemp Collection, 1781-1829: Letters of John Adams and John Quincy Adams, 1781-1829, Historical Society of Pennsylvania.

[47]   John Adams to Francis Adrian van der Kemp, 16 July 1816, Francis Adrian Van der Kemp Collection, 1781-1829: Letters of John Adams and John Quincy Adams, 1781-1829, Historical Society of Pennsylvania.

issues on both Continents." The outline clearly marked the mutual path toward popular sovereignty adopted by the patriots and the Americans. Unfortunately, the piece never made it past the planning stage.[48]

The tension between optimism and vexation with American memory is most clearly expressed in Van der Kemp's "A Dutch Symposium." Crafted originally in 1811, Van der Kemp went back to the document in 1814 with Dutch independence in mind.[49] Designed as a letter detailing a night among a group of Dutch Americans, the "Symposium" reflects the same themes as the oration and uses much the same style. Leading the conversation is a man named Frankfort, a thinly veiled Van der Kemp. After a brief opening, the letter delves right into the conversation, which, unsurprisingly, is about Dutch history and the consequences of renewed Dutch independence. As Van der Kemp cycled through his regular list of features uniting the United States and the Netherlands, he also expressed exasperation that the United States had never come to the aid of the Dutch during either the Patriot Revolt or Batavian Revolution as the Dutch had for them during the American Revolution. Invoking the immediate context of the War of 1812, he asked, "How could Americans ridicule, scoff at a nation, which never offended their vanity . . . never injured their commerce—impressed their saylors [sic]—burned their defenceless merchant men, or insulted them as a nation?" Instead, he argued, Americans showed "the blackest ingratitude towards the only nation, which sincerily [sic] and cordially interested herself in our cause, when we were fighting Great Britain for our Liberty—for our independence, our existence."[50]

Yet as with the *Oration*, Van der Kemp ended with the hope that the two nations would renew their relationship now that both had secured their independence. He added that the history of the Netherlands was the perfect education for Americans. The Dutch, he wrote, "give us a fresh proof that no Nation recovers its liberty twice under a Republican government," and Americans needed "to reap advantage from their

---

[48]   Francis A. van der Kemp to Thomas Jefferson, 10 February 1812, with Historical Synopsis, the Thomas Jefferson Papers Series 1. General Correspondence, 1651-1827, Library of Congress, available at http://hdl.loc.gov.loc.mss/mtj. mtjbib020830, accessed 27 January 2016.

[49]   Francis Adrian van der Kemp, "A Dutch Symposium," 1814, Buffalo and Erie County Historical Society Archives, A69-66, Francis Adrian Van der Kemp Papers, vol. 4: A Dutch Symposium. The 1811 version is located in the De Witt Clinton Papers, vol. 24, Rare Book & Manuscript Library, Columbia University in the city of New York.

[50]   Van der Kemp, "Symposium," 23.

example."[51] Urging Americans to explore the Dutch past for lessons was also a theme found in the *Oration* and the "Moral and Physical Causes of the Revolutionary Spirit." With the detailed attention paid to the history of the Netherlands and the history of New Netherland, it is clear that Van der Kemp intended these pieces to serve as instructional primers for American audiences largely ignorant of the Dutch past. In an effort to spread the information, he sent out copies of his recent work to his correspondents and several magazines across the country.[52]

All of this work reinvigorated Van der Kemp's scholarship, and it gave him a new and distinct purpose. He now sought to recapture the experience he had had in the 1790s, when everything reminded him of the interwoven history of the United States and the Dutch. Exposure to the forces of Dutch erasure forced Van der Kemp to acknowledge that Dutch American history was not an obvious context for most Americans and that work had to be done to combat those processes. The period after 1814 brought Van der Kemp back to his roots, to his scholarship on the Dutch American Atlantic, and to thinking of the Dutch as an illustrative example for Americans. It was under this mindset that he accepted the job of translating the colonial records of New Netherland. The Albany Records became the next project in Van der Kemp's long history of promoting the legacy of the Dutch in America.

Conclusion: the Albany Records

Van der Kemp took immense pride in his opportunity and felt a heavy responsibility to restore New Netherland to a place of prominence for posterity. As he labored, the records consumed his correspondence—there was hardly a letter between 1818 and 1822 that did not mention them. Often, the letter would be entirely about his most recent findings. With only a few of the volumes remaining, the letters present the best picture of the Albany Records. The image of New Netherland that emerged from Van der Kemp's account was of a multicultural society based on the pursuit of political and religious

---

51 Van der Kemp, "Symposium," 29-30.
52 For the "Symposium," see Francis Adrian van der Kemp to Andrews Norton, 12 May 1814, Van der Kemp Collection, New York Historical Society; Francis Adrian van der Kemp to John Adams, 17 December 1814, microfilm edition of the Adams Family Papers, reel 421, Massachusetts Historical Society. For the outline, see Van der Kemp to Jefferson, 10 Feb 1812. For the *Oration*, see De Witt Clinton to Francis Adrian van der Kemp, 30 May 1814, De Witt Clinton Papers, vol. 17, Rare Book & Manuscript Library, Columbia University in the city of New York; Andrews Norton to Francis Adrian van der Kemp, 24 June 1814, Van der Kemp Collection, New York Historical Society.

liberty. It was a society that sought creative and adaptive solutions to the problems of diversity and conflicting levels of authority. In Van der Kemp's hands, New Netherland ceased to be a caricature and became the progenitor of New York and the bedrock upon which contemporary New York has been built.[53]

In the years after completing the records, Van der Kemp continued to discuss his work, especially with Adams. Both men realized that the records were but a first step to correcting the historical record. As the distance from the Revolution increased, the Americans who had welcomed the Van der Kemps to the United States began to die and their memories of Dutch involvement with them. With the completion of the translations, Adams "hope[d] the Knickerbockers in America will be excited to assert the dignity of their nation" but admitted Americans' "low estimation in which we have held the importance of their connection with us." But Adams maintained that the treaty between the Netherlands and the United States had been a turning point in the American Revolution, and "in some future day, it may be thought of more importance."[54] If Americans, however, wrote Adams, particularly his own family, "do not recognize the obligations of this country to Holland, it will prove them an ignorance, inattention, and ingratitude unworthy of their name."[55] Works such as the records were needed to combat the lack of awareness, promote more research on the Dutch in America, and prevent Americans from forgetting their debt.

With the records housed at the capitol in Albany for anyone to access, Van der Kemp took his biggest and most public step toward countering the negligence of Dutch history in New York. Scholars who wanted to study the Dutch but did not read the language now had a powerful, albeit imperfect, resource. The records contained a picture of New Netherland and a full-throated defense of the Dutch influence in American history. It was a history that most Americans had never encountered and one that spoke to many of the same themes in the current literature on New Netherland.[56]

---

[53] A more detailed description of the contents of the records and of Van der Kemp's correspondence can be found in Van Cleave, "Rescuing the Albany Records."

[54] John Adams to Francis Adrian van der Kemp, 3 January 1823, Francis Adrian Van der Kemp Collection, 1781-1829: Letters of John Adams and John Quincy Adams, 1781-1829, Historical Society of Pennsylvania.

[55] John Adams to Francis Adrian van der Kemp, 4 February 1823, Francis Adrian Van der Kemp Collection, 1781-1829: Letters of John Adams and John Quincy Adams, 1781-1829, Historical Society of Pennsylvania.

[56] For some general examples, see Joyce D. Goodfriend, ed., *Revisiting New Netherland: Perspectives on Early Dutch America* (Leiden: Brill, 2005); Shorto, *The Island at the Center of the World.*

The potential value of Van der Kemp's Albany Records for Dutch American history was well known at the time as well as today, which helps to account for why scholars have rightly pointed to the deep flaws of Van der Kemp's translations. It is why histories of the attempts to translate the New Netherland documents usually begin with Van der Kemp's failure.[57] But the effect of framing Van der Kemp's work as worthless has both neglected his intentions with the translations and, as importantly, obscured his other contributions to the history of Dutch America. While the official work on the Albany Records began in 1818, the origins and inspiration for studying the interconnected history between the Dutch and America date back to 1781 in the Netherlands, when Van der Kemp met John Adams and turned his full attention to the American Revolution. From then on, Van der Kemp sought to educate the Dutch and then Americans about their shared histories.

The Albany Records not only represent the final product in a lifetime of scholarship but also reflect the importance of the Early American Republic for studying the Dutch presence in America. Occupying the historical gap between the colony and the later nineteenth-century immigration, the Early American Republic at times gets overlooked in Dutch American histories.[58] The long history of

[57] The work of translating the Dutch colonial records and the over-twelve-thousand documents continues to this day with the work of the scholars in the New Netherland Research Center under the direction of Dr. Charles Gehring and Dr. Janny Venema.

[58] There are of course some notable exceptions. The Dutch-owned Holland Land Company has received attention, see Paul D. Evans, the *Holland Land Company* (Fairfield, NJ: Augustus M. Kelley, 1924, reprint 1979); Charles E. Brooks, *Frontier Settlement and Market Revolution: the Holland Land Purchase* (Ithaca: Cornell University Press, 1996). Of particular note are works examining the role of the Reformed faith and the Reformed Dutch Church and works tracing the continued presence of the Dutch from the colonial period, see Firth Haring Fabend, *Zion on the Hudson: Dutch New York and New Jersey in the Age of Revivals* (New Brunswick: Rutgers University Press, 2000); Fabend, *A Dutch Family in the Middle Colonies, 1660-1800* (New Brunswick: Rutgers University Press, 1991); for an earlier period, see Randall Balmer, *A Perfect Babel of Confusion: Dutch Religion and English Culture in the Middle Colonies* (New York: Oxford, 1989); for a later period, see James D. Bratt, *Dutch Calvinism in Modern America: A History of a Conservative Subculture* (Grand Rapids: Eerdmans, 1984). In addition to tracing the continued influence, another vein of scholarship examines the use of Dutch history by Americans, particularly Washington Irving and John Lothrop Motley. But tellingly, in recent overviews of Dutch-American relations, the Early American Republic and particularly the years of Van der Kemp's life in the United States, 1788-1829, received scant attention. Most of the chapters covering the nineteenth century focus on events after 1830. Hans Krabbendam, Cornelis A. van Minnen, and Giles Scott-Smith, eds., *Four Centuries of Dutch-American Relations, 1609-2009* (Albany: SUNY Press, 2009); Goodfriend, Schmidt, and Stott, eds., *Going Dutch: The Dutch Presence in America, 1609-2009*.

the Albany Records helps to provide a bridge between the two most prominent periods of Dutch American history, as does Van der Kemp's own history. His life in New York emerged from Dutch connections. He farmed on a parcel of land granted from the Holland Land Company in a town named Oldenbarneveld. He founded the United Protestant Religious Society and later the Reformed Christian Church based on principles he developed in the Netherlands, not the United States. Despite the similarity in name, it was not part of the Reformed Dutch Church, one the most significant Dutch institutions in North America. Given Van der Kemp's own struggles against the Reformed Church while in the Netherlands, the name could certainly be read as a tongue-in-cheek reference to the prominent Dutch faith, but it was also a reminder of the complicated history of religious tolerance in the Netherlands and the United States. Regardless, the Reformed Christian Church, which continues to hold services to this day as the Unitarian Church of Barneveld, stands as yet another reflection of the myriad ways the Dutch interconnect with America.

Van der Kemp's life of scholarship that led him to work on the Albany Records helps us to recognize the continued role of the Dutch in the creation of the United States and is a testament to his importance for understanding that history. The Dutch and Dutch Americans continued to build, shape, and reshape the American landscape and, along with it, American culture. Van der Kemp was not a ghost haunting upstate New York, but rather a fulcrum between the impact of the Dutch past and advancement of the Dutch American future.

CHAPTER 12

Contemplating, Complicating, and Comparing the Scenes: Elkanah Watson and William Elliot Griffis Connect Dutch America to the Netherlands

Babs Boter

View of the Exchange in Amsterdam, Hermanus Petrus Schouten, 1780
(*courtesy Leiden University Library, PK-P-136.259*)

259

Framing

In the spring of 1784, during his tour of the Netherlands, twenty-six-year-old American Elkanah Watson visited the Amsterdam stock exchange. This bourse was built in 1611, right at the center of the Dutch Republic of Europe and of the world.[1] Watson offers the following autobiographical account:

> I retired into one corner to contemplate the scene, which led me to compare this exchange to a glass beehive I saw at the famous Wildman's at the foot of the Highgate hill [in London], which was to all intents Amsterdam change [*sic*] in miniature. The buzz was the same—the eagerness of the bees crowding into the hive and their industry and ardour to collect the honey—was all the same—but it would be rather illiberal to carry the idea so far as to suppose them all a set of insects, in general actuated by nothing beyond the ideas of a bee, who trips from flower to flower and roams abroad in the wide world to suck in the sweets of every plant with no other view than to lay in a winter's stock for *his dear self*—which *in conscience* is the main spring that moves us sons of commerce, particularly in large cities.[2]

This excerpt exemplifies three typical features of travel accounts discussed by Carl Thompson in *Travel Writing*.[3] The first one is the emphasis on practices of looking.[4] The quotation includes references to voyeurism (watching from the corner), exhibition and transparency (the see-through hive put on display), and sightseeing (Highgate Hill in London, where Daniel Wildman performed as a famous bee tamer). Second, the account draws on an analogy—a literary device that, according to Thompson, can often be found in travel writing. Both the bee and the human trader take care of themselves by stocking honey/money, and both undertake traveling, exploring, and "roam[ing] abroad in the wide world."[5] Third, as Thompson claims for each travel account,

---

[1]   Inger Leemans, "De Beurs als bijenkorf: Naar een natuurwetenschap van economie en samenleving, rond 1700," Inaugural Lecture, Vrije Universiteit, Amsterdam, 28 October 2011.

[2]   Elkanah Watson, *A Tour in Holland in MDCCLXXXIV* / By an American (Worcester, MA: Isaiah Thomas, 1790), 120; italics in the original.

[3]   Carl Thompson, *Travel Writing* (New York: Routledge, 2011).

[4]   Ibid., 64. Tim Youngs claims that travel writing "deals with encounter and observation." Tim Youngs, *The Cambridge Introduction to Travel Writing* (Cambridge, NY: Cambridge University Press, 2013), 166.

[5]   Watson, *A Tour in Holland*, 120.

this one also discloses "something of the culture from which that writer emerged" and reveals who the traveller is and what his or her values, preoccupations, and assumptions are.[6]

Indeed, the quotation presents Watson in various ways via his autobiographical narrator.[7] First of all, he positions himself as a traveller who has visited the London tourist site of Highgate Hill and who is now visiting the Amsterdam bourse. Inger Leemans asserts that this building had been a touristic site since its construction.[8] Watson's reference to himself validates his experience and authority as a traveller. Second, the quotation suggests that his earlier London outing mediates this new encounter and that this traveler also experienced other framing encounters with strange places and objects. Third, the first-person narrator seems to be the sort of traveler who, upon entering a commercial tourist site, distances himself and is careful not to intrude. He creates a certain kind of *proximity*.[9] Fourth, the narrator seems to surreptitiously insert a critical idea into his description of the exchange, for example, traders are selfish hoarders of honey/money. Finally, his contemplation is a trigger to jointly classify himself and his audience as "sons of commerce," which hints at a possible complicity and complication. Practically all "sons" are selfish insects.

We may be familiar with other literary depictions of stock markets where animals stand in for traders and where the description

---

[6]   Thompson, *Travel Writing*, 10. Other critics have made similar claims. Referring to the traveling first-person narrator, Tim Youngs explains that he or she "not only looks at those who inhabit the places through which he or she passes but views them in ways that throw light on his or her own anxieties and desires and . . . of the home culture," Youngs, *The Cambridge Introduction*, 173.

[7]   Strictly speaking, following Gérard Genette, Mieke Bal, and other narratologists, the travel text's narrator is *not* the same as the traveller. We need to make a distinction between the identifiable social actor Elkanah Watson, who travelled and wrote, and the travel account's I-narrator, who has a distinct textual or narrative function. For the sake of readability, however, I will use Elkanah Watson (or William Elliot Griffis) for both traveller and narrator. The context will make clear whether I am referring to the actor or the narrator. Gérard Genette, *Narrative Discourse: An Essay in Method* (Ithaca, NY: Cornell University Press, 1983); Mieke Bal, *Narratology: Introduction to the Theory of Narrative* (Toronto: University of Toronto Press, 1985).

[8]   *Inger Leemans, "The Nature of the Economy: A Cultural History of Stock Trade," paper presented at the Fourteenth International Congress for Eighteenth-Century Studies in Rotterdam, 27-31 July 2015.*

[9]   The British historian, Leif Jerram, has coined and theorized the term "proximity," which involves most importantly distance to the "other." Leif Jerram, "Space! A useless category for historical analysis?" lecture for Spui25, University of Amsterdam, 22 May 2015. See also: Leif Jerram, "Space: A useless category for historical analysis?" *History and Theory. Studies in the Philosophy of History* 52, no. 3 (2013) 400-419.

of the seeming chaos and madness mocks the financial workings of the exchange. Most notable perhaps is Pierre Boulle's description of the stock exchange in *Planet of the Apes*,[10] in which traveler and journalist Ulysse Mérou, "obsessed by significant comparisons" when exploring the Simian planet, visits the stock exchange. It is "a large building, outwardly imbued with a strange atmosphere created by a vague buzz of voices." The "buzz" of course implicitly echoes the bee metaphor of Watson's text. Inside, Ulysse finds himself fixed in place against a column, observing from a distance the "screaming, gesticulating, and running" mass of monkeys. In this "hubbub of infernal exclamations, shouts, [and] cries," all monkeys wear a similar mask, "the mask of madness."[11] Ulysse's fixity, proximity, and confusion seem to echo Watson's text.

Of course, this text was published two centuries after Watson visited the Amsterdam exchange. But it may be possible that Watson had read Dutch poet Joost van den Vondel's 1655 poem about the stock exchange as a beehive, including the chaos of business and the anxious search for profit.[12] Watson worked in Albany at some time and was familiar with the Dutch history of that place. It may also be likely that he was familiar with the 1723 poem of the Flemish writer, Roeland van Leuve, which, likewise, brings attention to the beehive features of the exchange. Van Leuve points out that the exchange does not represent a normal exchange of goods: apart from order and organization, it displays a quick pace, passion, a desire for profit, and animal spirit.[13] It is plausible, of course, that if Watson was *not* aware of Vondel's or Van Leuve's use of the bee metaphor, other authors had introduced the allegory to him. In that case, his contemplation of the beehive-like stock exchange was mediated.

The concept of mediation has been theorized by various critics in the fields of literary and cultural studies. Dean MacCannell states that a sightseer's first contact with a sight "is not the sight itself but with some representation of that very sight."[14] This representation he

---

[10] Pierre Boulle, *La Planète des Singes* (Random House, 1963), trans. into English, *Planet of the Apes* (Vanguard Press, 1963).

[11] Boulle, *Planet of the Apes*, 160-61.

[12] Inger Leemans, "De beurs als bijenkorf: naar een natuurwetenschap van economie en samenleving, rond 1700," Inaugural Lecture, Vrije Universiteit, Amsterdam, 28 October 2011.

[13] Ibid.

[14] Dean MacCannell, *The Tourist: A New Theory of the Leisure Class* (Berkeley: University of California Press, 1999 [1976]), 110.

calls a "marker," which he defines as "any information about a sight, including that found in travel books, museum guides, stories told by persons who have visited it, art history texts and lectures, 'dissertations' and so forth."[15] Steve Clark uses the term of "pre-formation" when discussing the ways in which travellers are culturally prepared prior to their visit and refers to a "sense of re-encounter rather than discovery."[16] Sara Ahmed has also theorized such mediation and framing. Her focus is on the encounter with the stranger, but we could possibly replace that human stranger with a strange place or an object like the bourse. Ahmed explains that any encounter with the cultural other "is mediated." It is "not simply about two persons [or one person and one object, the traveller and the bourse] facing each other." Any encounter "presupposes other faces, other encounters of facing, other bodies, other spaces, and other times."[17] So if we want to understand how such strange encounters work in travel texts, we should note all references to histories read, pictures observed, maps looked at, earlier travel experiences, and other travellers' descriptions.

Elkanah Watson and William Elliot Griffis, the two American travelers to the Netherlands whose travel narratives are the focus of this essay, likewise underwent such "pre-formation." They relied on a framework that was based both on their acquaintance with representations of the landscape, history, and cultural traditions of their home country and with those of the Netherlands. In their travel texts they make a point of indicating which documents they have studied and what guidebooks and informants they have consulted; in this way, they emphasize their reliability and knowledgeability as travel writers. This secures the American reader's trust in, and understanding of, at least part of their frame. This essay will examine how the authors, negotiating with that very framework, construct double portraits, presenting themselves as well as the Dutch, their country, and their culture.

---

[15] Annette Stott, *Holland Mania: The Unknown Dutch Period in American Art & Culture* (Woodstock, NY: Overlook Press, 1998). It is possible, for example, that Griffis may have been familiar with illustrations showing Dutch costumes, as in *The Art Amateur* (July 1887). Mentioned in Stott, 39.

[16] Steve Clark, "Transatlantic Crossings: Recent British Travel Writing on the United States," in *Travel Writing and Empire: Postcolonial Theory in Transit*, ed. Steve Clark (London: Zed Books, 1999), 213.

[17] Sara Ahmed, *Strange Encounters: Embodied Others in Post-Coloniality* (New York: Routledge, 2000), 7.

Introducing two travellers

The two authors whose travel accounts are studied here were not Dutch Americans, but they reference Dutch America in their writings about the Netherlands. Elkanah Watson (1758-1842), from Plymouth, Massachusetts, travelled to France in 1779 in order to deliver money to Benjamin Franklin, who at that time, was one of the American representatives in Paris. One month later, Watson opened a mercantile house in Nantes, started to travel around the country, and made an attempt to learn French. Watson's business was successful, but the economic depression of 1783 forced him and his business partners into bankruptcy. Having financially recovered, Watson took up travelling through the Netherlands and England.

Even though Watson would later write in *A Tour in Holland*, we will see that he was ignorant about the Netherlands; we do know that before travelling in the Netherlands, Watson had become acquainted with the wealthy gentleman, Robert Morris, from Philadelphia, who dealt with Dutch loans to America and who was a chief agent in America for Dutch bankers. While in the Netherlands, during the spring and early summer of 1784, Watson became acquainted with John Adams, the first American ambassador to the Netherlands and later the second president of the United States, who turned out to be one of Griffis's informants and guides, one instance of which is when they jointly visited Huis ten Bosch.[18] Watson returned to America at the end of 1784 and in 1789 moved to Albany, New York, where he invested in land and business and established the State Bank of Albany in 1803.

France, Holland, and England were clearly not Watson's first or only travel destinations; in *A Tour in Holland*, Watson claims that, prior to his European journey, he had already travelled through the United States. He also refers to his "experience in the broad world."[19] But his travels to Europe, and especially the Netherlands, had a lasting impact on Watson, both personally and professionally. Having been impressed and inspired by the waterways in the Netherlands, in Albany, Watson formed a company to build locks and canals. While in Albany, he studied the history of the colonial Dutch and at one point visited the country house of Amsterdam-based John de Neuville. Based on journals he had

[18]   http://www.nysl.nysed.gov/msscfa/sc13294.htm; Herbert H. Rowen, "American Travelers in Holland through Two Centuries," in *A Bilateral Centennial: A History of Dutch-American Relations, 1782-1982. European Contributions to American Studies* 5 (Amsterdam: Meulenhoff, 1982), 617-40.

[19]   Watson, *A Tour in Holland*, 66.

kept since his twenties, Watson started writing his autobiography in 1821, when he was sixty-three years old. It was completed, edited, and published as *Men and the Times of the Revolution; or Memoirs of Elkanah Watson* (1856), by one of his sons, historian Winslow Cossoul Watson.

William Elliot Griffis (1843-1928) was born in Philadelphia, Pennsylvania, one year after Watson died. He was a teacher, orientalist, and minister. He made numerous trips to Europe, primarily to visit the Netherlands. He was a prolific author and wrote about six books on the Netherlands, two of which are: *The American in Holland: Sentimental Rambles in the Eleven Provinces of the Netherlands* (1899) and *The Story of New Netherland: The Dutch in America* (1909).[20] Griffis first became aware of Dutch American culture when studying at Rutgers College, which was affiliated with the Dutch Reformed Church. His on-campus friendships with Dutch American young men piqued his interest in the study of Dutch influence in United States history.[21] Having graduated with a master of arts from Rutgers College in 1869, Griffis visited the Netherlands during a tour of Europe with his sister. It was the first of ultimately eleven journeys to the Netherlands.

In 1877 Griffis was licensed by the Manhattan Congregational Association and called to the First Reformed Church of Schenectady as the congregation's sixteenth minister. Griffis would remain a member of the Dutch Reformed Church for twenty-five years. In the following years, around the two hundredth anniversary of First Reformed Church of Schenectady, Griffis became an authority on the Dutch in America through his study of the Dutch archives in Schenectady and Albany. In 1890, during the commemorations of the bicentennial of the Schenectady Massacre, Griffis returned to Schenectady to present an address at the First Reformed Church. In 1898 Griffis attended the Congress of Diplomatic History in the Netherlands, as well as the festivities related to the enthronement of Queen Wilhelmina.

After his retirement, Griffis devoted time and energy to advocating the marking of historical sites both in the Netherlands and in Dutch America. In 1906 he participated in the placement of the Pilgrim Memorial at Delfshaven, the Netherlands, and installed five bronze

---

[20]   William Elliot Griffis, *The American in Holland: Sentimental Rambles in the Eleven Provinces of the Netherlands* (Boston: Houghton, Mifflin, 1899); *The Story of New Netherland: The Dutch in America* (Boston: Houghton Mifflin, 1909). The first title was based on five voyages to the Netherlands, see: Annette Stott, *Holland Mania*, 88. The second text was related to the celebrations of the tricentennial of Hudson sailing up the Hudson.

[21]   Stott, *Holland Mania*, 97.

historical tablets in the Netherlands, including a Van Curler plaque in Nijkerk. Van Curler had been the focus of Griffis's biographical study for some time. A Van Curler plaque was also installed in Schenectady's Stockade at Union and North Church Streets, dedicated 29 September 1909.[22] Griffis was able to read Dutch, as he describes reading *Elsevier's Maandschrift* during his travels through the Netherlands and was engaged in research at the provincial archives of Overijssel in the city of Zwolle.[23] He was one of four Americans elected to the Netherlands Society of Letters in Leiden. In his preface to *Young People's History of Holland*, he claims that

> Every American should know the history of the Netherlands, the fatherland of millions of Americans, and the storehouse of precedents in federal government from which those who made our nation borrowed most freely. Nowhere in Europe, except in England, can one find the origin of so much that is deepest and best in our national life—including the highest jewel of civilization, religious liberty—as in Holland, as John Adams and Benjamin Franklin long ago confessed.[24]

To date, scholars have placed Watson and Griffis mostly in an historical and political context and have focused on the ways in which these two travellers historicize the Netherlands and New Netherland.[25] This essay will use a more literary and semiotic approach. The two texts are from different centuries, have different aims, and show different styles. Still they seem to employ very similar narrative strategies and techniques to create a Dutch American double portrait.

Of the two, Griffis most often boasts of his many travel experiences and refers to the documents he has studied. Watson confesses his "total ignorance" of Holland and the Dutch and relates he has in vain tried to find "some good description of that artificial country."[26] Although

---

[22]   The above biographical information was kindly offered to the author by Ms. Laura Linder on 30 September 2015.

[23]   Griffis, *The American in Holland*, 167, 198.

[24]   https://archive.org/details/youngpeopleshis01grifgoog, p. vii.

[25]   See for instance: Alfons Lammers, *De jachtvelden van het geluk: reizen door historisch Amerika* (Amsterdam: Balans, 1998), 133; Annette Stott, "Images of Dutchness in the United States," in *Four Centuries of Dutch-American Relations, 1609-2009*, ed. Hans Krabbendam, Cornelis A. van Minnen, Giles Scott-Smith (New York: Suny Press, 2009), 238-49, esp. 242. For "historicize," I use the online definitions: "to interpret something as a product of historical development" and "to render historic"; http://www.dictionary.com/browse/historicize.

[26]   Watson, *A Tour in Holland*, 13.

we should not take that claim at face value, it is clear that Griffis, much more than Watson, makes an attempt to identify the way in which he has prepared for his tour and account. Among the many references, Griffis points out a text by Baedeker, and he refers to John Lothrop Motley's *The Rise of the Dutch Republic*.[27] His later work, *The Story of New Netherland: The Dutch in America*, offers many more references, such as those drawn from popular art, proverbs, literature, "all Dutch history," "Leyden archives," and "records of the City Council."[28] Dutch Americans have served as his informants, and Griffis notes that he has met "the real people!" and claims he has lived with Dutch Americans for fourteen years.[29]

Griffis cites not only his sources of information but, pointing to a complicated frame of reference, he also makes comparisons with other countries. Visits to countries such as Japan and Egypt make up part of that frame. Dutch culture and habits reminded him of the Japanese and triggered his imagining himself "back in Japan."[30] Holland is "an Egypt-like, hollow land"; "the whole country is a sort of Egypt, very hollow and sandy."[31] But Griffis most often compares late nineteenth-century Holland, which he calls "Patria" or "the old home-land," to "Dutch America" or "New Netherland."[32]

This comparative rhetorical strategy served several purposes. First, it was part of an attempt to find common ground with his American readers. According to Carl Thompson, "The traveller must seek to attach unknown entities to known reference points and familiar frameworks of meaning and understanding."[33] Thompson calls this the principle of attachment. Griffis and Watson both tried to cater to their respective audiences by finding ways to "attach" to them. They explain to their American readers the difference in geographical size or scale. In *A Tour in Holland*, when describing the Zuiderzee, Watson explains, "This famous lake would be only ranked as a pond in America, where nature forms every thing [*sic*] upon a broad scale—here it is thought more of

---

27 Griffis, *The American in Holland*, 5, 86. He also refers to Motley in his 1909 text, 121.
28 Griffis, *The Story of New Netherland*, 161, 23. Griffis has also studied Dutch "fads and fashions" on paintings, in stories within picture frames, and on Delftware exhibited in New Netherland, 197.
29 Griffis, *The Story of New Netherland*, 259, x-xi.
30 Griffis, *The American in Holland*, 17, 84. For comparisons with Japan, see also: Griffis, *The American in Holland*, 108, 114, 171, 183, and Griffis, *The Story of New Netherland*, 196.
31 Griffis, *The Story of New Netherland*, 3, 34; see also: 135.
32 Griffis, *The American in Holland*, 8-9.
33 Thompson, *Travel Writing*, 67.

than we think of our Lake Superiour, which is capable of receiving three such republicks [*sic*] upon its area."[34] Griffis refers to a southern Dutch province, and he states that "In area, North Brabant is exactly the size of Delaware."[35] In addition, Griffis, at one point, compares the weather in the Netherlands to "Colorado sunshine" and ignores racial categories when equating the white poor of the Dutch province of Drenthe to the free "negroes in Virginia."[36]

Second, equating Holland and America helped substantiate Griffis's arguments in the historical debate about the "English versus Dutch influence in early New York."[37] That meant that in his project of "recounting" Washington Irving's description of the colonial Dutch, satirical though it was, Griffis perhaps emphasized that common ground more than he otherwise would have done.[38] Among his comparisons of Holland and America in colonial times are these two: looking at a Dutch farmer on his horse, he is reminded of "an early American colonist going to church,"[39] and referring to the town of Hoogeveen, the Netherlands, he writes, "What memories were recalled of old Schenectady, when, on the year's opening morning, the white sugar cookies, duly stamped and moulded in Dutch decorations of knights, birds, flowers, and sentimental symbols were bestowed freely on the children who called at the doors!"[40]

Third, comparisons with the home country (more or less deliberately) express the author's personal and nostalgic national engagement with it and help construct his persona as travel writer.[41] Describing a particular Dutch landscape, he states that he, as "an American," is "*remind*[ed] of New Orleans." In another instance, he "*thought of* the adobe houses and 'sod shacks' on our own prairies." When Griffis arrives at the Rhine valley, he "can almost *imagine* [he is] looking at the natural splendors of [his] own native Pennsylvania."[42]

---

[34] Watson, *A Tour in Holland*, 112-13.

[35] Griffis, *The American in Holland*, 239.

[36] Ibid., 94, 137. In another text, Griffis does likewise, as he compares Rembrandt to Lincoln. See: William Elliot Griffis, "Rembrandt: Interpreter of the Twentieth Century Essay," *The North American Review* 183, no. 596 (July 1906), 102.

[37] Stott, *Holland Mania*, 94.

[38] Ibid.

[39] Griffis, *The American in Holland*, 117.

[40] Ibid., 140.

[41] I use Mineke Bosch's definition of "persona" as theorized in "Persona en de performance van identiteit: Parallelle ontwikkelingen in de nieuwe biografische geschiedschrijving van gender en van wetenschap," *Tijdschrift voor biografie* 1, no. 3 (Fall 2012), 10-21.

[42] Griffis, *The American in Holland*, 144, 163, 185. Italics added.

In his descriptions of the Netherlands, Watson inserts a three-page-long account of his earlier tour of the United States, that ends with an expression of his pride in the superior United States landscape, history, and culture.[43]

The italicized references to memory and the imagination in the three examples from Griffis's text often turn up in travel writing and carry connotations of the visual. Both Watson and Griffis in their travel narratives emphasize the significance of the practice of looking. They relate their own joyful inspections and reflections and in turn create picturesque and painterly texts that are meant to energize and stimulate their readers and to invite them to come and participate in the celebration of looking.[44] This representation of, as well as invitation to, an indulgence in the spectral is clear from the following account of Griffis's visit to Haarlem: "My eyes feast on an ocean of color. On this early June morning, myriad blooms of most gorgeous hue sparkle with innumerable prismatics as the sun's rays strike the dewdrops on their petals."[45] Griffis and Watson may have assumed their readers' knowledge of Dutch art, as well as their willingness to have a new look at it.

Ekphrasis: occasions for visualization[46]

Ekphrasis is the verbal representation of visual representation. A narrow definition of the term limits it to a minor literary grenre: poems on works of art. A broader definition of the term, introduced and used by W. J. T. Mitchell, I would like to use here: "A set description intended to bring person, place, picture [sic] before the mind's eye."[47] Mitchell also coined the term ekphrastic hope, which occurs when language can make us see through the imagination or metaphor. This ekphrastic hope overcomes a phase of the "impossibility of ekphrasis"[48] or the impossibility of visualizing something in a text. This is what seems to engage Watson and Griffis.

---

[43]   Watson, *A Tour in Holland*, 45-47.

[44]   I make use of the term "painterly" as defined in Joyce Goggin and Erinç Salor, "Romance and Commerce: Imagining Global Amsterdam in the Contemporary Historical Novel," in *Imagining Global Amsterdam: History, Culture, and Geography in a World City*, ed. Marco de Waard (Amsterdam: Amsterdam University Press, 2012), 83-99. I use "looking" as defined by Kaja Silverman in *The Threshold of the Visible World* (New York: Routledge, 1996).

[45]   Griffis, *The American in Holland*, 34.

[46]   I borrow Mitchell's use of "occasion for visualization." W. J. T. Mitchell, *Picture Theory: Essays on Verbal and Visual Representation* (Chicago: University of Chicago Press, 1994), 77.

[47]   George Saintsbury in Mitchell, 153.

[48]   Mitchell, 152.

In the accounts of the two travellers, I have found five different levels of ekphrasis. The simplest and perhaps most obvious form appears, for instance, when Watson relates coming across a variety of paintings while travelling in Holland. They fit into an already established framework: the author states that he is familiar with the "sacred and historical pieces, some landscapes and portraits" of artists such as Raphael, Rubens, and Holbein.[49] In line with Goggin and Salor, we could say that the Netherlands has come to the author "through a museumized collective memory comprised of [works by] famous Dutch painters."[50]

A related form of ekphrasis occurs when the travel writers seem to identify with the visual artists whose work they admire and know. They note the visual artists' sources of inspiration. In Harderwijk, in the market place or at his hotel, where a group of farmers meet, Griffis claims he "enjoyed as a good an opportunity as ever Rembrandt had, to study Dutch faces in repose."[51] In Friesland, Griffis associates himself with yet another painter when he states, "I could look upon the sea which Mesdag so loves to paint and enjoy the breezes."[52] Griffis is doing more than relating himself to Rembrandt and Mesdag. He also seems to invite his readers to imagine (1) the Dutch market, hotel, or sea; (2) Rembrandt, Mesdag, and Griffis finding inspiration at those respective locations; and (3) the final visual products of such visits: Rembrandt's portraits, Mesdag's sea paintings, and Griffis's writings. Griffis may have been aware of the fact that, by the time he was writing his travel account, his readers would be familiar with Mesdag. According to Annette Stott, "After 1865 wealthy Americans started to seriously collect paintings by Rembrandt, Hals, Vermeer, and many lesser known Dutch artists . . . for those who could not afford to buy expensive oil paintings, magazine articles and reproduction prints, as well as oil copies of famous Dutch

49   Watson, *A Tour in Holland*, 91.
50   Goggin and Salor, "Romance and Commerce," 92.
51   Griffis, *The American in Holland*, 205. Griffis wrote an essay on the Dutch painter, Rembandt, which also suggests his identification with the painter. The Orientalist Griffis writes: "[Rembrandt] searched long and deep after whatever of Orientalism was then accessible in books or in objects brought by the ships from afar," Griffis, *The Story of New Netherland*, 99, 102-3. Griffis describes Boughton's colonial Dutch paintings of the 1880s and early 1890s as follows: "One can easily see that he has drawn his faces and figures of magistrates from the classic canvases of Rembrandt, Hals, Van der Helst, etc." Quoted in Stott, *Holland Mania*, 106.
52   Griffis, *The American in Holland*, 83.

paintings were readily available."[53] Stott discusses other authors who write as if they were painting the artists George Boughton, George Hitchcock, and Edward Penfield. According to Stott, "Soon tourists began to describe their Dutch travels in terms of the illustrations and paintings they had seen before departure."[54]

A third somewhat more concealed manifestation of ekphrasis takes place when the narrator/traveller becomes more involved in the practice of painting himself, as when he compares a Dutch scene with a painting, using the device of the simile. Griffis's text offers the following example: "The scene was grandly impressive, appearing in the twilight like a colossal etching."[55] In Watson's text, we come across the following simile: "The city [of Rotterdam] appeared like a highly finished and curious picture below us; and the country beyond, a delightful background, cultivated like a continued [*sic*] garden, all the way to our horizon."[56] In these descriptions, especially the latter ("continued garden"), the narrator seems to become a painter himself. Indeed, Watson claims that he was "born with a painter's soul."[57] That is even more evident when Watson compares a Dutch scene not to a piece of art but to an American scene: "The *lofty oaks* seemed to be so *promiscuously thrown together* that it revived in my breast a lively picture of many such situations I had seen in the course of my tour through the United States of America, some years since.[58] As we have seen above, the reference to memory and the imagination ("revived"; "had seen"; "some years since") is strongly related to the visual ("lively picture").

Fourth, although both narrators occasionally point to their work as that of (literary) artists (for example, when Watson states he is "paint[ing] the contrast of objects in strong colours"[59]), they also indicate their active involvement in more concealed forms of ekphrasis. Griffis describes a winter landscape as follows: "On these [sleighs] sit the fat-cheeked beauties of Friesland, while Jan, with his long curved skates, ribbed wollen clothes, warm cap, and hot pipe, pushes the steel runners over the glassy ice."[60] Asking his reader to form a mental picture, Griffis locates himself among the company of Dutch artists

53   Stott, "Images of Dutchness in the United States," 241.
54   *Holland Mania*, 132.
55   Griffis, *The American in Holland*, 229.
56   Watson, *A Tour in Holland*, 38.
57   Ibid., 43, 78-79.
58   Ibid., 81; italics added.
59   Ibid., 18.
60   Griffis, *The American in Holland*, 83.

and identifies his audience as visitors to the Dutch winter landscapes and viewers of painted winter scenes. Like Griffis, Watson is skillful at putting his readers to work when he asks them to imagine: "I will endeavor to give you a general idea at once of the principal cities in Holland. *Imagine* yourself traversing one of these cities. . . . *Hold fast to* these grand outlines, and *suppose* yourself immersed in a crowd of industrious mortals, all in pursuit of wealth, and you can easily *trace*, by your fireside, most of the towns in the Seven Provinces."[61] Watson provides a frame for his readers and invites them to imagine. In conclusion, Griffis and Watson give form to the ekphrastic hope that W. J. T. Mitchell introduced. In various ways, both visualize the Dutch and their landscape in their written text and, with that, inform, appeal to, and invigorate their (American) audience.

Limitations and possibilities of looking

Although Watson and Griffis celebrate the practices of looking, they also point out the limitations and complications of those very practices. First of all, they may feel at a loss having to portray in words the country that they visit. Watson states that "[the elegant Dutch old houses] cannot be easily described but must be seen in order to be properly conceived of."[62] This does not, of course, just reflect the actual inability of the writer to portray the scene but also replicates a trope often found in travel writing. Carl Thompson discusses this tendency of travel writers to claim their inability to describe certain scenes, for example, that of Niagara Falls.

The authors may also, more indirectly, refer to the complex workings of the practice of looking. They do this in several ways. First, using one example from Watson and one from Griffis, I will point out how how both travel writers are aware that looking can produce confusion. Visiting Rotterdam, Watson writes, "We *penetrated* with our eyes into the heart of this beautiful city, through two or three avenues as we passed, which *shewed us* such a singular *confusion* of masts, spires, trees, canals, and houses, all jumbled together."[63] Although the travel writer has some kind of agency ("penetrated"), he has also been tricked by the imposed disarray of various sights ("shewed"; "confusion"). When Griffis explicitly refers to a painting by Jan Steen, he finishes his

---

61   Watson, *A Tour in Holland*, 34-35.
62   Ibid., 29.
63   Ibid., 33.

description with an ironic twist indicating his awareness of a possible mix-up between the original and its representations: "Standing mirrored in the stream by the roadside are three cows, superb in form, and glossy in hide, lifting up their frontlets like stately creatures. We exclaim at once, 'There is the original of Jan Steen's picture which we saw at the Hague.' Yet, where are the small boys swimming?"[64]

Second, both authors suggest how their looking is almost literally framed. In Watson's text, trees play a significant role in disabling or enabling the traveler to see. In Rotterdam, a line of trees that is planted along the river *"half* deprived us of the sight of the most magnificent houses."[65] Trees, however, may become pictures themselves, framed by reflecting surfaces. Travelling in a Dutch *trekschuit*, a boat pulled by a horse, he experiences "a sublime scene in the night to view the effect of the moon upon the country, through a double row of trees planted on the banks of the river."[66] The trees thus function as a frame.

Watson has returned to his cabin on the *trekschuit*, he "spent the night upon cushions on a bench, sometimes viewing the country *from the cabin windows* by a fair moon light and reading occasionally."[67] The repeated references to objects that frame his view (*trekschuit*, window) are significant. They easily combine with very implicit references to the various discourses that inform Watson's writing, as is betrayed by his choice of words: "penetrate," possibly coming from a familiar discourse on exploration; "sublime scene," conceivably originating from the literary genre of travel writing; and "effect of the moon upon the country," perhaps borrowed from a contemporary fine arts discourse.[68] Thus Watson's readers end up looking at a traveller who himself is framed but who also actively partakes in the act of framing. This reminds one of the concept of the mise-en-abyme, a technique that is evoked when Watson introduces the Dutch *spionnetje*. He explains, "It had an odd appearance to us, to see reflecting glasses hitched upon the outside of the most genteel windows, so that Madam (Mavrow) can set

---

64 Griffis, *The American in Holland*, 185. To make matters more complicated, the painting Griffis refers to is not a Jan Steen but a Paulus Potter.

65 Watson, *A Tour in Holland*, 32; italics in the original.

66 Ibid., 153.

67 Ibid., 152.

68 I use Michel Foucault's definition of discourse here, as introduced and discussed by Sara Mills: "A discourse is a regulated set of statements which combine with others in predictable ways. Discourse is regulated by a set of rules which lead to the distribution and circulation of certain utterances and statements." See Sara Mills, *Michel Foucault*, (London: Routledge, 2003), 54.

[*sic*] unobserved by her window and reconnoitre at her ease every object passing up and down the streets."[69] Thus Watson is imagining that the lady is looking at the passers-by, one of whom is Watson.

Griffis seems to have a similar interest in framing. Riding in a carriage near the town of Rolde in the province of Drenthe, Griffis sits so close to a farmer and his wife that he is able to describe the wife as "young, bright-eyed, and with bulging red cheeks." He explains: "The golden skull-cap of the farmer's bride was so dazzlingly bright that it furnished me with a mirror in which I could see reflected the whole landscape. The trees, the birds, the patches of blue sky, and the moving clouds were all visible as in a camera, and I could tell what was behind me without turning my head."[70] Griffis, like Watson, references an object that frames the skull-cap and indirectly the camera. Again this frame combines well with another frame that we can find hiding in the text: the fine arts discourse Griffis refers to when describing Dutch painting. The figure of the mise-en-abyme returns in Griffis's description of his encounter with the American painter Amy Cross (1856-1939), who is from Milwaukee and who visits the Dutch village of Nunspeet. Cross pays her "humble friends" for posing, to depict "life among the lowly."[71]

Griffis describes what the painter is looking at and gives an indirect presentation of life among the lowly. "In one corner, where the mother sits, her face prematurely wrinkled, and every wrinkle a furrow of experience telling of a sorrow, is the spinning-wheel." Then after a rather lengthy and painterly description, Griffis suddenly steps out of the frame of the painter and into the home and, resembling a tour guide at a tourist spot, describes the set-up: "The bed is in the closet. Stepping outside into the rear room on the left, we find the cow and the sheep" who look up at Griffis. When the painter friend has finished the oil painting depicting the poor family's home, Griffis is glad to have seen "the original" first before seeing "the copy in oil painting,"[72] suggesting that originals are better than representations. The difference between Cross's portrait, as shown above, which was exhibited at the National Academy of Design in 1897, and Griffis's literary depiction is striking. The oil painting hardly looks like "life among the lowly."

Griffis's own painterly images leap from many pages of his travel account. A close reading of one scene, in which Griffis sits to rest on a

---

69   Watson, *A Tour in Holland*, 29-30.
70   Griffis, *The American in Holland*, 133.
71   Ibid., 194; Stott mentions the artist's name in *Holland Mania*, 57.
72   Ibid., 194-95.

Amy Cross,
Weighing the Bread
(*courtesy Patrick Jolly
Fine Art*)

dike west of Flushing, discloses his triple vision of the surroundings: like a painter, he first describes the calm sea, then moves on to imagine (and ask his readers to visualize) a winter storm, and finally he remembers "old times," in which the streets were flooded, and people had to wait for six weeks for "a change of winds."[73] The reader is even offered a fourth image: a picture of "The Maid of the Dikes."[74]

When visiting the Brederode castle, a similarly layered image evolves: "I pictured the children playing here . . . the mirth of summer serenade or of winter night's skating on the moonlighted moat." Then he moves on (or rather, back in time) to imagine the following: "I thought of the sieges and sorties, the bloodshed." The contemporary Brederode castle is the location where the narrator describes himself as lounging dreamily and having his serving of coffee: "I sat under the superb old trees."[75] The reader is offered a multiple-layered imagery. Just as Griffis himself refers to the idea of the palimpsest, the Dutch landscape carries several traces, one on top of the other, to indicate different historical events.

---

[73] Ibid., 284.
[74] Griffis, *The American in Holland*, 284-85.
[75] Ibid., 44.

Griffis points out similarities by referring to paintings, stating that the interiors in Dutch America were just like the canvases "from Ostade to Israels," or that the marriage rituals of the Dutch in America are "as full of realism as is a canvas of Rembrandt or Jan Steen."[76] Interestingly, Griffis here seems to copy the American painter George Boughton, who, like Griffis, linked the Netherlands and the United States in his work: Griffis states that for the depiction of magistrates in his colonial Dutch paintings of the 1880s and early 1890s, Boughton draws from Rembrandt, van Hals, and Van de Helst, "while those of the young women and men in the humbler walks of life are reproductions of his own sketches from life in the Holland of to-day."[77]

Simple painterly descriptions may have political messages, such as Griffis observing wheatfields on the first of July: "Down under the gold, the red poppies fling out their scarlett splendors, and the blue corn-flower moves lightly in the wind."[78] But there is more to it than that. Griffis also discovers the white blossoms of the potato and completes the picture by referring to the three colors of the Dutch and American flags. Thus the painterly text seems to have a political undertone that tries to connect the United States to Holland, which seems to have been the purpose of the trip. Griffis likewise sketches for us, almost as a Dutch painter, the fireplace scenes of Dutch America:

> In winter the long evenings were given up to stories, finger games, with lullaby for baby and pipe for papa, and then, at the right time, cider, apples, nuts, and refreshments as desired. For the real old folks, the hearth was the place of memory, but for the young, it was the seed-bed of dreams. In the darting tongues of the blaze and the deep glow of the embers, lad and lassie saw the castles of the future and the aged pictures of the past.[79]

Griffis here nostalgically imagines or dreams of the old Dutch in America who in their turn are dreaming of their old home.

Griffis and Watson were not merely writing personal travel narratives. They were not just engaged in "representing the self" or

---

[76] Griffis, *The Story of New Netherland*, 168, 170. Griffis uses strikingly similar phrasing when describing costumed figures in the parade on the day of the inauguration of Queen Wilhelmina, 6 September 1898: "Warriors and statesmen, stadholders and kings . . . in living pictures that had apparently just left the canvas and frames of Rembrandt and Jan Steen, marched by," Griffis, *The American in Holland*, 391.

[77] William Elliot Griffis, "George H. Boughton, the Painter of New England Puritanism," *New England Magazine* n.s. 15 (December 1896), 501.

[78] Griffis, *The American in Holland*, 184.

[79] Griffis, *The Story of New Netherland*, 167.

"reporting the world," which are two of the models that Carl Thompson employs when analyzing travel writing.[80] The two American travellers were constructing a link between the Netherlands and Dutch America. They were able to do so because they had, even before their travels to the Netherlands, built a framework from which they explored the Dutch landscape, people, and their culture. Visiting Dutch towns, they noted reminders of the Dutch heritage as represented in the American places they came from. Part of this narrative strategy must have been a result of particular travel writing conventions and of their wish to reach a specific American audience. But both travel writers seemed to have felt a personal need to emphasize American-Dutch connections. For Watson this may have been triggered more by commercial and techological motives than for Griffis. Watson's interest in land speculation, banking business, and the promotion of canals differed of course from Griffis's more scholarly and religious affinities with the Dutch. By complicating their own practices of looking, by offering powerful painterly images of Dutch scenes, and by putting forward possible visual frames for their readers, both, however, left us with especially rich sources demonstrating American-Dutch ties.

[80]   The two phrases are the titles of chapters in Thompson's text and frame the many examples he offers of travel writing.

Contributors

Henk Aay, PhD, Clark University; Senior Research Fellow, Van Raalte Institute, Hope College; professor of geography and environmental studies and Meijer Chair Emeritus in Dutch Language and Culture, Calvin College. Henk is currently taking the lead on an atlas of Dutch American history and culture.

Anthonia Boersema-Bremmer, MA, graduated in Dutch language and literature from Utrecht University and in cultural studies from Open University, the Netherlands.

Jan J. Boersema, PhD, University of Groningen, the Netherlands; professor of principles of environmental sciences, the Institute of Environmental Sciences, Leiden University. His most recent book is *The Survival of Easter Island, Dwindling Resources and Cultural Resilience* (2011).

Babs Boter, PhD, has a background in history (Leiden University) and American studies (University of Minnesota). She is assistant professor of literature in English at Vrije Universiteit Amsterdam. Her research focuses on travel narratives, life writing, and transnationalism.

Pieter Hovens, PhD, studied anthropology at Radboud University, Nijmegen, the Netherlands and first nations studies at the University of British Columbia, Canada. He was a policy advisor for the Dutch government on minorities, volunteering, and citizenship education. Currently he is curator of the North American Department at the National Museum of World Cultures (Leiden).

Hans Krabbendam, PhD, Leiden University; director of the Catholic Documentation Center, Radboud University, the Netherlands; formerly assistant director of the Roosevelt Study Center in Middelburg, the Netherlands. Author of numerous articles and books, among others, *Freedom on the Horizon: Dutch Immigration to America, 1840-1940* (2009).

Erin Kramer is a PhD candidate in history at the University of Wisconsin-Madison.

Nella Kennedy, MA, art history, University of Iowa; Senior Research Fellow, Van Raalte Institute, in which capacity she has translated numerous documents, written articles, and has been a coeditor of three AADAS conference volumes. She has frequently been a guest curator at the Holland Museum.

Earl Wm. (Bill) Kennedy, ThD, American church history, Princeton Theological Seminary; Senior Research Fellow, Van Raalte Institute; and professor of religion emeritus, Northwestern College, Iowa. Author of many articles, with forthcoming publication of *A Commentary on the Minutes of the Classis of Holland, 1848-1876. A Detailed Record of Persons and Issues, Civil and Religious, in the Dutch Colony of Holland, Michigan.*

Andrew Stahlhut, PhD, Lehigh University in history; adjunct professor of history at the Wescoe School of Muhlenberg College and project associate at Lehigh University's special collections. He has published in *de Halve Maen*, Journal of the Holland Society of New York.

Robert P. Swierenga, PhD, University of Iowa; research professor, Van Raalte Institute, Hope College; professor emeritus of history, Kent State University; and author and editor of numerous books, most recently *Holland, Michigan: From Dutch Colony to Dynamic City* (2014) and *Park Township Centennial History, 1915-2015: "Holland's Water Playground," Ottawa County, Michigan* (2015).

Leon van den Broeke, PhD, assistant professor of religion, law and society/church polity, faculty of theology, Vrije Universiteit Amsterdam; chair of the Center for Religion and Law, Vrije Universiteit Amsterdam; assistant professor church polity at the Theologische Universiteit Kampen, the Netherlands.

Peter D. Van Cleave, PhD History; instructor in history in the School of Historical, Philosophical, and Religious Studies at Arizona State University. He is working on a history of Francis Adrian van der Kemp and the political and religious environments of the Dutch American Atlantic during the early republic.

Index

283